Natalie & R.J.

Other Books by Warren G. Harris

GABLE & LOMBARD
THE OTHER MARILYN
CARY GRANT: A TOUCH OF ELEGANCE

Warren G. Harris

Natalie & R.J.

Hollywood's Star-Crossed Lovers

A DOLPHIN BOOK
Doubleday
NEW YORK   LONDON   TORONTO   SYDNEY

A Dolphin Book
Published by Doubleday, a division of
Bantam Doubleday Dell Publishing Group, Inc.,
666 Fifth Avenue, New York, New York 10103

Dolphin and the portrayal of two dolphins
are trademarks of Doubleday, a division of
Bantam Doubleday Dell Publishing Group, Inc.

Library of Congress Cataloging-in-Publication Data

Harris, Warren G.
Natalie & R.J.

"A Dolphin book."
Filmography: p. 221
Includes index.
1. Wood, Natalie.   2. Wagner, Robert, 1930–
3. Motion picture actors and actresses—United States—
Biography. I. Title.
PN2287.W59H37   1988   791.43'028'0922 [B]   87–30127

ISBN 0-385-23691-3
First Edition
July 1988

BG

For Barry McGoffin,
Who should have been here

Contents

Prologue

IN THE ANNALS of Hollywood marriages, Natalie Wood and Robert John Wagner hold a unique place. The young movie stars fell in love, got married and, just when everything seemed perfect, their lives came apart and they divorced. More than a decade later, after unsuccessful marriages to others, their love flamed anew.

In 1972, Natalie and R.J. remarried and repeated their vows to remain together "till death do us part." This time they did.

On November 27, 1981, the day after the national Thanksgiving holiday, the Wagners set off on a weekend cruise aboard their sixty-foot power yacht, *Splendour*. A buzz of recognition spread among the people who spotted them arriving at the dock in Marina del Rey.

No other woman had her winsome combination of bouncing shoulder-length hair, pert upturned nose and soulful black-coffee eyes. Despite the encroachments of middle age, he still looked very much the personification of Prince Valiant. Tourists who'd never seen the couple close up before couldn't get over how petite she was. He towered over her.

Two less familiar men accompanied the Wagners. The tall thin one with the disconcerting, almost sinister appearance was Christopher Walken, currently working as Natalie's leading man in a sci-fi thriller called *Brainstorm*. Bearded Dennis Davern served as skipper of the *Splendour* and also doubled as cook, butler and bodyguard.

A native New Yorker, Walken had seen little of the sights along the Pacific coast, so Natalie and R.J. had invited him on a tour of the area around Santa Catalina Island, situated twenty-two miles off Los Angeles and famous for its primeval landscape, flying fish and barking seals. With R.J. behind the steering wheel, they headed first for Avalon, the former gambling and entertainment resort that inspired one of the biggest song hits of all time.

After the *Splendour* dropped anchor in the harbor, Dennis Davern took the Wagners and Walken to shore in the *Valiant,* a motorized dinghy named after "Prince Valiant," one of R.J.'s most famous roles. While Davern returned to the ship to prepare dinner, the Wagners and their guest wandered around for a couple of hours. They visited the fanciful art deco casino built by the Wrigley chewing gum magnate and window-shopped in the small town's multitude of boutiques and souvenir stores.

Waiting for Davern to come to pick them up, the trio stopped for drinks at El Galleon restaurant. Natalie had a beer, then switched to margaritas and started getting tipsy, the waiter claimed later. "She turned very argumentative and tried to talk the others into staying in town for the evening. But her husband finally persuaded her to return to the boat," he said.

Natalie apparently sobered up during the ride back to the *Splendour* in the bracing sea air. "We had dinner and everything was peaceful until Natalie and Chris started talking about *Brainstorm,*" Davern recalled. "R.J. felt left out and didn't like it. Suddenly, he announced that he wanted to move the boat to Isthmus Cove on the other side of the island."

R.J.'s decision may not have been as hot-tempered as it seemed. Rain had been falling intermittently since they left Marina del Rey that morning. Weather broadcasts carried a storm alert.

Natalie disagreed with her husband. Having sailed that same course many times, she feared that if a storm hit before they reached the shelter of Isthmus Cove they'd be in worse danger than they were now. But R.J. went up to the bridge and started gunning the engines in spite of her protests.

Flying into a rage, Natalie said that, unless R.J. desisted, she intended to spend the night in a hotel in Avalon. Davern tried to reason with him, but to no avail. Finally, R.J. told Davern to take Natalie ashore in the *Valiant* and to stay with her for protection.

Christopher Walken remained on the *Splendour* with R.J. According to Davern, Walken had started to feel seasick and had already retired for the night.

Natalie and Davern checked into the Pavillion Lodge, where she booked two rooms with her American Express card and ordered champagne sent up. Davern claimed later that he never used his room. They sat talking in Natalie's room, she on the bed and he on the floor, until the wine ran out and they fell asleep.

The next morning Natalie felt in a conciliatory mood and sent Davern to check the location of the *Splendour*. R.J. also must have had second thoughts, for the yacht was still moored in the same spot. Natalie and Davern returned in the dinghy and over breakfast everybody decided that the cruise would continue despite the still inclement weather.

This time with Natalie's approval, they headed for Isthmus Cove after all so that Walken could see more of the natural splendors of Catalina. Nearly ninety percent of the island, which is twenty-one miles long and eight miles wide, is owned by the Santa Catalina Conservancy. A herd of four hundred buffalo roams free among its thousands of wildlife inhabitants.

When the *Splendour* reached its destination, R.J. dropped anchor among numerous other vessels that were out for the long holiday weekend. The area was a popular gathering spot for the sailing crowd because of its proximity to the tiny community of Two Harbors. Once an outpost for the Union Army during the Civil War, it now consisted of a yacht club, a general store and a self-proclaimed "world famous" restaurant called Doug's Harbor Reef Saloon.

Right after lunch, Natalie insisted on taking Walken into Two Harbors to point out some of the spots where Hollywood studios used to shoot exteriors for their jungle and seafaring epics during the 1920s and '30s. R.J. intended to go along, but Natalie talked him out of it. Proud of her ability to navigate the dinghy by herself, she wanted to prove to Walken that her husband wasn't the only sailor in the family.

Natalie and Walken were gone all afternoon. Later, a number of boaters remembered seeing Natalie and a male companion "buzzing" past them in the dinghy. Some patrons of Doug's Harbor Reef Saloon recalled seeing Natalie and Walken drinking and talking at the bar for several hours.

By dusk, Natalie and Walken hadn't returned to the *Splendour*. R.J. started to get very tense. Around six o'clock he said to Davern, "It's getting to be dinnertime, maybe we should go ashore." He radioed for a water taxi to come to pick them up.

Since the Harbor Reef Saloon was the town's only eatery, R.J. and Davern headed straight there. "When we walked in, Natalie and Chris were sitting at the bar and looking very cozy," Davern said later. "R.J. made a reservation for eight o'clock dinner and he convinced Chris and Natalie to leave their bar stools so we could all sit at a cocktail table together.

"But when they sat down, Natalie stayed next to Walken. They both had a good buzz on, and she was flirting with him constantly."

If R.J. disapproved of Natalie's behavior, his attitude mellowed after he had a few drinks himself. A couple of diners who were fans of the Wagners sent two bottles of champagne to their table. By the time the foursome moved into the dining room, all were in a festive mood, according to restaurant manager Don Whiting, who'd known Natalie and R.J. for years.

"After they placed their food orders, they didn't like the wine list, so they sent Dennis Davern back to the yacht for some of their own bottles," Whiting said.

Providing background music that night was Jack Wright, an accordionist known as "Gypsy John." The Wagners and their companions clapped along as he played some Irish jigs and then complied with Natalie's request for "Somewhere My Love." Besides its obvious romantic appeal, the love theme from *Dr. Zhivago* always had a special meaning for her because of her Russian ancestry.

As time passed and the wine continued to flow, the atmosphere at the Wagners' table grew tense.

"Natalie was drunk and she was definitely being flirtatious with Christopher Walken. She was giving him suggestive looks, snuggling close and caressing his shoulder. R.J. looked very upset," said Don Whiting.

Around ten o'clock the Wagners began to argue. R.J. wanted to return to the *Splendour*, but Natalie insisted on staying.

When people at surrounding tables started to stare, R.J. said to her, "Let's do this in private, not here in front of strangers."

Paying the sixty-five-dollar tab with a hundred-dollar bill, R.J. told the waiter to keep the change. As the quartet got up to leave, they followed Natalie's example by swallowing the last of their wine and then smashing the empty glasses against the wall in the Russian tradition.

They were all noticeably drunk as they made their way down the dock to board the dinghy. "Due to the rain, the dock was very slippery and Natalie fell a couple of times," said Don Whiting. As a part-time member of the area's Harbor Patrol, he phoned the officer on duty to keep an eye out for the *Valiant* and make sure that its occupants got back safely to the *Splendour*.

Natalie and Walken sat together in the stern of the dinghy, R.J. and Davern in the bow. Curtis Craig of the Harbor Patrol, who tailed after them, said later that he could hear everybody laughing as they reached the yacht and climbed on board around eleven o'clock.

It was probably the last time that anyone except her husband and their two companions saw Natalie Wood alive. At seven-thirty the next morning her body was found floating face down in an isolated cove less than a mile from the *Splendour*'s mooring.

Two young children were left motherless. The story-book romance that had seemingly beaten all the odds against endurance had suddenly ended in tragedy and mystery.

ONE

Chance Meeting

THE SPRING of 1950 wasn't the best time for a girl to choose a future husband. President Truman had just ordered the Atomic Energy Commission to rush-develop a hydrogen bomb. And if America's scientists didn't blow up the world first, the war brewing in divided Korea threatened to have a similar catastrophic effect.

But in Hollywood, U.S.A., the dream factories carried on regardless. Just outside Beverly Hills at 20th Century-Fox, Betty Grable, Bette Davis, Tyrone Power, Clifton Webb, June Haver, Anne Baxter, James Stewart, Linda Darnell, Richard Widmark, Gene Tierney, Gregory Peck and Ann Sheridan drifted in and out, working in such films as *My Blue Heaven*, *All About Eve*, *The Gun Fighter* and *An American Guerrilla in the Philippines*.

For every star there were ten times as many supporting players and extras roaming the lot. Two of them just happened to be a veteran eleven-year-old actress and a new twenty-year-old contractee who was making his first Fox film. Gawky and pig-tailed, she had temporary braces on her teeth for her role as James Stewart and Barbara Hale's daughter in *The Jackpot*. Bronzed and crew-cutted, he wore Marine fatigues for *Halls of Montezuma*.

"I was walking to the commissary with my mother and I saw Robert Wagner heading toward me," Natalie Wood remem-bered. "As he passed, I turned around and gaped. As soon as I caught my breath, I whispered to my mother, 'When I grow up, I'm going to marry him.'"

After lunch Natalie insisted that her mother take her to the publicity department so that she could get a glossy 8 × 10 photograph of her new crush. Carefully and lovingly, she car-ried it home and hung it in her bedroom. It was always the last thing she looked at before she switched the light off to go to sleep.

Robert John Wagner, Jr., was born in Detroit, Michigan, cap-ital of the American automotive industry, on February 10, 1930. Since his father already answered to "Bob" and the fam-ily abhorred the nickname "Junior," he became known as R.J., initials that also happen to be the abbreviation for "junior" in reverse.

Although R.J. comes from a well-to-do family, it hadn't al-ways been that way. "My father was a self-made man, born in Kalamazoo, Michigan. He went through the eighth grade and then started hawking newspapers in the street," R.J. said.

Moving up to peddling everything from underwear to elec-trical plugs, R.J.'s father earned a respectable fortune, lost it in the 1929 stock market crash and then made it back again selling paint to Detroit's auto manufacturers. Somewhere along the way he met and married office stenographer Hazel Boe (nick-named "Chatty" for her talkative ways). The couple had one other child, Mary Lou, R.J.'s senior by four years.

Crazy as it may seem, Robert Wagner was addressed and de-livered to Hollywood at the tender age of seven. In 1937 his father became a manufacturer's representative in the steel busi-ness and transferred operations to industrially booming Los Angeles. So that he would get there for the start of the new school term, R.J. was dispatched by himself in advance of the rest of the family, via the Atchison, Topeka & Santa Fe Railway.

With a tag tied to his coat that read "Deliver this boy to Mrs. Pierce, Hollywood Military Academy, Hollywood, California," R.J. arrived at the Detroit terminal hand in hand with his father, who boosted him up the Pullman-car steps and tipped the porter ten dollars to make sure that he reached his destination safely.

As soon as the train pulled out, R.J. ripped off the shipping label and enjoyed the benefits of being a rich man's son. For the trip, his father had given him his own checking account, out of which he had to pay all his expenses and school tuition. During a stopover in Albuquerque, R.J. popped into a souvenir shop to buy an antique revolver to protect himself against imagined onslaughts by savage Indians and masked bandits as the train continued its way through the wild West.

California proved to be paradise for the sports-crazy boy, who shuttled between the family's new home overlooking the Bel-Air Country Club and a weekend retreat in the San Fernando Valley where he had his own pinto pony to ride. At school he was an athletic standout—captain of the baseball team, a member of championship swimming and tennis squads, and a trophy-winning horseman.

But as a scholar R.J. proved woefully indifferent. By his own account, he was a hellion who dropped in and out of nine schools before graduating from high school at nineteen. A former teacher at Black-Foxe Military Academy recalled that R.J. "could do anything—except study." He was expelled from another military school for "lack of application" and for starting a one-cadet rebellion against marching and discipline.

His adventurous personality involved him in one spirited escapade after another. With his BB gun, he shot out all the lights in the locker room of the Bel-Air Country Club, which proved particularly embarrassing to his father, a member of the board of directors. Another time R.J. purchased a secondhand motorcycle, neglecting to acquire either a certificate of ownership or a license. He wound up in the Beverly Hills police station, suspected of possessing stolen goods.

Just weeks after arriving in California, seven-year-old R.J.

made his acting debut in a Hollywood Military Academy production of *The Courtship of Miles Standish.* To his extreme discomfiture, he played Priscilla Alden, in blond curls and a long dress. A few months later he felt more at ease portraying his own sex as the crippled Tiny Tim in the school's Christmas show.

By that time R.J. had also met his first movie star. "Fred Astaire's son was a classmate, and I used to play at his house," R.J. said. "Fred was wonderful to me. Little did we know that thirty years later we'd be acting as father and son in *It Takes a Thief.*"

Given the environment, it was almost impossible for R.J. *not* to contract movie fever. Many of his schoolmates were children of actors, writers, directors, producers and studio executives. His first dates were with daughters of stars: Alan Ladd's Carol Lee, Harold Lloyd's Gloria, Joan Bennett's Melinda and Gloria Swanson's Michelle, most of whom also had acting ambitions.

"I never wanted to be anything but an actor," R.J. once said. "Christ, what more could you ask for? This is a wonderful, wonderful business, getting to make people smile, taking them out of their lives for a little while. Of course, I wasn't doing that yet. I was just a nice-looking kid hanging around doing movie-star impersonations."

When not at school, R.J. was either sitting in a movie theater or climbing over studio walls to watch them being made. "And when I was at home I was usually in my bedroom acting out scenes from whatever I'd seen that day," he said.

R.J.'s father, however, started preparing him for a business career. "When R.J. was very young I made a deal with him," Wagner, Sr., said. "Every dollar he earned himself, I would match. It turned out to be a pretty expensive arrangement. R.J. was a real hustler. He kept a little notebook and jotted down every dime he made."

While growing up, R.J. always had a part-time or summer job. Starting out by shining shoes, he also delivered papers, sold magazine subscriptions, set pins in bowling alleys, currycombed horses, washed dishes, dusted private airplanes at Clover Field and sold automobiles on the UCLA campus. But the job he enjoyed most was caddying at the Bel-Air Country

Club golf links, situated just across the way from the Wagner residence.

Like MGM, the club had "more stars than there are in heaven" on the membership rolls. Working for them at the rate of seven dollars a day, R.J. got to rub elbows with the likes of Clark Gable, Cary Grant, Bing Crosby, Alan Ladd and Gary Cooper.

Randolph Scott, another of his employers, said: "You couldn't help liking R.J., but he wasn't the best caddy in the world. You could be right in the middle of a backswing and he'd break out with some question about the picture business."

In 1949, R.J. ended his scholastic career upon graduating from St. Monica's High School, where he was one of the few non-Catholic students (the Wagner family belonged to the Unity faith, which is similar to Christian Science). During R.J.'s final semester a priest-teacher of chemistry and physics gave him extra tutoring on alloys and the processing of steel, to prepare him for a job in his father's business.

That summer R.J. was sent East to learn the steel business first hand, everything from furnacing and milling to warehousing and marketing. Returning to Los Angeles, he took over a desk in his father's office, soliciting new accounts. Receiving a monthly retainer of $200, he was also promised a share in the profits at the end of the year.

R.J. lasted six months. For his father, it meant the fulfillment of a dream to have his son following in his footsteps. Approaching sixty, he intended to turn the business over to R.J. when he retired.

But R.J. was miserable. He wanted another kind of life. His heart was within those studio walls and sound stages he had to pass on the way to work every day. Finally he confronted Wagner, Sr., and confessed his unhappiness.

"I was pretty selfish," R.J. remembered. "I didn't really think about what a blow it would be to Dad. He had so many plans for the two of us. He was disappointed all right, but *how* disappointed he didn't let on. Even though I'm sure he hoped it would prove just a whim, when I asked him to give me a year off to pursue a career as an actor, he agreed. If he hadn't, I could have become embittered and resentful, and he could have changed my whole life."

Part of the deal that R.J. made with Wagner, Sr., was that the latter would help him out financially while he tried to establish himself. R.J. eventually piled up a debt to his father of $4,000 (equivalent to about $50,000 today), all of which he later repaid.

There being almost as many tall, handsome and inexperienced star hopefuls in Hollywood as oranges on the trees, R.J. had little that distinguished him from the rest of the crop. But he did have determination and some influential friends.

"Clark Gable—'The King' himself—was the man who really got me into the movies," R.J. said. "I used to caddy for him. He was my idol. I worshiped him. He was the one who talked to me, advised me and helped me. And when he saw I was really serious about an acting career he took me to MGM to meet Billy Grady, who was head of casting."

Gable's introduction led nowhere beyond a bit part in MGM's *The Happy Years*, a nostalgic comedy-drama about a prep school, based on Owen Johnson's popular Lawrenceville stories. One of the lesser efforts of master director William Wellman, it had no major stars in the cast. Juvenile actors Dean Stockwell, Darryl Hickman and Scotty Beckett played the leading roles.

R.J. had such an insignificant part that he not only didn't receive billing but was also unrecognizable. In his only scene he participated in a baseball game and wore a catcher's mask that completely covered his face. It was definitely not the kind of scene-stealing moment from which stars are sometimes made. All that R.J. received was a smidgen of before-the-camera experience and one day's pay of $37.50, which he promptly spent on a membership card in the Screen Actors Guild.

R.J.'s first breakthrough came when he was "discovered" while dining with his parents at their favorite Beverly Hills hangout, the Gourmet. His fondness for jazz and pop music had caused him to become friendly with Lew Spence, the restaurant's resident piano player. On this particular evening R.J. went over to chat with Spence and ended up clowning and singing along with him.

If it could happen to Lana Turner at a soda fountain counter, why not Robert Wagner in a cocktail lounge? One of the patrons that night happened to be Henry Willson, an agent for Famous Artists and a former talent scout for producer David

O. Selznick. Willson was captivated by R.J.'s impromptu performance and invited him to come to his office the next day to discuss a representation deal.

Willson, when later asked what had impressed him about R.J. that night, said, "The changing expressions on his face. I watched his face mirror every thought and word—that, together with his looks and bright, clean-cut personality. I saw a sincerity and a relaxed quality that would come right across the screen. Given the opportunity, I was sure he couldn't miss."

Since Henry Willson was homosexual (years later the scandal press called him "the man who corrupted Rock Hudson"), his interest in R.J. may have been more than just professional. Whether that entered into it or not, R.J.'s career definitely started to zoom after he signed with Famous Artists and placed himself under Willson's guidance.

Although he'd recommended it for some of his other clients, Willson didn't urge R.J. to change his name. Willson's creations included "Rock Hudson" for Roy Scherer, "Tab Hunter" for Art Gelien, "Tony Curtis" for Bernie Schwartz, "Rory Calhoun" for Francis Durgin and "Guy Madison" for Robert Moseley. But "Robert Wagner" had a classical ring and R.J. felt glad about retaining it. If he wasn't going to follow in his father's footsteps in business, he could at least perpetuate his name on theater marquees.

To determine R.J.'s capabilities, Willson sent him to MGM to test for director Fred Zinnemann, who was looking for an unknown to team with newcomer Pier Angeli in *Teresa*, the story of a returning World War II veteran and his Italian bride.

The shell-shocked soldier was supposed to be psychoneurotic. "I was so nervous making my first screen test that all I really had to do was act natural," R.J. remembered.

After a hundred and fifty actors were tested, the results had to be shipped to New York for screening by MGM's home-office executives before the final choice could be made. In the meantime, Henry Willson got a copy of R.J.'s test and sent it to 20th Century-Fox, which always needed raw recruits to develop as its established stars faded and were put out to pasture.

In R.J.'s dashing handsomeness, Fox potentate Darryl F. Zanuck thought he detected something of Tyrone Power, who, at thirty-six, had started to show signs of declining popularity as the studio's top leading man. Approaching twenty, R.J. was roughly the same age as Power had been when he joined Fox in the 1930s.

Never one to gamble for high stakes except while playing poker with his mogul cronies, Zanuck offered R.J. a ninety-day option on a seven-year contract, starting at seventy-five dollars a week. Although R.J. could earn more than that caddying at the Bel Air Country Club, he was happy to take it when he received the crushing news that another newcomer, John Ericson, got the role he'd been after in *Teresa.*

While it seemed as if R.J. had sold himself into bondage, it wasn't a bad deal for a novice. Like most of the major studios since the 1920s, 20th Century-Fox operated under a mass-production system that was part factory and part training school. Young contractees like R.J. were given rigorous training in nearly everything: acting, singing, dancing, swimming, fencing, archery, tumbling, boxing, horseback riding, whatever. At Fox, the men also had to learn to fire a machine gun because the studio made so many war movies.

During his ninety-day trial period R.J. worked mainly as a "test boy." As he remembered it: "I was the guy they always used when the studio was making screen tests of new actresses. And believe me, no job is more dead-end than that. The only interesting thing that came out of it was when they were testing a new kid and asked me to do a couple of scenes with her. Her name was Marilyn Monroe."

Fox dramatic coach Helena Sorrell worked with R.J. from the day he signed on. Seeing her as the key to his future, R.J. haunted her office. Often just to get him out of her hair, she used him in about a hundred tests with other hopefuls. It was a good way for him to acquire poise before the cameras and to practice voice projection. "At first he used his voice so poorly that I had to pretend to be hard of hearing to get him to speak up," Sorrell said.

In March 1950, R.J. made a qualifying screen test of his own with actress Patricia Knox. Zanuck and the production staff were impressed enough to pick up his option and assign him to a small role in the patriotic flag-waver *Halls of Montezuma.* Ironically, R.J. was already a member of the Marine Reserves, which he joined after graduating from high school to avoid being drafted into full-time military service.

In his first two years at Fox, R.J. played a spectrum of roles, all but two in military uniform. He was a Marine buck private in *Halls of Montezuma* . . . a Navy underwater demolition swimmer in *The Frogmen* . . . Claudette Colbert's junior exec son-in-law in *Let's Make It Legal* . . . a Marine company clerk in John Ford's James Cagney-Dan Dailey remake of *What Price Glory?* . . . a Marine band musician and inventor of the sousaphone tuba in the John Philip Sousa bio-musical *Stars and Stripes Forever* . . . the driver of a six-horse stagecoach in *The Silver Whip.*

Right or wrong for the part, R.J. took whatever came along in order to survive under the studio system. "It was a struggle because I wasn't the only young hopeful being groomed for stardom," he recalled. "There were two hundred and fifty of us, all earning the princely starting sum of seventy-five dollars a week and all equally good-looking. One of the little tortures the studio used in case you got out of hand was to have another guy who looked just like you standing around as a reminder that you were easily replaceable. And the cold fact was—you were!"

R.J. took his obligation to the studio very seriously. Right from the beginning, he developed a reputation for diligence and a cooperative spirit, an eagerness to please. Everybody liked him: fellow actors, producers, directors, executives. At no time was he ever accused of being difficult or uncooperative à la Marlon Brando, James Dean and Montgomery Clift.

On the other hand, nobody thought he possessed the talent of those actors. Robert Wagner seemed just another WASP-faced pretty boy who still had a lot to learn if he was ever going to make it into the top ranks.

In 1952, R.J.'s career finally ignited with a small role in *With a Song in My Heart,* a lavish Technicolor musical based on the life of singer Jane Froman, who was permanently crippled in a plane crash while entertaining the troops during World War II.

R.J.'s scenes numbered only two, both with Susan Hayward as Jane Froman. In the first one, R.J. was a shy GI to whom Hayward sings "Embraceable You" in a New York nightclub scene. Later in the film, R.J. and Hayward meet again, only by this time he's a patient in a military hospital. The familiar sound of her singing suddenly and miraculously snaps him out of shellshock.

"It was a tremendously moving moment because it was a true incident," R.J. said later. "The trouble was, I didn't know very much what I was doing. The director, Walter Lang, told me, 'Just watch her.' He reminded me of a trick they always used with Rin Tin Tin. When they wanted the dog's ears to perk up, they'd have a guy standing off camera with a cat in a bag, which was let loose at the crucial moment."

For Robert Wagner, Susan Hayward proved the perfect "cat." "When she started to work, I automatically responded," he said. "What she did was produce a whole reaction in me. I couldn't say to myself, 'Now I have to get tears in my eyes,' because I didn't know how to do that. Susan must have realized it because, my God, she was so helpful. When she sang 'I'll Walk Alone' to me, I got so caught up in the moment that the tears just came. It got to her, too, because after it was over she ran to her dressing room and just fell apart."

Released during the darkest moments of the Korean War, *With a Song in My Heart* hit a sensitive nerve with movie audiences and became a box-office smash. R.J.'s two brief scenes got a disproportionate amount of attention and approval.

"Mothers who saw the picture apparently thought of their sons in service overseas; wives thought of husbands; girls thought of sweethearts," R.J. said.

"After the opening, the fan mail poured in—I guess five thousand letters a week—and I became a bobby-sox idol along with Tony Curtis, Tab Hunter and Rock Hudson. We were *the* guys," he laughed, looking back on it years later.

Women of all ages were suddenly captivated by Robert Wagner. They fell in love with his boyish smile, his perplexed brow, his youthfulness that seemed to need soothing and assurance. Before he knew it, he had a national fan club with 250,000 members and a monthly newsletter called the *Wagner World.*

Fox's publicity department, which up to then had had a tough time getting coverage for R.J. in the fan magazines, suddenly became deluged with requests for interviews and photographs. Also came the first questions about his personal life. What kind of women did he like? Was he dating anyone special?

If so, how soon were they getting married? All rather prim and proper, but that's the way it was in the 1950s.

The truth was that R.J. found himself too wrapped up in his career for a serious emotional involvement. If he wanted a bed partner, he didn't have to look very far. Actresses, extras and secretaries camped outside his dressing-room door.

The nearest thing to a steady girl friend was Mary Frances Reynolds, better known as Debbie and two years younger than R.J. They first met during their schooldays, when she belonged to the cheerleading squad at Burbank High. Now she was a contract player at MGM. Like R.J. at Fox, she wasn't a star but definitely on the way to becoming one.

"Debbie and R.J. were a perfect match," said mutual friend Gene Kelly. "She was the Girl Next Door and he was the All-American Boy. Although they were in their twenties, they were simple, fun-loving kids. Both of them still lived at home with their parents."

Realizing the publicity value of such a coupling, the press agents at 20th Century-Fox and MGM encouraged R.J. and Debbie to go around together, hoping it would develop into a serious romance that would make hot copy for the gossip columnists and fan magazines. In the end it fizzled, reportedly because Debbie tried to coerce R.J. into matrimony.

"Debbie was a member of what Hedda and Louella used to call the 'No Necking League,' which was a polite way of saying 'No Sex Before Marriage.' She wouldn't sleep with R.J. unless he married her. R.J. considered that sexual blackmail, so Debbie eventually gave up on him and had better luck with Eddie Fisher," said a veteran publicist.

In 1953, at the age of twenty-three, R.J. finally took an apartment of his own in Beverly Hills when his father decided to semiretire and bought a new house in La Jolla, a resort town a hundred and twenty miles from Los Angeles. Now earning $350 a week, R.J. adopted the lifestyle of a bachelor playboy but always shied away from talking about his escapades.

"If I go out with one woman a few times, it's considered a romance. If I date a lot of girls, then I'm a Casanova. It's one of those 'heads-you-win, tails-I-lose' deals. I don't think it's anybody's business what I do," R.J. said at a time when he was often seen on the town with starlet Lori Nelson or his boss's daughter, Susan Zanuck.

Sometimes R.J. got involved in some curious relationships. While making *Titanic,* he became very chummy with forty-six-year-old Barbara Stanwyck, one of the stars of the epic sea tragedy. R.J. was dazzled by Stanwyck's distinguished career and looked to her for professional guidance. She seemed happy to provide it.

Insiders were not too surprised when an affair developed. Divorced the previous year from Robert Taylor (who left her for a much younger German actress named Ursula Thiess), Stanwyck still carried a torch, spending many of her lonely hours with men who resembled her ex-husband. Robert Wagner was very much in the Robert Taylor mold: a boyish innocence combined with a beautiful face and physique. R.J. was also in his early twenties, the same age Taylor had been when Stanwyck fell in love with him.

Darryl F. Zanuck exploded when his studio spies tipped him to what was going on. With R.J. on the verge of becoming a major romantic star, a liaison with an imperious silver-haired divorcee old enough to be his mother was hardly likely to please his fans or to perpetuate his clean-cut image.

Zanuck summoned R.J. to his office to remind him of the morals clause in his contract. It stipulated that Robert Wagner could be dismissed for conduct that "will tend to shock, insult, or offend the community or ridicule public morals or decency, or prejudice 20th Century-Fox or the motion picture industry in general."

Unfortunately, gossip about R.J. and Stanwyck had already started. The International News Service had just sent out a wirephoto of them supposedly having a wild night at the Mocambo. To make it appear even more scandalous, the photograph had been retouched by cutting out Clifton Webb and several other people from the *Titanic* cast who shared the table with them.

Before any more damage could be done, Fox's publicity chief, Harry Brand, arranged for R.J. to telephone Louella Parsons with a gallant denial of the rumors. "All this talk has definitely hurt my chances for a real friendship with a fine woman and a great actress," R.J. said. "She is a sensitive lady beneath that tough outer shell. She's changed my whole approach to my work, made me want to learn the business completely. It means a lot when someone takes time with a newcomer, especially when it's Barbara Stanwyck."

To further quell the talk, Fox matched up R.J. with sexy starlet Terry Moore, another contractee causing the studio similar problems, only in her case the older lover was multimillionaire Howard Hughes. Conveniently, R.J. and Moore were about to start working together in *Beneath the Twelve-Mile Reef.* When they were sent to Tarpon Springs, Florida, for location scenes, the publicity department really did a number on them.

"From the moment the first photographer snapped R.J.'s picture with me, we became America's sweethearts," Terry Moore recalled. "Nothing could have been further from the truth. R.J. was madly in love with Barbara Stanwyck and I had Howard. He called me every night and R.J. called Barbara. Looking back, it seems to have been such a waste to have been in a romantic place like that with R.J. and both of us pining away for other people."

In a matter of days, newspapers across the country carried a headline bulletin that Robert Wagner and Terry Moore were engaged to be married.

"Phone calls and telegrams came pouring in," Moore said. "The first ones I received were from my girl friends, Debbie Reynolds and Susan Zanuck. I knew they'd much rather wring my neck because each of them had a huge crush on R.J. His parents couldn't understand why they hadn't been told about our plans. Barbara Stanwyck and Howard Hughes must have been the only two people in the world who knew the story wasn't true."

Beneath the Twelve-Mile Reef was intended to be Robert Wagner's breakthrough movie, the first time that Fox assigned him to the central starring role in one of its high-budgeted "A" productions.

With tremendous fanfare, the studio had just introduced CinemaScope, a giant wide-screen process designed to lure the lost audience away from their 12-inch TV tubes. *Reef* was only the third film made in the process (preceded by *The Robe* and *How to Marry a Millionaire*). As a major selling point, advertising proudly boasted of the first underwater photography using the anamorphic lens!

Unfortunately for R.J., his portrayal of a Greek-American sponge diver became one of the 1950s' best examples of glorious miscasting. With his hair dyed jet black and permed into tight curls, he had to spend an hour in the beauty parlor every morning before starting work.

Although Walter Winchell called R.J.'s performance the most convincing since Frank Sinatra in *The Kissing Bandit*, *Beneath the Twelve-Mile Reef* grossed $4 million and certainly didn't lose him any admirers. The Fox publicity department claimed that he now received more fan mail than Marilyn Monroe, the queen of the lot. During a single month in 1953 he was featured on the covers of seven magazines.

R.J.'s popularity gave him bargaining power that he didn't have before. His agent, Henry Willson, negotiated a new Fox contract starting at $1,250 a week, a hefty increase from R.J.'s previous $350. To celebrate the deal, Darryl Zanuck personally selected R.J. for a role that he seemed born to play, and that also earned him a second nickname: Prince Valiant.

Based on an exquisitely drawn comic strip by Harold R. Foster that had been running in newspapers since 1937, *Prince Valiant* marked both the high and low points of R.J.'s entire movie career. In theory, the $3 million CinemaScope spectacle about King Arthur's reign could have done for Robert Wagner what *Gone With the Wind* did for his friend Clark Gable. Prince Valiant was every bit as famous and indelible a character as Rhett Butler.

But the similarity ended there. R.J. still had a long way to go before he acquired Gable's competency or charisma. And the script, though written by the revered Dudley Nichols (whose credits included *Stagecoach* and *The Informer*), hardly measured up to the cerebral standards of Edgar Rice Burroughs, let alone Margaret Mitchell.

The ineffably confusing plot concerned Prince Valiant's efforts to restore his father, Augar, the Christian king of Scandia, to his throne and become a knight of the Round Table. "Robert Wagner reads his lines in a vacant monotone and wears a long Dutch bob and a jerkin with the skittish air of a man trying to be funny in a lady's hat," said *The New Yorker*'s critic. "If Mr.

Wagner is preposterous, his colleagues aren't what you would call a help."

Janet Leigh, R.J.'s leading lady, remembers him "good-naturedly submitting to the indignity of being with the ladies in the hair department every morning to don his Prince Valiant pageboy wig. Our director, Henry Hathaway, ragged R.J. a bit much. But on reflection I decided he was really helping him, protecting him, tugging on every string, pulling out all stops, making him better than he thought he was."

While *Prince Valiant* struck gold at the box office and earned him legions of new fans among children and adolescents, R.J. never lived it down. "During production, all the young Method-trained actors used to drop by the set for a good howl, watching me with my body stocking, rubber-padded calves and magical singing sword," R.J. said. "Dean Martin was walking around the lot one day and bumped into me while I was wearing the wig and full regalia. He talked to me for ten minutes before he realized I wasn't Jane Wyman."

In the spring of 1954, R.J. won *Photoplay* magazine's coveted Gold Medal Award as "Fastest Rising Star of the Year," placing him in company with Alan Ladd and Marilyn Monroe, who were that year's picks in the established star category.

Although 20th Century-Fox was reluctant to hand R.J. another demanding star vehicle like *Prince Valiant*, Zanuck decided to give him a chance to prove what he could do by casting him in an offbeat dramatic role as Spencer Tracy's half-breed son in *Broken Lance*. A remake of the studio's 1949 *House of Strangers*, the CinemaScope super Western was more like *King Lear of the Plains*, pitting an aging cattle baron against his children for the control of his empire.

During location work in Arizona, R.J. established one of the most important friendships of his life with tough, sardonic Spencer Tracy. Already white-haired at fifty-four, Tracy perhaps saw R.J. as what his own son, John, might have become had he not been born incurably deaf.

"Spence became my old friend, my mentor, and the man I thought of as a second father," R.J. remembered. "I'm a lucky fellow: a great man touched my life deeply. I was a mere lad in the shadow of this giant, but Spencer Tracy influenced me, inspired me and gave me a sense of self-esteem. Everything I know about working hard and having standards I learned from him. 'You've got to grow,' he kept saying. 'You mustn't stand still.' "

On the set, R.J. watched Tracy like a hawk. In advance of their scenes together, Tracy would coach him and R.J. tried hard to please. "I was desperate to be an actor," he said. "I could mimic all the greats—Gable, Cagney, Cary Grant—but I kept doing things the way I thought *they'd* do it. Spence kept saying, 'Don't act; just be yourself,' but it took me a helluva long time to learn that."

Meanwhile, R.J. found himself falling in love with costar Jean Peters. Four years younger, she was a fetching brunette whom 20th Century-Fox developed as a replacement for the similarly named Gene Tierney and Jeanne Crain. Like Terry Moore, Peters belonged to Howard Hughes's farflung harem, but she apparently didn't consider herself to be his exclusive property.

"Hughes was maniacally jealous," said director Edward Dmytryk. "When Jean wasn't working, she had to stick to her quarters in case he telephoned. R.J. was with her constantly. He had a place of his own, but it was a waste of the studio's money because he was rarely there. God knows what would have happened if Hughes had taken his private plane and flown in for a surprise visit, but he never did."

The affair reportedly continued very discreetly after R.J. and Jean Peters returned to Los Angeles. Ultimately, Howard Hughes got wind of what was going on and threatened R.J. with career extinction and worse if it didn't stop immediately. To prevent Peters from succumbing to further temptations, Hughes subsequently married her. Giving up her career, she lived under private guard in a bungalow at the Beverly Hills Hotel until their divorce in 1971.

When *Broken Lance* was released in August 1954, R.J. received his best reviews yet. "Robert Wagner's brooding, sullen portrayal of the half-breed son marks his arrival in the ranks of mature actors," said the influential Hollywood *Reporter*. "Gone are the statuesque poses of ego. His love scenes are notable for the fact that he is a romantic-looking man who doesn't try to look hammily romantic."

To capitalize on his success in *Broken Lance*, Fox assigned R.J.

to another epic Western, *White Feather*, portraying a government agent trying to make peace with warring Cheyennes. One of countless imitations of Fox's 1950 classic, *Broken Arrow*, it had nothing new to say on the problems of racial prejudice or the maltreatment of the American Indian. With a poor script, uninspired direction and removed from the influence of Spencer Tracy, R.J.'s performance suffered noticeably.

White Feather also brought bad luck. While working on location under primitive conditions near Durango, Mexico, R.J. came down with severe amebic dysentery. Because of lack of adequate treatment at the onset, he kept having recurrences, lost twenty-five pounds and was unable to work for more than a year.

R.J.'s illness cost him a role that might have established him as a swashbuckler in the Tyrone Power-Errol Flynn mold. Darryl Zanuck purchased the screen rights to Thomas B. Costain's best-seller, *Lord Vanity*, as a vehicle for R.J., but the project was shelved until he recuperated. By that time Zanuck had resigned as studio head to become an independent producer for Fox, based in Europe. His successor, Buddy Adler, had no enthusiasm for *Lord Vanity* or Robert Wagner, it seemed.

"After Zanuck resigned," R.J. said, "I was left there as the perennial juvenile with a tennis racket in one hand and a beach ball in the other. And they never let me grow up. If I went in and complained, they'd say: 'What the hell are you beefing about? You're getting $2,000 a week and working. There are hundreds of kids out there doing nothing.' "

Since Buddy Adler seemed in no rush to put R.J. back to work, friends came to his rescue. Robert L. Jacks, a former Zanuck aide who moved over to United Artists as an independent producer, arranged to "borrow" R.J., Joanne Woodward, Jeffrey Hunter and Virginia Leith for a film he had originally planned to make at Fox. Entitled *A Kiss Before Dying*, it was based on a well-reviewed chiller by Ira Levin, who years later wrote the classic *Rosemary's Baby*.

The producer must have had a lot of confidence in Robert Wagner's acting ability; the leading role of a ruthless psychopathic killer had originally been intended for Montgomery Clift. Surprisingly, R.J. rose to the challenge and gave a superb performance, although he never received much credit for it.

Owing to a glut of similar fare on television, the movie received poor distribution, playing the bottom of double bills in many places.

Spencer Tracy again proved his friendship by insisting that Paramount Pictures hire R.J. to appear with him in *The Mountain*, Tracy's first free-lance project after ending his twenty-one-year association with MGM.

R.J. felt deeply honored when Tracy arranged for him to get costar billing above the title, but the older man also had a selfish motive for doing that. Besides a $200,000 salary, Tracy was getting a share of the profits. With a fan idol like Robert Wagner playing opposite him, the movie seemed more likely to attract the younger and larger audience who considered Spencer Tracy a dinosaur of the pretelevision age.

Based on a novel by Henri Troyat, *The Mountain* gave R.J. another chance to break out of stereotyping with an unsympathetic role. As Tracy's younger brother, he persuades the retired mountaineer to help him rescue the passengers of a crashed airliner high up in the Alps. Following a perilous climb, it turns out that R.J. is only interested in looting the wreckage and intends to leave the sole survivor to die because he wants no witnesses.

Filming *The Mountain* on location at Mont Blanc, near the French village of Chamonix, turned out to be a three-month ordeal for R.J. and Tracy because of the altitude and all the climbing involved. "Tracy took it like a soldier, but R.J. was always bitching that the director was working them too hard," the unit publicist recalled. "Finally, Tracy got fed up with listening to him and said, 'Young man, you ought to get down on your knees every night and thank God you work in the most overpaid business in the world."

Although *The Mountain* turned out to be a critical and box-office dud, an incident took place during production that forged an even closer bond between R.J. and Tracy. When two people face death together and live to tell about it, there's a special communion far beyond mere friendship.

"Spence used to say it was the worst thing that ever happened to him, and it was the same for me," R.J. remembered. "There was this *téléphérique* that went up to the mountain. It's the largest single-span cable railway in the world, with no pylons along the way. I was afraid to go on it, so Spence said, 'Look, we'll ride up together.' Halfway there, with a drop of three thousand feet below us, it slid off the track! The front end went up and banged the cable. We just hung there in space. I was sure we were going to drop."

When the engineers at the summit discovered what had happened, they sent down a work car, which was nothing more than an exposed platform. "We were supposed to get out of our car and climb into the other one with three thousand feet of nothing underneath," R.J. said. "We couldn't do it. We were frightened out of our wits that we'd never make it. Even if we hadn't slipped during the transfer, we couldn't have clung to that platform for the several miles to the top. We hung there for forty-five minutes with our car swaying in the wind. A woman and a couple of young kids were there, and a so-called conductor. What a conductor does in a *téléphérique* I can't imagine.

"Spence was numb—just staring into the void below. Finally, they succeeded in backing the car onto the cable again. Inch by inch. I thought the car was going to cut the cable in half. But they managed to balance us and suddenly up we went. Spence had signed a pledge not to drink until the production was over, but we both had a stiff one as soon as we got off."

The Mountain holds a special place in the love affair that developed between R.J. and Natalie Wood. It was the movie he took her to see on their very first date.

TWO

Natasha

ROBERT WAGNER *chose* to be an actor, but Natalie Wood got forced into it at an early age to help support an indigent family of four.

She was born in San Francisco, California, on July 20, 1938. Her real name was Natasha Nikolaevna Zacharenko, but it became Natasha Gurdin after her Russian father, Nikolai Zacharenko, took up American citizenship as Nicholas Gurdin.

Born in Vladivostok, Gurdin left Russia as a youth when his family fled to China during the Communist Revolution. But his parents were so poor that they sent him and a brother to Canada to be raised by relatives. He eventually moved to San Francisco, where he eked out a living as a carpenter and day laborer.

Natasha's mother, the former Maria Kuleff, originally came from Siberia. Expert at weaving tales, she claimed alternately to be the daughter of gypsies and of landowning aristocrats, but she probably had the same kind of impoverished background as Nicholas Gurdin.

The difference was that Maria arrived in America with a two-year-old daughter, Olga, and a husband who soon abandoned them for another woman. After getting a divorce, Maria married Nicholas Gurdin in 1937.

When Natasha arrived the following year, the baby caused such a strain on the family's finances that they were forced to move from San Francisco to the small inland city of Santa Rosa. Although the Great Depression had supposedly lifted, the Gurdins lived in near poverty among other immigrants who, like themselves, could barely speak English.

In her youth, Maria Gurdin had dreamed of becoming an actress or ballet dancer with one of the great Moscow theater companies. Given the family's needy circumstances, it's not surprising that she began to transfer those ambitions to her youngest daughter.

Natasha had "star quality" written all over her. At four she was an adorable pigtailed pixie, only two feet tall and weighing thirty-five pounds. Her enormous dark eyes perfectly mirrored her happy, mischievous personality.

For lack of funds beyond the twenty-five cents it took to get both of them into the Santa Rosa movie houses, Natasha's only professional training was watching Hollywood child stars from her mother's lap.

"My mother used to tell me that the cameraman who pointed his lens out at the audience at the end of the Paramount newsreel was taking my picture. I'd pose and smile like he was going to make me famous or something. I believed everything my mother told me," Natalie Wood remembered.

Since the Gurdins couldn't even afford bus fare to San Francisco, let alone Los Angeles, who knows what direction Natasha's life would have taken if a 20th Century-Fox production unit hadn't come to Santa Rosa in the spring of 1943 to film scenes for *Happy Land*, which starred Don Ameche and Frances Dee.

The inspirational tearjerker took place in Iowa, showing how Middle America was learning to cope with the hardships and tragedies of World War II. But Fox saved money and travel time by shooting the exteriors in Santa Rosa, which had already proved its effectiveness as a small-town setting in Alfred Hitchcock's *Shadow of a Doubt*.

When *Happy Land* director Irving Pichel issued a casting call for localites to work as extras, Maria Gurdin rushed there with Natasha. They arrived early enough that both of them were among the fifty hired for a dollar a day.

"During a work break, my mother took me over to where Irving Pichel was sitting and practically dumped me in his lap," Natalie recalled. "She had told me beforehand exactly what to do. I curtsied for him and then I went into a little song and dance. I don't think he thought I was Shirley Temple, but he was impressed enough to give me a bit part in the picture."

Pichel asked if Natasha could cry on cue. "Of course she can," lied Maria Gurdin, who wasn't about to lose such an opportunity or the extra five dollars that went with it.

Luckily, it was a situation that any child could relate to. Natasha had to lick an ice cream cone, accidentally drop it and then burst into tears. She did it perfectly on the first take. As a reward, she got to eat two more cones that had been made up in case she flubbed it.

And so, just a few weeks before her fifth birthday, Natasha Gurdin made her acting debut in what turned out to be fifteen seconds of screen time when *Happy Land* was released at the Thanksgiving holiday in November 1943. It wasn't enough to send Hollywood agents rushing to Santa Rosa to sign her up, but it did result in a rather bizarre offer from the movie's director.

"Irving Pichel took a liking to me and wanted to adopt me," Natalie remembered. "My mother thought he was joking, of course, and said, 'Oh, sure! You can have her whenever you please!' Several weeks later Pichel turned up at the house with a couple of attorneys and adoption papers drawn up. My mother was mortified, and my father was furious. Pichel really expected to take me home with him that day."

Pichel was bitterly disappointed. But when he left Santa Rosa he promised the Gurdins that, if another part came along that suited Natasha, he would definitely contact them. For two years he corresponded with the family and sent Natasha gifts.

In the summer of 1945, just as the end of World War II seemed imminent, Pichel finally kept his word when International Pictures signed him to direct *Tomorrow Is Forever.* The RKO release concerns a war veteran who, mistakenly reported killed in action, comes home to find his wife married to another man. Starring Orson Welles, Claudette Colbert and George Brent, the tearjerker had a major part for a child actress as an orphan refugee caught up in the romantic triangle.

When Irving Pichel telephoned Maria Gurdin to ask her to bring Natasha for a screen test, Maria overreacted and packed the whole family off to Los Angeles to live. Her husband opposed the whole idea, but he lacked the backbone to stand up to his wife's overpowering ambition to make Natasha a star.

Surprise of surprises, Natasha flunked the screen test. Now two years more sophisticated than when she made *Happy Land,* she needed more than a dropped ice cream cone to make her cry when Pichel told her to. She just couldn't do it. Sadly disappointed, the director sent her home and started looking for another girl.

After two days of weeping and wailing over what would become of the Gurdin family, Maria returned to the studio via an unguarded back entrance, barged into Pichel's office and told him the score. Feeling pity for her, he agreed to a second test.

Natasha became paralyzed with fright. If she failed a second time, it not only meant the end of everything, but her mother would never forgive her.

Trying to be helpful, her teenage stepsister, Olga, suggested a trick that she'd learned in the high school dramatic society. She reminded Natasha of a moment several years earlier when their dog got killed by a car while crossing the road. Although Olga had told her to avert her eyes from the pitiful scene, Natasha looked anyway and started to bawl.

"When Mr. Pichel tells you to cry, try to relive that experience and the tears will come as naturally as the rain," Olga said.

The advice worked. Natasha got the part, but at what further damage to her psyche for having to recall such a horrifying and traumatic incident?

From that time on, they never had to blow camphor in her eyes to make her cry, as they did with some other child actors. "Mother would remind me about my dog being run over or tell me some other sad story. She made me do emotion memories, which was actually the Method, though I didn't know that at the time. She would get me all worked up and say to the director: 'She's ready. Start shooting,' " Natalie recalled.

Soon after *Tomorrow Is Forever* started filming, William Goetz, head of International Pictures, came on the set and told Natasha, "From now on, your name will be Natalie Wood." He explained that Natalie was a close American approximation of Natasha. The surname had been chosen in honor of his close friend and business associate, director Sam Wood.

"I didn't mind 'Natalie,' but I hated 'Wood,' " she recalled. "It didn't suggest a nice image to me. It made me think of a block of wood. I asked if it couldn't be Woods. Then I could think of trees and forests. Goetz just laughed. 'Don't fret,' he said. 'When you see "Natalie Wood" up in lights, you'll love it!' "

With her name changed, Natalie Wood quickly established a reputation as a scene-stealer, first with Orson Welles. "She was so good, she was terrifying," Welles said later. "She was *professional* when I first saw her. I guess she was born professional, and yet she was also so innocently childlike. At the studio, she used to play with my valet, Shorty, a midget who was the only person on the set smaller than she was."

Before *Tomorrow Is Forever* was even released, America's most read magazine, *Life*, ran a two-page article about Natalie, describing her as "Hollywood's latest wonder child." Photos showed her romping topless in her underpants with a pet kitten.

After a preview of the movie, Louella Parsons wrote, "As a tiny refugee, Natalie Wood gives a remarkable performance for a child. She eats your heart out." Parsons' archrival, Hedda Hopper, reported that at least four studios were clamoring to sign Natalie to a long-term contract on the strength of her performance.

But before that could happen International Pictures exercised an option in Natalie's contract by signing her to a seven-year deal, starting at $350 a week. Since International didn't make that many movies, William Goetz started "loaning" Natalie to other companies, running her asking price up to $1,000 a week within a couple of years.

After directing Natalie in *Tomorrow Is Forever*, Irving Pichel hired her again for Paramount's *The Bride Wore Boots*, with Barbara Stanwyck and Robert Cummings. Then Natalie went to 20th Century-Fox to play Gene Tierney's daughter in *The Ghost and Mrs. Muir* and stayed on to make a family comedy called *It's Only Human* with Maureen O'Hara, John Payne and Edmund Gwenn.

"Nobody at Fox thought much of the picture or the title, so they changed it to *The Miracle on 34th Street* and dumped it on the market in the middle of the summer, which seemed the worst possible time for a fantasy about Santa Claus," Natalie remembered. "But the public loved it. The studio had everything riding on *Forever Amber*, which failed abominably at the box office, while this little black and white film made millions and became a classic."

As the confirmed nonbeliever in Santa Claus, Natalie seemed to touch more hearts than any child star since Margaret O'Brien in *Journey for Margaret* during the early days of World War II. By November 1947 she was so popular that Macy's invited her to appear in the department store's annual Thanksgiving Day parade. The trip to New York was her first direct contact with the public and she hated it.

"Everybody pulled on my pigtails and all I got to eat was chicken salad for breakfast, lunch and dinner," she said when she got home.

By that time Natalie was nine years old. Her formal education consisted of attending the schools of whatever studio she happened to be working at. California law stipulated that from first grade to age eighteen a young actor had to spend three hours of every workday in the classroom.

"I always felt guilty when I knew the crew was sitting around waiting for me to finish my three hours," Natalie recalled. "As soon as the teacher let us go, I ran to the set as fast as I could."

Natalie was a straight A student and reportedly one of the few child actors to excel at arithmetic, which in later life helped her to manage money very well.

"In all my years in the business, I never met a smarter moppet," said Joseph L. Mankiewicz, who directed Natalie in *The Ghost and Mrs. Muir* in 1947. "When I first met her, I asked her if she could read the script. With great authority, she said, 'Yes.' I asked her if she could spell, and she nodded again. Then I really threw her a curve and I asked her to spell Mankiewicz. She did! After that, we continued the game every morning."

Natalie became a creature whose life was totally controlled by two forces—her mother and the studios. "I couldn't even go to the bathroom alone. My mother or the state social worker who was required to be on the set always went with me," she said.

"I spent practically all of my time in the company of adults. I was very withdrawn, very shy. I did what I was told and I tried not to disappoint anybody. I knew I had a duty to perform, and I was trained to follow orders."

Natalie's mother became known as one of Hollywood's most dedicated stage mothers, rivaled in protective ferocity only by Elizabeth Taylor's. Stern and shrewd, Maria Gurdin scrutinized scripts, haggled over fees and dressed Natalie to look even more childish than she was in order to give her career a longer lease on life.

Until Natalie was well into her teens, her mother expected her to curtsy for adults as if being presented to the tsar. Mrs. Gurdin turned their modest suburban home in Sherman Oaks into a sort of shrine to Natalie Wood. There were photographs of her everywhere, stacks of scrapbooks of press clippings. Every night Maria lighted candles in front of an oil-painted portrait of Natalie that hung over the living-room fireplace.

Mrs. Gurdin never permitted anything to stand in the way of Natalie's career. When her third daughter, Svetlana, was born in 1946, Maria started taking the baby to the studios within the week. Olga, the daughter of Maria's previous marriage, had to be sent to live with her father in northern California because her mother no longer had any time for her.

Natalie's father was still the family's chief support. According to California's Coogan Law (passed after child star Jackie Coogan's mother and stepfather bilked him of millions in earnings), part of Natalie's income had to be put in trust until she was twenty-one. The balance could only be used for expenses of which she was the primary beneficiary.

To keep the rest of the brood clothed and fed, Nicholas Gurdin worked as a studio carpenter, woodcarver and propmaker. Needless to say, he obtained those jobs through the intercession of his wife, who, in turn, owed any power she had to the fact that she was Natalie Wood's mother.

Being made subservient to both wife *and* daughter turned Gurdin into an aloof, uncommunicative man. He would sit alone in a corner at night reading the old Russian books from his childhood. Eventually he became a heavy drinker who vented his frustrations by erupting into violent rages and smashing the furniture and china. Often Mrs. Gurdin had to take the children to a motel and spend the night there until he sobered up.

All that Nicholas Gurdin ever talked about was moving the family back to Santa Rosa. "Why don't we quit while we're ahead?" he used to say. Obviously he saw that as the only way of restoring himself to a position of dominance in the family.

But Maria Gurdin would never let that happen as long as Natalie could get work in Hollywood. After her success in *Miracle on 34th Street*, she made from two to four movies a year. Dubbed "The Pigtail Kid" by the fan magazines, she played the archetypal daughter or little sister: funny, endearing or bratty, depending on the role.

"Because I was petite, I could pass for younger than I was," Natalie said. "When I was eleven, I could still play a nine-year-old. When I was thirteen, I could seem eleven."

In the truest sense, she was not a child *star*. No big starring vehicles were built around Natalie Wood, which undoubtedly helped her when she later switched over to adult roles. She would not be considered a has-been at sixteen, as Shirley Temple, Margaret O'Brien and Peggy Ann Garner were.

"I was never typed, I projected no special image like Shirley Temple, for example. And so, when I grew up, the public didn't expect me to look the same as I did as a child. As my personality matured and changed, the public seemed to accept that change and didn't compare me to the youngster I was," Natalie remembered.

In the ten-year period between the ages of four and fourteen, Natalie made nineteen movies, most of which weren't particularly memorable but at least provided opportunities to work with and learn from major stars like James Stewart, Irene

Dunne, Margaret Sullavan, Bing Crosby, Jane Wyman, Fred MacMurray and Rex Harrison.

Two of those early movies also left indelible scars. At age eight, while making the family programmer *Driftwood* at second-string Republic Pictures, Natalie accidentally fell off a wooden bridge onto the concrete studio floor, seriously injuring her left wrist.

Because the bone was distended, the attending physician recommended surgery, but Natalie's Russian mother, who had a peasant's fear of doctors and hospitals, refused. As a consequence, Natalie had a permanent deformity which she always covered with jewelry or long sleeves. Although it could hardly have been as noticeable as precursor Deanna Durbin's deformed right arm, it caused Natalie needless psychological trauma for the rest of her life.

Natalie always believed that her fear of deep water started at fourteen, when she portrayed Bette Davis' daughter in *The Star*, a 20th Century-Fox drama about a fading movie queen trying for a comeback. In one of her scenes Natalie had to dive off a yacht and swim to a raft. She'd been promised a stunt double, but director Stuart Heisler reneged in the interest of realism and ordered Natalie to do it herself.

"I went into hysterics that must have been heard all the way to Catalina," Natalie recalled. "Bette Davis heard me screaming and came out of her dressing trailer to find out what the commotion was. It was the only time I ever saw Bette's legendary temperament surface, and it was not in her behalf. When she discovered what was going on, she shouted at the director, 'If you make Natalie do that, I'll walk off the picture. Who do you think she is, Johnny Weissmuller?' A double was sent for pretty fast."

By the time of *The Star*, Natalie had reached the so-called "awkward age," not quite a young woman but not a child either. Parts were becoming difficult to obtain. Luckily, Revue Productions signed her for a weekly TV comedy series, "Pride of the Family," which premiered on the ABC network in October 1953.

Portraying the daughter of Paul Hartman and Fay Wray, Natalie earned $400 a week. Although she could get more per week in movies, it worked out to about the same thing because there were no lulls between assignments.

"The show was pretty bad," Natalie said, "but it kept me steadily employed for a year. By the time it was over, I was ready for grown-up roles."

That first adult part came right afterward, also on television, when Natalie appeared in an adaptation of Sherwood Anderson's *I Am a Fool* on "General Electric Theatre," the CBS anthology series hosted by Ronald Reagan. While many people assume that Natalie's association with James Dean started with *Rebel Without a Cause*, it actually began a year earlier, in that half-hour teleplay. Dean, then twenty-three, gave Natalie, sixteen, her first on-screen kiss.

Natalie never forgot her introduction to James Dean, which took place during rehearsals in a former warehouse in downtown Los Angeles. "Except for Jimmy, everybody arrived on time," she said. "There was a loading platform elevated about six feet above the floor where we were all assembled. Jimmy suddenly pulled in there on his motorcycle, peered down at all of us, parked and then leaped down because there were no steps.

"He was wearing an old tattered T-shirt and blue jeans, with a safety pin holding his fly together. He was already somewhat of a legend among young actors and exactly what I expected, a junior version of Marlon Brando. He mumbled so you could hardly hear what he was saying, and he seemed very exotic and eccentric and attractive."

When the lunch break came, everybody wandered off and Natalie started looking for a place to eat. Suddenly she glanced around and discovered Dean following her.

"He asked me if I wanted to have lunch and I said sure. 'Hop on the motorcycle,' he said. I was thrilled," Natalie said. "We went speeding off to some greasy spoon. While we were eating, I could tell he was trying to remember something. Then, in the middle of his sandwich, he said, 'I know you. You're a child actor.' I said that was true, but it was a lot better than acting like a child. He didn't get it for a moment. Then he started to laugh, and I laughed too. And that's how a wonderful friendship began."

Although James Dean very quickly became a major influence

on Natalie Wood, they apparently were never romantically involved. Natalie always denied it, and their friends believed her.

"Natalie was too young for Jimmy, and she was also the wrong sex," said an actor friend. "Jimmy's much-publicized affairs with Pier Angeli and Ursula Andress were purely platonic, cover-ups for his homosexuality. Among the S&M leather crowd, he was known as 'The Human Ashtray,' an explanation of which is better left to the imagination."

On the strength of her television work, Natalie was signed to a contract by Warner Brothers. By coincidence, it also happened to be the new home lot of James Dean.

"Like every other studio in town, we were desperate to develop new stars who would appeal to the younger crowd, who were about the only people attending movies anymore," said Warner executive William Orr. "Natalie had a pleasing personality. She came across as hip and sharp, without being overbearing or offensive. Teenage girls could accept her as one of their own. Boys would regard her as the kind of girl friend they'd like for a steady."

In the beginning Warner Brothers didn't know what to do with Natalie, first casting her as a young bleached blond Helen of Troy (sexpot Virginia Mayo played the adult woman) in *The Silver Chalice*. The biblical epic about the Greek craftsman who made the cup used by Jesus at the Last Supper marked TV and stage actor Paul Newman's movie debut. It turned out so disastrously that it almost ended his film career before it started. When the bomb premiered on television years later, Newman took ads in the trade papers apologizing for its dreadfulness and his own embarrassing performance.

After *The Silver Chalice*, Warners "loaned" Natalie to Universal for the Rock Hudson-Anne Baxter Western soap opera, *One Desire*, which was important only because it marked the professional debut of Natalie's eight-year-old sister, Svetlana Gurdin, in a bit part. Their mother had started to mold a new puppet once Natalie became old enough to assert her independence. To make sure that no one missed the family connection, Svetlana became known as Lana Wood.

In March 1955, Natalie finally got her big chance by being cast opposite James Dean in *Rebel Without a Cause*, a landmark movie that might never have been produced had it not been for an "act of God."

Elizabeth Taylor, then married to Michael Wilding, became pregnant, so Warner Brothers had to postpone the start of *Giant*, which she had been scheduled to make with Dean and Rock Hudson. But Dean created such a sensation in his first major movie role in *East of Eden* that the studio wanted to put him back to work as soon as possible. The quickest way was to reactivate a property it had once nearly filmed with Marlon Brando, the star to whom Dean was most often compared.

Surprisingly, although Natalie was a Warner Brothers contractee, she wasn't the original choice for the role of Dean's sensitive, misunderstood girl friend in *Rebel Without a Cause*.

"When we were going down a list of names, I eliminated Natalie because she had been a child actress. As far as I was concerned, the only child actress who ever made it as an adult was Helen Hayes," said director Nicholas Ray. "So we tested everybody from Debbie Reynolds to Jayne Mansfield, who was a hallucination on the part of the casting department. When she came in, we didn't even put film in the camera."

Meanwhile, Natalie heard about this major role being unfilled and began to campaign for it by hanging around outside Ray's office. Finally the director asked her in for an interview but he wasn't terribly impressed.

"When I walked Nat to the door afterward," Ray recalled, "I noticed that outside waiting for her was this tough-looking kid with a fresh scar across his face, so I said, 'We'll talk again.' She seemed to be on that kind of trip."

At home a few nights later, Nicholas Ray received an urgent phone call from actor Dennis Hopper, who'd already been cast in the movie and had just gotten involved in a car crash while out driving with Natalie and a couple of other friends. They were being held at the Van Nuys police station. Hopper wanted Ray to come there immediately with a doctor because Natalie had suffered a concussion.

"When I got there, my doctor and Natalie's parents had just arrived," Nicholas Ray said. "Her mother, whom I'd known for years because she was always hanging around the studios, runs up to me and says, 'Oh, Nick, what happened? You know this is no good for her father, he's just getting over a heart attack.' No questions about how's Natalie or anything.

"Then my doctor comes out after examining her and says that Natalie's okay, but that she wants to talk to me first before her parents are allowed in. So I go in and Nat is lying down on a couch. Before I can say anything, she grabs me, pulls me close and whispers in my ear, 'You see that son of a bitch?' And she's pointing to the precinct doctor. 'Well, he called me a juvenile delinquent! Now do I get the part?' "

Of course she did, and very quickly the forty-three-year-old Nicholas Ray became the most important person in Natalie's life. A former screenwriter and stage director, Ray had only been directing films since 1949 but had developed a cult following with the socially conscious *They Live by Night* and the bizarre Joan Crawford Western, *Johnny Guitar.*

"Nick Ray was able to judge someone almost like a psychiatrist and say things to that person which were meaningful to them," Natalie said later. "Nick gave me a career, in a sense, because up to that time, although I'd worked a lot, it was kid stuff, really. And by giving me that chance, he also gave me a kind of insight and point of view of my work. Because he regarded me as an actress with a meaningful contribution to make, I felt better about myself and better about my work, and I learned to stand up to the studio about some of the choices they wanted to make for me. So, in a way, I guess he taught me to be more of a rebel, which benefited me tremendously."

Natalie also became romantically smitten with Nicholas Ray, who was her senior by twenty-eight years and divorced from actress Gloria Grahame. "Nick was the great love of Nat's life, at least for the ten weeks that they were working together," Dennis Hopper recalled.

"Every time she'd come home after being out late with Nick, there'd be screaming by her parents, and she'd run out of the house crying. There wasn't much they could do about it though, because Nat was bringing most of the money into the house," Hopper said. "Eventually Nick broke it off in the gentlest way he could. The relationship had nowhere to go—a middle-aged man and a girl who was still jail bait."

Because he believed it would help their performances, Nicholas Ray encouraged the young actors in the cast to hang out together. Natalie became sort of the moll in a group that consisted of James Dean, Sal Mineo, Dennis Hopper and Nick Adams, all of whom seriously aspired to being the next Great American Actor. At last she'd found the world she'd been unconsciously seeking.

"They were the gods," Natalie recalled. "I just wanted to be exactly like them. What we used to talk about was how unhappy we were. Whoever was the unhappiest, whoever came closest to suicide the night before, he was the winner."

Making *Rebel Without a Cause* created serious problems for Natalie at home. "My parents didn't approve of the people I was hanging out with," she said. "They hated the script and didn't want me to do it. They thought it presented parents in a very bad light."

But Natalie stuck to her guns. She wanted to change her image, to raise the level of her work, and she succeeded. The film eventually made her a full-fledged star, an actress to be reckoned with, at the ripe old age of seventeen.

While making *Rebel Without a Cause*, Natalie was getting ready to graduate from Van Nuys High School. For years she'd looked forward to the moment when she could walk across the school stage and receive her diploma like any other kid.

But when the big moment finally arrived, Warner Brothers recognized the publicity value and sent press agents, photographers and newsreel cameramen. Natalie's private triumph was violated and she burst into tears.

"It's no wonder that I broke out in a big way," Natalie recalled. Suddenly she was running wild, starting with burning some of her teachers in effigy in the backyard barbecue pit to celebrate her emancipation. She also sent a box of cigarette butts to the high school principal, who'd once reprimanded her for trying to smoke in class.

If Natalie seemed to be turning into a real-life *Rebel Without a Cause*, she had some of the wind knocked out of her sails on September 30, 1955. That night, while speeding to a sports car rally in Salinas, California, James Dean died instantly in the collision of his silver Porsche with another auto on Highway 41 near Paso Robles.

Natalie reacted as if she were the widow, telling reporters, "Our feelings for each other were the kind that come rarely to a man and woman. I'll never forget Jimmy." For years afterward she wore a gold love bracelet that he once gave her on one ankle. At home, she always kept a sculptured bust of Dean on prominent display.

Although Warner Brothers hadn't planned it that way, *Rebel Without a Cause* entered release just four days after the twenty-four-year-old actor's death, setting off the greatest wave of Hollywood cult worship since Rudolph Valentino.

Natalie became one of the main beneficiaries of the movie's tremendous popularity. Millions of teenagers not only identified with the alienated heroine but also transferred some of their pent-up emotions about James Dean to Natalie Wood. Girls copied her hairstyle, makeup and clothes. Boys put her on a pedestal as the ideal sweetheart.

Natalie received a 1955 Academy Award nomination as Best Supporting Actress for her performance. Her parents bought her a silver fox stole to wear to the presentation ceremony but she never got a chance to show it off to the national TV audience. The Oscar went to Jo Van Fleet for *East of Eden* (the other nominees were Betsy Blair in *Marty*, Peggy Lee in *Pete Kelly's Blues* and Marisa Pavan in *The Rose Tattoo*). Natalie had also gone prepared to accept the statuette for James Dean if he'd won in the Best Actor category (for his debut film, *East of Eden*), but Ernest Borgnine copped it for *Marty*.

Despite a huge upsurge in Natalie's fan mail, Warner Brothers was caught unprepared. She'd already been cast in a small though pivotal role in John Ford's *The Searchers*, as a girl kidnapped by Indians and long sought after by her uncle, John Wayne. Although hailed as one of Ford's greatest Westerns, it showed Natalie to little advantage. She appeared only in the last scenes, with sister Lana Wood playing her as a child earlier on.

By the time Natalie finished *The Searchers*, the studio attempted to cash in on the success of *Rebel Without a Cause* by teaming her with another darling of the teen set, twenty-four-year-old Tab Hunter. Ads for the Western romance, *The Burning Hills*, described it as a scorcher, with "today's hottest teenage star team flaming with the fire of first love."

Jack Warner hoped to build Natalie Wood and Tab Hunter into a regular team, so the publicity department worked overtime trying to get coverage for them by fostering an off-screen romance for the benefit of the fan magazines. Although Natalie and Hunter often went out together socially and her mother liked him the best of all her swains, nothing serious developed, reportedly because he fancied another of her pals, Sal Mineo.

Encouraged by Natalie's Oscar nomination, the studio decided she was ready for more adult emotional roles and next assigned her to *A Cry in the Night*. Playing the kidnapped daughter of police lieutenant Edmond O'Brien, she spent most of the crime melodrama trying to avoid being raped by psychopath Raymond Burr.

As undoubtedly intended, Natalie shocked the Hedda Hopper-Louella Parsons-Sheilah Graham circuit when she started keeping steady company with Raymond Burr, who was twenty-one years older and who also outweighed her by about two hundred pounds. Known around Hollywood as a bon vivant and "perennial bachelor" (a euphemism for "possibly gay"), he introduced Natalie to the world of gourmet restaurants and bohemian night spots.

The underage gamine turned up everywhere with the foppishly dressed hulk. Waiters served her straight ginger ale with a wink. She had arranged beforehand to have it spiked with vodka or bourbon.

"We had escargots for dinner last night," she raved to Hedda Hopper when the latter asked for the inside story on rumors that she intended to marry Burr. "We have a plan, but it's in the future. I don't see anyone now except Raymond—except when he's out of town, of course. But we do have a definite understanding."

The understanding lasted about a month. Burr made the mistake of being *in* town too much. The dating became routine. Natalie wanted the excitement of being involved with a sophisticated older man, but also the freedom to change companions as often as her restless moods demanded.

Fan magazines called her a "wild girl," clucking with delighted dismay over her antics in articles like "Is Natalie Riding for a Fall?" and "How Natalie Plays with Fire and Never Gets Burned." Off screen, she looked the part in low-cut dresses, heavy makeup, gaudy jewelry and dark glasses, an appearance that she kept in modifying degrees throughout her life. She always wore ultra-high stiletto heels to compensate for her five-feet-two inch height.

Aided by the Warner publicity machine, Natalie was turning into the Hollywood embodiment of the discordant sociosexual rhythms of her generation. If girls growing up in dreary suburbs wanted to look and behave like Natalie Wood, it was because she seemed to be the fulfillment of the promise of happiness which everyone went to California looking for. She became as much a part of their lives as drive-ins, surfers, necking and hot-rodding.

THREE

Love in Bloom

IN THE SUMMER of 1956, Natalie started working on a second movie with Tab Hunter. Although *The Burning Hills* was still unreleased, Warner Brothers had so thoroughly saturated the fan magazines and gossip columns with propaganda about "the screen's most sizzling star-team" that it made good business sense to have a follow-up ready if the public responded favorably to the pairing.

This time it was a contemporary romantic comedy, *The Girl He Left Behind*, with Natalie, of course, in the title role. Hunter played her rich, spoiled-rotten suitor; suddenly drafted into the peacetime Army, he emerges a "real" man and proves himself a worthy match.

With most of the movie focusing on Hunter's experiences in boot camp, Natalie had only two weeks of actual work. For the rest of the time, her contract required her to be on standby for press interviews, photo sittings or whatever else the publicity department arranged for her. One day they delegated her to represent Warner Brothers at a charity luncheon being held at the Beverly Wilshire Hotel.

Among many other celebrities attending was Robert Wagner. Suddenly he found a photographer from *Photoplay* tapping him on the shoulder and asking if he'd pose for a few candids with Natalie Wood. He'd be delighted, provided it was okay with Miss Wood. It was. They moved to an uncrowded corner of the room and chatted briefly while flashbulbs flared. Nothing more than shoptalk about their current movies, his being *Between Heaven and Hell* with Terry Moore and Broderick Crawford.

Not a dazzling beginning for a romance, but a spark had definitely been struck. Remembering the moment, R.J. said, "Natalie was so beautiful—those eyes. I fell head over heels in love with her, the way they wrote about it in songs."

Yet he hesitated about pursuing her, fearful of the age difference between them. Natalie was still a teenager, while he was well into his twenties. His previous lovers were his own age or older, as in the case of Barbara Stanwyck.

But R.J. couldn't erase Natalie from his thoughts. Finally he obtained her telephone number from Nick Adams and called for a date. He had to attend a preview of *The Mountain,* his new picture with Spencer Tracy. Would she like to go with him?

Natalie couldn't believe it when Wagner told her that the preview was July 20, which happened to be her eighteenth birthday. How lucky can a girl get? she wondered. Robert Wagner for a birthday present! Should she tell him of her childhood crush? She decided not to, lest he consider her a sexual pushover should it get around to that.

But it didn't, not for a long time. "I positively couldn't stand R.J. when we first started dating," Natalie recalled. "He kept lecturing me, talking to me like a Dutch uncle. He used to say things like 'Who do you think you are, anyhow—the Queen of Sheba?' 'What makes you think you've got some kind of built-in guarantee that you're going to remain a Hollywood hotshot? You'd better buckle down to work. Forget all those gossip column notices about what a grand femme fatale you are, and learn your trade.' He was right, of course, and that made me detest him all the more."

"I was a different type than Natalie was used to," R.J. once said. "Remember, I was eight years older than she was. She was still playing Bing Crosby's daughter when I was out at Pebble Beach playing golf with Bing. When we first met, she was running around with the Jimmy Dean disciples, part of the young rebel movement. Me, I was around what you might call the old guard of Hollywood. Tyrone Power, Clifton Webb, Barbara Stanwyck, Bogie and Lauren Bacall, Gary Cooper. This was a whole new world to her. Hell, Gilbert Roland took us to the bullfights down in Mexico. She'd never known anything like that."

In the beginning the dates were casual and infrequent. "There was a long line outside of Natalie's door, and it took a fellow a helluva long time to get to the front door and knock," R.J. said. Chief among his rivals was Scott Marlowe, an Actors Studio alumnus who, despite being hyped as "the next James Dean," had so far landed only a few minor movie and TV roles.

"Scott is the great love of my life," Natalie breathlessly informed Louella Parsons. "I hope to marry him someday. I can now. I'm of legal age and don't even have to have a welfare worker on the set anymore."

Marlowe, however, was soon replaced by playboy Lance Reventlow, the only child of Woolworth heiress Barbara Hutton. But before you could whistle "I Found a Million Dollar Baby in the 5 and 10 Cent Store," Natalie also started running around with actors Robert Vaughan and John Ireland. The latter coupling raised more than a few eyebrows among the bluestockings. Besides being old enough to be Natalie's father, Ireland also had a reputation as the best-endowed cocksman in Hollywood.

Then along came Elvis the Pelvis. Much to the despair of fifteen million teeny-boppers, it appeared for a while that Natalie Wood would become the first Mrs. Elvis Presley. He was then twenty-one, three years older than Natalie, and had just finished making his first movie, *Love Me Tender.*

Not surprisingly, the Tennessee bumpkin fell hopelessly in love with his leading lady, flame-haired sexpot Debra Paget. But neither Paget nor her domineering stage mother could stand Elvis, so the romance died aborning.

Nick Adams, who had a knack for ingratiating himself with

people who had the power to get him jobs, had become one of Elvis' closest buddies. To help him forget Debra Paget's rejection, Adams introduced Elvis to Natalie. She was dazzled, not so much by Elvis himself as by the Presley phenomenon. Without question, he was the biggest star to burst from the pop music field since Frank Sinatra in the early 1940s. What a boost to her ego and to Natalie Wood's public image to become the love object of the King of Rock 'n' Roll.

Suddenly Natalie was racing all over town on the back of Elvis' motorcycle, holding on to him for dear life. Because he was the antithesis of the hip, rebellious crowd she generally palled around with, she found him fascinating.

"Elvis was so square," Natalie remembered. "We'd go to P. C. Brown's ice cream parlor and have hot fudge sundaes, or to Hamburger Hamlet for a burger and Coke. He didn't drink, he didn't swear. He didn't even smoke. It was like having the date that I never had in high school. I thought it was really wild."

Elvis' deep-rooted piousness also amazed Natalie. "I'd never been around anyone who was that religious," she said. "He felt he had been given this gift, this talent, by God. He didn't take it for granted. He thought it was something that he had to protect. He had to be nice to people, otherwise God would take it all away."

In November 1956, Natalie got into trouble at Warner Brothers by claiming to be ill and canceling a highly publicized appearance at the Hollywood Bowl, standing up 15,000 teenagers from the Young Men's Christian Association who were supposed to crown her queen of their annual harvest festival. Instead, Natalie boarded a plane with Elvis Presley and flew to Memphis to meet his family.

But if a wedding was in the offing, plans were quickly aborted by Gladys Presley, Elvis' maniacally possessive mother. She made absolutely certain that the lovebirds never had a moment alone together while they were at the Presley homestead. When the couple did manage to escape on Elvis' gargantuan Harley Davidson, he seemed only interested in exhibiting her like a prize Kewpie doll to an endless array of kissing cousins and high school cronies.

Natalie had intended to stay a week in Memphis, but two

days were all she could tolerate before she sneaked a telephone call to her mother in Los Angeles.

"Get me out of this and fast," Natalie said. "Ring me right back and pretend somebody's dying or something."

The ruse worked, but it also ended the affair, if it could be termed that. "Elvis can sing, but he can't do much else," Natalie told her family when she got home.

Although her relationship with Elvis was presumably never consummated sexually, Natalie earned a million dollars' worth of publicity from it. More importantly, it ignited the jealousy of Robert Wagner, who wasn't one of Elvis' greatest fans. They'd met while Presley filmed *Love Me Tender* at 20th Century-Fox. Always one of the studio's fair-haired boys until then, R.J. resented the preferential treatment accorded Elvis. The bosses saw him as a sort of greaseball Messiah who would raise Fox from the box-office doldrums.

Soon after Natalie returned from Memphis, R.J. phoned and wanted to know if she was really serious about "that creep." Natalie said it was none of his damn business but that she still had a few open dates in her engagement book. Did he have something specific in mind?

As a matter of fact he did. R.J. couldn't contain his pride over the new boat he'd just bought, *My Lady*, which he kept docked at Newport Beach. If Natalie would meet him there one night, he'd take her out for a moonlight sail.

Natalie had a terrible sense of direction and usually got lost whenever she had any place important to go. But this time she arrived at Newport Beach in her white Thunderbird convertible without a snag.

"How I ever found it I'll never know, but I'm glad I did," Natalie remembered. She'd never been out on the water alone with a man before. She was bewitched, by the romantic setting and especially by R.J., who lost all his inhibitions to the sea air. One thing led to another and, to use a quaint expression that Natalie favored, they "locked limbs" for the first time. Forever after, they celebrated the date—December 6, 1956—as the most important one in their association.

They had fallen madly in love. "We felt very strongly about each other—needed each other," R.J. said. "It was an intense and marvelous relationship."

Still, they decided to keep steady company for a while before making a rush decision that might be regretted later. Both were already married to their careers. It would have been a mistake to pretend otherwise.

But secrets of any kind, especially romantic ones, are impossible to keep in Hollywood. It wasn't long before Natalie Wood and Robert Wagner became a main topic of gossip in the movie colony. Warner Brothers looked favorably on the match because they thought Natalie had been playing too fast and loose with a constantly changing cast of lovers. Publicists at 20th Century-Fox also jumped on the bandwagon. They had been running out of ways to get space for R.J., who hadn't exactly been Errol Flynn in the love department.

But what really launched the romance into Hedda and Louella's proverbial Seventh Heaven were the fan magazines, which then numbered over a dozen, all with similar-sounding names like *Photoplay, Modern Screen, Motion Picture, Silver Screen, Movieland, Movie Life,* et cetera. Although the fanzines were starting to take a more realistic attitude toward Hollywood as a result of competition from *Confidential* and similar muckraking periodicals, they still followed a gushy, moonlight-and-roses line that dated back to the silent era.

Every decade had its real-life courtships and marriages between stars. In the twenties the biggest headline grabbers were Mary Pickford and Douglas Fairbanks, and Vilma Banky and Rod La Rocque. In the thirties, it was Clark Gable and Carole Lombard, and Robert Taylor and Barbara Stanwyck. The forties brought Humphrey Bogart and Lauren Bacall, and June Allyson and Dick Powell. Natalie Wood and Robert Wagner capped the fifties, following in the path of Janet Leigh and Tony Curtis and Debbie Reynolds and Eddie Fisher.

It had been two years since Debbie and Eddie settled down to apparent domestic bliss. Millions of single girls, new brides and bored housewives who purchased most of the fan magazines sold in America needed a new starrified couple to focus their hopes and dreams on. Natalie and R.J. were *it!*

For the principals themselves, it couldn't have happened at a more propitious time. Had it not been for the landslide of romantic publicity, Natalie Wood and Robert Wagner might have ended on the scrap heap of fifties has-beens, along with Ty

Hardin, Lori Nelson, John Smith, Diane Varsi, John Kerr, Tina Louise and many other young stars whose careers bottomed out along with the decade. They were making one turkey after another. In a business where the philosophy has always been "You're only as good as your last picture," both definitely had reason to worry.

R.J. took whatever assignments 20th Century-Fox threw his way. Usually the movies were instantly forgettable, as in the case of *Between Heaven and Hell*, where he played a spoiled Southerner serving World War II duty among a group of hard-boiled veterans known as the Hellfighters of the Pacific.

But then came an opportunity that R.J. hoped would turn his career around. It was a role that might have gone to James Dean if he'd still been alive, that of America's most famous outlaw, Jesse James.

R.J. saw a good-luck omen in the fact that his friend Tyrone Power scored his first big success playing the same part in Fox's 1939 *Jesse James*. Nunnally Johnson's old screenplay was revised to portray Jesse as less sympathetic than before, more violent and neurotic, hence the new title, *The True Story of Jesse James*. R.J.'s frequent costar, Jeffrey Hunter, played brother Frank James (Henry Fonda played Frank in the original).

Since the goal was a *Rebel Without a Cause* in cowboy boots, the studio hired the same director, Nicholas Ray, which caused problems for R.J. First, Ray had once been Natalie's lover, so R.J. resented him for that. Second, Ray swore by the Method, an improvisational approach completely alien to R.J., who'd always counted on his directors to tell him exactly what to do.

Meanwhile Natalie also had career problems, the most serious being her age. At eighteen, she still looked like a kid dressed up in Mom's clothes when required to play against type. To cast her as an adult, sexy woman was still rushing it.

When *The Burning Hills* was released, critics parboiled both the movie and Natalie's teaming with Tab Hunter. *Time* magazine snickered that "Tab and Natalie speak pidgin English to each other and sleep out on the prairie without a chaperone." *Newsweek* dubbed them "the most electrifying screen combo to come along since Marjorie Main and Percy Kilbride [Ma and Pa Kettle]."

Thanks to the huge advance publicity buildup, *The Burning*

Hills did satisfactory business. But once the public had seen Natalie and Tab strut their stuff, few were interested in returning for a second look when *The Girl He Left Behind* was launched a few months later. The movie wound up as the bottom half of double bills and marked the farewell appearance of the Wood-Hunter team.

Warner Brothers didn't know what to do with Natalie next, so they used her as marquee dressing in what amounted to a supporting role in a patriotic flag-waver about America's newest superfortress, *Bombers B-52*. In the few scenes that took place on the ground, Natalie portrayed the overly protected daughter of master mechanic Karl Malden, who tries to stop her from marrying Air Force colonel Efrem Zimbalist, Jr.

While Natalie endured the making of that eventual turkey, she heard that Warners had purchased the rights to Herman Wouk's bestseller, *Marjorie Morningstar*. Rarely since Scarlett O'Hara had a fictional heroine so captivated readers as the Jewish "princess" who rebels against the conventions of her religious upbringing by opting for a career as an actress over marriage and raising a family.

Natalie phoned her agent and insisted that she had to be Marjorie Morningstar. She was the right age and the right type: no one under Warner contract was more suitable or more deserving, she believed. Jack Warner, however, disagreed. He intended to "borrow" Elizabeth Taylor from MGM. Failing that, Audrey Hepburn from Paramount, or Susan Strasberg from RKO.

Natalie wouldn't give up. Learning that Herman Wouk had to approve the choice of the actress who played Marjorie Morningstar, she instructed her agent to set up a meeting with him so that she could plead her case.

That the author happened to reside in New York City didn't deter her. With her agent in tow, Natalie flew there at her own expense. A luncheon meeting was held at "21." Wouk couldn't have been friendlier and seemed to like her very much. She returned to Los Angeles convinced that she had the part.

A few days later Natalie broke down in tears when she learned that Wouk had filed a negative report: a delightful young woman, but definitely *not* Marjorie Morningstar.

She was even more disappointed when R.J. told her to forget

the whole thing. Another role just as good or even better would come along, he said. It was their first serious disagreement, and it left Natalie more determined than ever.

"Just to show R.J., I waged a campaign until I convinced Jack Warner that I was the only girl who could play Marjorie Morningstar," she recalled.

Milton Sperling was the producer assigned to *Marjorie Morningstar*. When negotiations for Elizabeth Taylor and other stars fell through, he decided to launch a nationwide talent hunt for an unknown actress, à la *Gone With the Wind*.

Natalie freaked out when she heard about it. How dare Warner Brothers do such a thing when they had Marjorie Morningstar right under their own roof? She rushed to Jack Warner's office, barged into his inner sanctum and demanded that he at least grant her the courtesy of a screen test. Warner admired her spunk and the test was made.

"Jack Warner wanted the test to include all the key scenes," said director Irving Rapper. "I told him it would take three days. I used the best cameraman and cutter that I could find. Natalie was great! She'd say, 'Are you sure it's right? Are you sure we don't need another take?' After seeing the test, I called Jack and said, 'You have a star!' When Herman Wouk saw it, he threw his yarmulke in the air!"

More than a year had passed since Warners purchased *Marjorie Morningstar*. Everybody who had a stake in the movie wanted to get it produced while the book was still selling like hotcakes (4.5 million hardcover and paperback copies so far). By taking a chance on Natalie Wood, they weren't risking that much and were also saving a bundle. Her Warner salary was still only $750 a week. A major star hired from the outside would have cost the studio at least $25,000 a week.

Although she thought that Warners was taking unfair advantage of her monetarily, Natalie felt on cloud nine. Then R.J. had to go and spoil it all by dropping a bombshell of his own. 20th Century-Fox was sending him to Japan for at least two months to make a spy thriller, *Stopover Tokyo*. Believe it or not, he would be taking over a role intended for John Wayne, who was stranded indefinitely in North Africa with a trouble-racked epic called *Legend of the Lost*.

Natalie was very upset. She'd been counting on R.J. being

around for moral support while she prepared for *Marjorie Morningstar*, which promised to be the toughest role she'd ever undertaken.

As she described her reaction: " 'That's just great,' I told him. 'Maybe you could manage to stay a while longer?' R.J. said that if he could manage it he certainly would, because there wouldn't be any chance of his running into me in Japan, even accidentally. Oh, we could be a couple of dolls when we were in fighting moods."

Out of fear of upsetting her even more, R.J. refrained from telling Natalie another important detail. But she found out anyway, via a catty phone call from gossipmonger Hedda Hopper. How did Natalie feel about R.J. Wagner going off to Japan to make a movie with that well-known man killer, Joan Collins, as his leading lady? After Natalie caught her breath, her answer was unprintable.

It took a lot of cajoling before Natalie would speak to R.J. again. Finally he convinced her that he was going to Japan solely to make a movie and that there would be no hanky-panky. The fact that he was taking his mother and father along on the trip and that they'd be sharing a hotel suite with him seemed to indicate that he would have little time for anything but work and occasional sightseeing.

Her anger forgotten, Natalie decided to see R.J. off at Los Angeles Airport. She hadn't counted on Joan Collins and others connected with *Stopover Tokyo* being booked on the same flight. Collins arrived only seconds before departure time, arm in arm with her lover, Nicky Hilton, son of hotel tycoon Conrad Hilton. Natalie hoped that Hilton was accompanying Collins to Japan, but it turned out otherwise.

Making sure that Collins was watching, Natalie gave R.J. a searing farewell kiss, as if to say, "Hands off, bitch, if you know what's good for you!"

After everybody had boarded the flight, Natalie stayed to view the takeoff. "As the plane wheeled to the runway, I started to cry," she remembered. "All of a sudden those two months that R.J. was going to be away began to look like two centuries. That was when I knew that, for all the bickering, I really loved him."

Divided by six thousand miles, Natalie and R.J. both felt

terribly lonely. When he left, he promised to telephone her daily, but that didn't turn out to be as easy as he expected. It usually took hours to get a call through to Los Angeles. R.J. became a prisoner of his hotel suite, afraid to go out for fear he would miss his connection. The transpacific phone charges were astronomical. Eventually, most of his salary from *Stopover Tokyo* went to pay the bill.

Until she actually found herself in that position, Natalie had never stopped to consider how a girl of eighteen was supposed to fill her spare time during her steady boyfriend's absence. As a gorgeous up-and-coming movie star, it was unlikely that she would stay home nights embroidering pillowcases for her hope chest. Men never stopped calling her with invitations and propositions. She wasn't going to let too many of them pass her by. If R.J. didn't like it, well, she'd face that problem when he returned.

Natalie's most frequent escort turned out to be Nicky Hilton. Friends thought it was simply a matter of two people keeping each other company while their true loves, Robert Wagner and Joan Collins, were out of town. But it quickly developed into an affair.

Celebrity watchers spotted Natalie driving all over town in Hilton's sky-blue Lincoln Continental, while he careened around in her white Thunderbird. "Hollywood is the only place in the world where lovers swap sports cars instead of fraternity pins," columnist Sidney Skolsky quipped.

Nicky Hilton was thirty, three years older than Robert Wagner and Natalie's senior by more than a decade. Dark-featured and rakishly handsome, he was one of America's most conspicuous playboys, best known as the first man to become an ex-husband of Elizabeth Taylor. Although he held an executive position in his father's hotel conglomerate, he spent most of his time gambling, nightclubbing and courting beautiful women.

For Natalie, Nicky Hilton was a new experience, a type she'd never been involved with before. He doled out eye-popping presents like a chinchilla stole and an emerald bracelet. He took her to Las Vegas and taught her how to shoot craps. He gave her the champagne and caviar treatment at Ciro's and the Mocambo.

It didn't take long for R.J. to find out about Natalie and

Hilton. Unfortunately, he was stuck in Japan until the completion of *Stopover Tokyo,* so he couldn't very well hop on the next plane back to Los Angeles for a showdown. He didn't even discuss it with Natalie on the phone. Ordering her to stop seeing Hilton might only have the opposite effect.

But by the time R.J.'s sojurn ended, Natalie had come to her senses and dropped Nicky Hilton like the proverbial hot potato. She discovered that underneath that suave facade Hilton was a very unbalanced man who drank too much, despised Jews and "niggers," and was well on his way to becoming a drug addict.

The biggest turnoff, however, was a telephone call that Natalie received from Elizabeth Taylor, who became very upset over rumors that Natalie and Hilton were going to be married.

Now very happily wed to producer Mike Todd and expecting a baby, Taylor felt obligated to warn Natalie of what could happen if she became Mrs. Nicky Hilton. For all his other faults, Hilton was also a wife beater, Taylor claimed, citing an incident when he punched her in the stomach and caused her to have a miscarriage.

Although Taylor knew Robert Wagner only slightly, she considered him a decent sort, a man who, unlike Nicky Hilton, genuinely loved women and would make a good husband. "You two were made for each other," Taylor told Natalie. "You'd better grab him before somebody else does."

Natalie and R.J. picked up where they had left off as soon as he returned from Japan. So did Joan Collins and Nicky Hilton. The chroniclers of Hollywood romance were delighted. It touched off a "Battle of the *Femmes Fatales*" that waged for years between Natalie Wood and Joan Collins, if only in the imaginations of the fan magazine editors who perpetuated it.

Supposedly Natalie "lost" Nicky Hilton because Collins was more sexually experienced and could "out-woman" her at every turn. Never mind that Natalie's real reason for breaking with Hilton was that she caught on to his dangerous proclivities. Collins eventually did too. That didn't stop Hilton from becoming involved with droves of other women before he finally died from a drug overdose in 1969 at age forty-two.

For resuming with Natalie, R.J. had to take a lot of flak from associates who advised him to drop her because of the Nicky

Hilton affair. "I think R.J. realized that he ended up looking like a jerk, but he loved her so much that he didn't care what people thought," a friend said. "They both sort of glossed over it, pretended it never happened, which proved to be a big mistake later on. Natalie developed this sense that she could do anything and get away with it."

By this time Natalie was on the verge of starting *Marjorie Morningstar*. Her leading man had yet to be selected, but the field had been narrowed down to Montgomery Clift, Paul Newman and William Holden. Natalie would have been thrilled to have any of them play the part, that of a dashing summer theater director with dreams of becoming a Broadway playwright.

Imagine her disappointment when she ended up with Gene Kelly! Why? Nobody knew for sure, but it seemed a combination of the following: Kelly had a terrific agent, was willing to work cheaper than any of his competition and had once impressed Jack Warner by playing a similar role opposite Judy Garland in an MGM musical entitled *Summer Stock*.

Natalie had nothing against Gene Kelly personally—in fact they became lifelong friends—but his casting made about as much sense as it would have if Fred Astaire had played Rhett Butler.

But Natalie had a more serious problem worrying her. Part of *Marjorie Morningstar* would be shot on location near Schroon Lake in New York's Adirondack Mountains, which meant another lengthy separation from R.J. Not something that either wanted, but unavoidable unless . . .

Unless R.J. could also play a role in *Marjorie Morningstar*, which wasn't as farfetched as it seemed. Marjorie has a second man in her life, the one she finally marries after Noel Airman (the Gene Kelly character) realizes that the theater and his career will always be his first love.

R.J. considered it a terrific idea. Since 20th Century-Fox had nothing lined up for him at the moment, there should be no conflict, or so he thought. But Fox refused to loan his services to Warner Brothers, claiming that the part wasn't important enough for a "star" of R.J.'s caliber. It finally went to Warner contract player Martin Milner.

The lovers decided that R.J. would go East with Natalie anyway. She was also taking along her mother and younger sister, Lana, so R.J. left separately to avoid being involved in the publicity hoopla scheduled for her arrival at Schroon Lake. When her plane landed at Glens Falls airport, Natalie treated the country bumpkins to a rather incongruous display of Hollywood glamor. Wearing a strapless black sheath dress and a mink stole, she clutched three of her favorite stuffed tigers in her arms.

Natalie and her family stayed at Schroon Manor, a rambling old-timey hotel with a private beach and dozens of acres of forested grounds. Their huge, high-ceilinged suite had two bedrooms, one for Natalie and the other for Mrs. Gurdin and Lana. The day after they checked in, Natalie took R.J. as a roommate.

Realizing it was useless to object, her mother served them breakfast in bed each morning.

It was August 1957, the height of the tourist season in Schroon Lake. Natalie and R.J. couldn't go out for a stroll without attracting hordes of spectators. To Natalie's extreme annoyance, most of them were female teenagers trying to get as near to Robert Wagner as they possibly could. One day a hundred and fifty from a nearby girls' camp descended on them en masse. Natalie and R.J. escaped in a speed boat, with a band of photographers from the fan magazines in hot pursuit.

Natalie and R.J. had reached their absolute peak as Hollywood's most publicized sweethearts. Owing to the conventions of the era, you had to read between the lines to know that they were sleeping together. Had it become public knowledge, their careers might have been ruined. They would have been condemned by the press and pulpit and probably dismissed by their studios, for disobeying the morality clauses in their contracts.

The super-abundance of romantic puffery benefited Natalie's career more than R.J.'s. After he finished *Stopover Tokyo*, Fox kept him idle for six months before assigning him to *The Hunters*, a Korean War saga directed by former actor-crooner Dick Powell. It was becoming plain that R.J. had not turned out to be the box-office draw that Fox had once anticipated. *The Hunters* was mainly a vehicle for Robert Mitchum, then one of the most popular tough-guy stars. R.J. shared secondary billing with such other downsliding contractees as Richard Egan, Lee Philips and May Britt (a Swedish blonde who later became celebrated as the first Mrs. Sammy Davis, Jr.).

Natalie's career seemed to be on more solid ground. *Marjorie Morningstar* loomed as Warner Brothers' biggest hit in years; theater exhibitors clamored for it because of the enormous popularity of the book. Being the star of such a prestigious movie sent Natalie's stock soaring within the industry. Everybody wanted her for their next picture, but Frank Sinatra won.

The deal all but confirmed that Natalie Wood had landed in Hollywood's top ranks at last. She would be teamed with Sinatra *and* Tony Curtis, another ultra-hot star of the moment, in *Kings Go Forth*, Sinatra's independent production for United Artists release.

Natalie hardly slept while waiting for Jack Warner to decide whether or not to approve the loan-out. She could have hugged him when he consented, but affection turned to indignation when she discovered the terms of the arrangement.

Although United Artists had to pay Warner Brothers $75,000 for Natalie's services, she would still get her checks from the Warner payroll department at her usual contract rate of $750 a week. In other words, Warners would pocket $6,750 a week on the ten-week deal.

What infuriated Natalie even more was that, in order to "borrow" her, Frank Sinatra also had to pledge one of his future productions to Warner Brothers. The value of such a commitment had to be in the millions. No one knew then that it would turn out to be *Ocean's Eleven*, the biggest grosser of Sinatra's career.

Small wonder that Natalie began to feel like a slave who could be sold or traded at will. The practice had been going on in Hollywood for decades, especially at Warner Brothers, where Jack Warner was considered the Simon Legree of the industry. Like some earlier Warner stars, notably Bette Davis, James Cagney and Olivia de Havilland, it was only a matter of time before Natalie would be pushed to the breaking point and become a rebel *with* a cause.

Natalie had just started *Kings Go Forth* when 20th Century-Fox sent R.J. on a cross-country publicity tour in connection with the release of *Stopover Tokyo*. Realizing that R.J. had as little control over his career as she did, Natalie resigned herself to the fact that Joan Collins again would be traveling with R.J., chaperoned, of course, by Fox press agents. As it turned out, Natalie had nothing to worry about in the way of romantic competition. Collins by this time had dropped Nicky Hilton for a clandestine affair with producer George Englund, husband of actress Cloris Leachman.

By the end of the tour R.J. was in a despairing mood. *Stopover Tokyo* turned out to be another clinker, both for 20th Century-Fox and for R.J. personally. Based on one of John P. Marquand's "Mr. Moto" novels, it retained the plot but eliminated the Japanese master sleuth, replacing him with R.J. and Edmond O'Brien as a pair of American detectives who seemed straight out of *Naked City* and similar TV crime series popular at the time. It was a B programmer stretched to CinemaScope proportions, with lumbering action, flat characters and stolid acting. Fox lost $2 million on the movie.

R.J. realized it was time to put his foot down. A few more flops like *Stopover Tokyo* and he'd be in real trouble. He disliked the script Fox sent him for *The Hunters*, which presented no challenge for him personally.

"It was the usual kind of part for me, a one-dimensional boy," he recalled. "I told the studio if they wanted me to continue doing those kind of parts I didn't want to work there anymore. I'd do it only if they rewrote the character into a three-dimensional adult." Since other Fox contractees who might have suited the part were all involved with other projects, R.J.'s demands were met.

Natalie and R.J. had been keeping steady company now for almost a year. The avalanche of publicity surrounding the romance had reached the burning question stage of "When are Natalie and Bob going to get married?"

In the months since R.J.'s return from Japan, the relationship had grown stronger. The problems that both were experiencing in their careers created an additional bond of sympathy and understanding. Alone, they might have been miserable. Together, they gave each other comfort and nurtured dreams of a happy future in which they would be the most devoted, most successful couple that Hollywood had ever known.

December 6, 1957, was the first anniversary of Natalie and

R.J.'s "locking limbs." To celebrate, he made a dinner reservation at Romanoff's, *the* place to go for the movie aristocracy, which was run by a former New York garment worker who pretended kinship to the deposed Russian dynasty.

R.J. drove to Natalie's house to pick her up, bringing with him a bottle of Dom Perignon and two crystal champagne glasses. He poured them each some bubbly and proposed a toast to the exciting evening ahead.

As Natalie raised the glass to her lips she noticed something glittering at the bottom of it. Carefully sipping the champagne until it was nearly gone, she stuck her pinky in the glass and fished out a diamond and pearl ring.

"Read what's on the inside," R.J. said.

Holding the ring to the light, Natalie saw the inscription, "Marry me?" Her huge dark eyes brimmed over with teary rapture. No further answer was necessary.

FOUR

Married at Last

THE ENGAGEMENT lasted a mere three weeks. As soon as the news broke, reporters and columnists never stopped hounding Natalie and R.J. for wedding details. Had it been up to Louella Parsons, the nuptials of America's Sweethearts would have been thrown open to the public at the 25,000-seat Shrine Auditorium, with a ceremony outdazzling the one between Grace Kelly and Prince Rainier in Monaco the previous year.

Natalie and R.J. desired none of that. All they wanted was to sneak off quietly, as far away as possible, for a simple, dignified wedding.

Right after Christmas, while the Hollywood press corps was preoccupied with the annual glut of studio parties, the couple gathered together a few relatives and friends and headed for Phoenix, Arizona. Their final destination was the resort community of Scottsdale, in the so-called "Valley of the Sun," where R.J.'s parents now resided.

In order to get away, Natalie forfeited a trip to France to film exteriors for *Kings Go Forth*. As a wedding present, Frank Sinatra arranged for her scenes to be rewritten so that a double could play them. For the two weeks that entailed, her time was her own.

The wedding took place on Saturday afternoon, December 28. The night before, Nick Adams, part of the Los Angeles group, delivered R.J.'s wedding gift to Natalie. The heart-shaped diamond had a handwritten note attached: "I miss you. What are you doing tomorrow around one o'clock?"

Overwhelmed, Natalie sat down and scribbled a reply: "Darling, I'm not doing anything tomorrow. What do you say we get married?" She sent it back to R.J. with her wedding gift to him, which turned out to be a diamond stickpin.

Just before the next day's ceremony began, the doors of the Scottsdale Methodist Church were locked and barred. R.J. had personally seen to that in case someone blabbed the couple's secret to the press in neighboring Phoenix. The 500-seat church contained fewer than a dozen people, all clustered together in the front row.

Natalie had picked her closest girl friend, Barbara Gould, to be maid of honor. Nick Adams, Lana Wood and the married director-writer team of Richard Sale and Mary Loos (R.J.'s longtime associates at 20th Century-Fox) were the other attendants.

In the foyer the twenty-seven-year-old groom nervously waited for the signal to present himself at the altar. His father, serving as best man, reminded R.J. that he'd once bet him that he'd never get married before the age of thirty. R.J. reached into his pocket and forked over a hundred dollars.

In a room nearby the nineteen-year-old bride stood putting on a lace mantilla instead of the traditional veil. Her ankle-length gown was made of delicate white lace, encrusted with tiny seed pearls. Although she'd worn many beautiful costumes in movies, one glance in the mirror told her this was the most exquisite one of all.

The processional music started. Natalie's father, as usual, had consumed a bit too much vodka. To make sure that he didn't fall over, Natalie grabbed him firmly by the arm and ended up walking *him* down the aisle.

The double-ring ceremony lasted about twenty minutes. In the front pew Natalie and R.J.'s mothers seemed to be in a contest over who could cry the loudest and most copiously. When the minister finally told the groom to kiss the bride, the clinch lasted so long that their attendants broke out in giggles.

A small reception followed at Scottsdale's Valley Ho Hotel. Everybody got crocked, and as a result the newlyweds arrived at the railway station three minutes too late to catch their train for the honeymoon trip. Fortunately their chauffeur was a speed demon in the James Dean tradition. He piled Natalie and R.J. back into the limousine and zoomed off down the highway that ran parallel to the railroad tracks.

As soon as they caught up with the train, the driver started honking the car horn and blinking the headlights. Natalie and R.J. hung out the windows, shouting and waving at the engineer.

"Finally he saw us and stopped at an intersection," Natalie remembered. "We scrambled aboard with sixteen pieces of luggage."

With two weeks at their disposal, Natalie and R.J. weren't concerned about how long it took them to get anywhere, so a deluxe compartment on the Atchison, Topeka & Santa Fe's streamlined *Super Chief* made an ideal bridal suite. They never left it until Chicago, where they stopped over several days and then boarded another supertrain, the *Silver Streak*, for Miami and a five-day boat cruise around the Florida Keys.

When Natalie and R.J. arrived in Miami they found Nick Adams waiting for them. It was his opinion—one not shared by the newlyweds—that they'd be longing for company by that time. The couple hoped to lose Adams when their ship sailed, but the cruise was canceled on account of bad weather.

Instead, Nick Adams suggested that the three of them go to New York, which proved to be a big mistake. Natalie and R.J. became sitting ducks whenever they went out to a theater, restaurant or nightclub. Press photographers trailed them everywhere, taxi drivers honked their horns at them, fans camped in the lobby of their hotel.

The only one who enjoyed all the attention was their seemingly constant companion, Nick Adams. R.J. threw a tantrum when Dorothy Kilgallen, "The Voice of Broadway," insinuated in her gossip column that the Wagners and Adams were a *ménage à trois.* Natalie found the suggestion hilarious but agreed with R.J. that they should return to California and try to get some relaxation before their honeymoon time ran out.

For Natalie and R.J., the best part of the honeymoon was the finale, spent off the coast of Santa Catalina Island on his boat, *My Lady* (now jokingly referred to as *My Other Woman).* Dense fog prevailed for four days, so the couple just dropped anchor and devoted most of the time to lovemaking. Neither could have foreseen the tragedy that would occur near that very location twenty-three years later.

All too soon they had to return to work. After being inactive for nearly nine months, R.J. was delighted when 20th Century-Fox finally placed *The Hunters* before the cameras. Following its completion, the studio intended to use him in *In Love and War,* once again in military uniform but this time World War II instead of Korea. It started to look as if R.J. would beat John Wayne's record as the star with the most war movies to his credit.

As usual, Natalie had a feud going with Jack Warner. Right after she finished *Kings Go Forth,* Warner Brothers assigned her to a three-week publicity tour in conjunction with the release of *Marjorie Morningstar.*

Natalie blew up, since it meant being separated from R.J. She accused Jack Warner of trying to ruin her marriage. Warner threatened to suspend her if she didn't obey orders. Didn't she realize she was cutting her own throat by refusing to cooperate? *Marjorie Morningstar* was the biggest movie of her career; too much rode on its success.

Natalie wouldn't budge until they reached a compromise. She wound up going to New York to attend the premiere of *Marjorie Morningstar* at the prestigious Radio City Music Hall. During a five-day stay, she nearly collapsed under the strain of 117 press, radio and TV interviews. She spent her few spare moments on the long-distance phone with R.J., crying over how hard they were working her.

By the time she left New York, however, Natalie felt deliriously happy. *Marjorie Morningstar* had registered the biggest opening day's business in the twenty-six-year history of Radio City Music Hall, which, with 6,000 seats, was the largest movie showcase in the world.

A Warner publicist took her out in a hired limousine to show her the constant block-long line of people waiting to buy tickets, slowly snaking toward a marquee that had her name emblazoned on it. It was one of the most thrilling experiences of her life.

Within a week Natalie's euphoria turned to despair. It became painfully obvious that *Marjorie Morningstar* owed its record-breaking opening to the enormous popularity of Herman Wouk's book. Once that initial "want-to-see" subsided, business plummeted as the result of unfavorable reviews and word of mouth.

What should have been a turning point in Natalie's career proved to be a major setback. The one saving grace was that she had never been photographed more beautifully. Cinematographer Harry Stradling created a lighting procedure that Natalie insisted on for the rest of her career. A round cardboard cutout that Stradling called a "kukaloris" was put in front of the key light to create shadows. The camera was always up high, giving her face a very moody look.

But critics described her performance as perfunctory at best. *Time* magazine was especially severe, noting that "Natalie Wood, a great beauty, is something less than a great actress. Her most believable moment comes when Marjorie, despairing of Broadway acting fame, says mechanically, 'Sometimes I think I don't have any talent at all.' "

Yet *Marjorie Morningstar* might have survived such lambasting if its love story had been more enthralling. But there was no sexual combustion between Natalie and Gene Kelly, who seemed more suited to playing father and daughter. Also, by casting two gentiles in the leads and eliminating about ninety-five percent of the novel's ethnic background, Warner Brothers alienated the large Jewish audience that might have flocked to the movie had it remained true to the spirit of the book.

Natalie's experience with *Marjorie Morningstar* left her deeply depressed. The apathy with which the movie was received had smothered her chance for major stardom. She'd worked hard for a great triumph and was rewarded with failure.

The subsequent box-office flop of *Kings Go Forth* didn't improve matters. Critics savaged the World War II melodrama, in which Natalie portrayed a half-black French girl romanced by American soldiers Frank Sinatra and Tony Curtis. Natalie prefers Curtis. When he turns out to be a racial bigot, she tries to drown herself, but Sinatra saves her. After Curtis is killed in battle, Sinatra, minus one arm, returns to Natalie's village to propose marriage. It was a "Golden Turkey" movie that embarrassed everybody concerned.

Happily, Natalie had something to cushion the tremendous disappointments—a husband who adored her. While she healed her wounds and waited for Warner Brothers to come up with a new assignment, she hurled herself wholeheartedly into what for her was a totally new way of life as a wife and homemaker.

The Wagners' first home together was R.J.'s bachelor apartment in Beverly Hills. Since they both owned racks and racks of clothes, the living room soon took on the appearance of a walk-in closet. With no place to entertain company or even to sit and watch TV when they were alone, they started shopping around for a house.

Natalie and R.J. dreamed of a vintage villa in Beverly Hills but had to settle for a two-year-old split-level in Laurel Canyon. Situated high up in the Hollywood Hills, they could at least see Beverly Hills on a smog-free day. Anything more expensive would have put them seriously in debt. Together they earned about $2,000 a week. After taxes, agents' fees and other deductions, there wasn't enough left to pursue a Big Movie Star lifestyle.

Within six weeks of the Wagners' marriage, most of the fan magazines published photographs of the wedding festivities in Scottsdale. Since they'd made such an effort to avoid publicity, Natalie and R.J. were devastated. Even worse, they felt betrayed upon discovering that the pictures came from a photographer friend who earned about $10,000 in the deal. The so-called "friend" had been invited to the wedding with the understanding that any snapshots he took would be solely for a keepsake album for Natalie and R.J.'s personal use.

After that unpleasantness, Natalie and R.J. adopted a belligerent attitude toward the press, especially the fan magazines. Except when required to promote their movies, they tried to avoid personal publicity by pleading that they didn't want to go "the Debbie and Eddie route," an avenue of overhype where their every move would be reported and analyzed *ad nauseam*.

Having grown up in Hollywood, Natalie and R.J. knew all too well that the odds against a successful marriage between two movie stars were about a million to one. But they were determined to prove that theirs would be the jackpot exception.

"If you really want to, and you really try, you can do it," Natalie said at the time. "Actually, it's not the fact that both of you have careers per se which busts up so many Hollywood marriages. It's the refusal of one party to make the small sacrifices necessary for the other's career. In other words, selfishness. Any marriage manual will tell you that if two people have a similarity of interests they have a much greater chance for a successful marriage."

The couple made a pact that they would try to arrange work schedules so that they were never separated. "We've seen too often what happens when people are parted for just a little while," Natalie said. "It's a big danger, so why take the chance?"

R.J. agreed with her. "I don't think you can go into marriage with a negative approach," he said. "We're not thinking of whether we can make it. We're *going* to make it, and have fun at the same time. We're not perfect on the subject of marriage, but I think that if we're left alone to work things out we'll just be fine."

The Wagners' togetherness became a legend in its own time. Dubbing them "Love-Birds in a Celluloid Cage," Hedda Hopper gushed that "Bob and Natalie are young, beautiful, famous and so terribly in love that I'm sure any zillionaire in the land would gladly change places with them. Their happiness dazzles you; it's like coming too close to a high voltage light."

Hollywood seldom saw them on the restaurant and nightclub circuit. When the Wagners did go out socially, it was usually to attend an important event like the televised Academy Awards ceremonies.

In March 1958 they made their first public appearance as Mr. and Mrs. in the roles of "Oscar sitters," helping to hand out the gold-plated statuettes to the winners. Introducing them to the audience at the Pantages Theater, emcee David Niven called for "a great big close-up to beautify living rooms all over America."

Boating, R.J.'s great passion before they married, gave them an opportunity to escape by themselves. Natalie learned how to navigate, to operate the ship's radio, even to cook a simple meal. But though she liked to swim in a pool, she couldn't be induced to dive into the open sea. "It looks so dark down there, and I'm scared of fish," she said.

The Wagners' togetherness policy eventually caused a major explosion in Natalie's turbulent relationship with the Warner Brothers management. Once again Jack Warner intended to "loan" Natalie to United Artists, this time to costar with Kirk Douglas, Burt Lancaster and Laurence Olivier in George Bernard Shaw's *The Devil's Disciple*. Despite its setting of the American Revolutionary War, the film would be shot in England, where UA had millions in "frozen" earnings to spend, owing to government restrictions on the transfer of British funds abroad.

Natalie refused the assignment, which required staying in England for about three months. If R.J. hadn't been involved with making two pictures back to back at 20th Century-Fox, she would have accepted. What young actress in her right mind would pass up an opportunity to work with such a dynamic trio as Douglas, Lancaster and Olivier? But she couldn't be persuaded to go abroad without her husband.

Jack Warner blew his stack. Natalie's decision not only cost the studio the $100,000 that UA had offered for her services but also jinxed a deal whereby either Burt Lancaster or Kirk Douglas would have made a picture for Warner Brothers.

Since the studio had no project of its own ready for Natalie, Jack Warner saw a perfect opportunity to place her under "suspension." As long as she toed the mark, she was supposed to be paid $750 a week for forty weeks a year, whether Warner Brothers put her to work or not. But, by refusing to make *The Devil's Disciple*, she was judged to be in breach of contract. Warners could suspend her indefinitely without salary.

That effectively sent Natalie Wood's career into limbo. If she didn't work for Warner Brothers, she couldn't work anywhere. In order to make an outside deal, she had first to get permission from Jack Warner himself, an impossibility while they were at loggerheads.

Natalie's contract with Warner Brothers still had three years to run. Theoretically, she could be quarantined for the duration if peace wasn't restored.

Far from feeling conquered, Natalie considered suspension a necessary first step to obtaining better working conditions for herself. Her vanity told her that Natalie Wood was too valuable a property for Jack Warner to keep idle. Before she went back she wanted more money—at least $1,000 a week—plus a voice in choosing the roles she played. She also desired the right to make occasional outside pictures as a free agent, that is, without Warner Brothers interfering or sharing in her earnings.

R.J. supported Natalie all the way. Her predicament at Warner Brothers wasn't much different from his own situation at 20th Century-Fox, or, for that matter, from most of the young stars under contract to the major studios. If she won, it would make it easier for others to get similar concessions.

Had Natalie and R.J. known that her suspension would last a year and three months, perhaps they wouldn't have been so determined to stick it out. But in the beginning it seemed quite exciting and daringly antiestablishment.

Natalie treated suspension as a long-delayed vacation. Having worked more or less constantly since the age of four, she felt like a new person. She slept late in the morning, lunched with friends, spent long afternoons exploring the Beverly Hills boutiques and department stores.

With Natalie off the Warner payroll indefinitely, the couple gave up all thought of moving from Laurel Canyon to a more prestigious and expensive area like Beverly Hills or Bel Air. Trying to get by on R.J.'s salary alone proved difficult, so Natalie cashed in $27,000 worth of government bonds to help tide them over.

The money represented an accumulation of earnings that had been placed in trust for her as a child actor, a requirement of California law as a protection against unscrupulous parents and managers. Natalie wasn't supposed to collect the funds before her twenty-first birthday, still more than a year away. But the court waived that restriction because she was married and supposedly mature enough to know how to handle money wisely.

Once the novelty of being unemployed wore off, Natalie didn't know what to do with herself. Since she longed to have a baby, she thought it might be the right time to start one. But R.J. considered their present circumstances unsatisfactory and insisted on waiting until they were more financially and psychologically able to undertake the obligations of parenthood.

Partly to keep Natalie occupied and partly because it made good business sense, the couple formed a jointly named corporation, Rona Productions (*Ro*bert & *Na*talie), which would package movies for them to star in, both individually and perhaps even as a team.

Of course Rona couldn't actually make any deals until Natalie clarified her status at Warner Brothers. But in the meantime she could keep busy scouting for suitable properties, which might be books, plays or original scripts.

Temporarily frustrated in her work as an actress, Natalie started taking a greater interest in R.J.'s career. While he made *The Hunters*, she worked with him every evening, helping him to learn his lines and to perfect his performance for the next day's shoot. She also accompanied him to the studio and sat on the sidelines of the set, offering moral support.

But Natalie didn't stick by her husband's side just to be his acting coach. She was extremely jealous and suspicious of other women. Not that R.J. had given her cause to worry, but she knew all too well that, when two people were thrown into each other's arms for a love scene, it sometimes combusted into a "quickie" interlude in a dressing room.

When R.J. started filming *In Love and War*, Natalie made sure that she was on the set whenever he played scenes with Sheree North, the vivacious blonde who usually wound up with roles rejected by 20th Century-Fox's reigning sex bombs, Marilyn Monroe and Jayne Mansfield.

Natalie seethed green one day when the script required R.J. to pinion Sheree North against the wall and kiss her passionately. Glaring at them from over the cameraman's shoulder, Natalie proved such a distraction that North finally shouted at her, "Don't worry, honey, I've got one of my own at home!"

But Natalie never gave up. Whether for togetherness or to

prevent any romantic hanky-panky from taking place, she made sure that R.J. took her with him when he had to go to Hawaii for two weeks of location shooting for the movie.

R.J.'s career was looking up. Critics would soon point out that he had done his best work to date as the brash, bebopping jet pilot in *The Hunters* and as the naive Irish-American boy from the wrong side of the tracks in *In Love and War*. Was the new dimension to his talent attributable to the maturation process of marriage and the influence of Natalie Wood? No one could tell for sure.

Initially Natalie didn't seem bothered by the upsurge in R.J.'s career while hers stood still. But as the months dragged by and she continued on the Warner suspension list, she was no longer the happy young wife depicted in the fan magazines. She became frightened and insecure, prone to lying awake nights and wondering why in hell she felt so miserable.

The quickest remedy for at least part of Natalie's dilemma was sleeping pills. But, with visions of his wife joining the seemingly endless ranks of celebrity drug abusers, R.J. succeeded in breaking her of the habit before it really had a chance to become one.

Then Natalie did something that R.J. considered equally dangerous. She consulted a psychiatrist! "I just couldn't stomach the notion of Natalie running off to a shrink," R.J. recalled. "I suppose I considered it a reflection on me. We were married only a short time and my wife says she needs a psychiatrist!"

As for Natalie herself, "My unhappiness was a complete mystery," she said. "I loved my husband. We were in good health. According to the press, we had everything one could desire, but all I felt was torment. I was unable to make a decision of any kind. People had told me what to do all my life, and now I was expected to function as an adult woman."

Psychoanalysis became the most important thing in Natalie's life. She had a session every day. While unemployed, it was certainly a more beneficial way of filling the void than hanging around R.J.'s movie sets. In fact some of her friends joked that, if Natalie had to choose between hopping onto the psychiatrist's couch or into bed with R.J., her husband would be the loser.

"What analysis did for me was to help me clarify what I

wanted to do," Natalie recalled. "And when I started figuring out what I wanted, it didn't make me more self-centered, it made me less self-centered.

"Analysis made me look at things," she continued. "Right after R.J. and I were married, I started to decorate our house. I'd never thought about furniture or things like that. All I'd thought about was acting, and whether I got the part or not. When the decorator said, 'What about the coffee table?' I realized I'd never even noticed what goes on a coffee table. I'd never looked. I didn't have any opinion about the kind of furniture I wanted.

"I'd always been so worried about being shy, or what people were going to think of me, or what I was going to say, that I'd never notice anything when I entered a room. Later on, as I got a little inner security, I felt I was discovering windows where I could see out. I became aware of how other people lived and what their homes were like."

Natalie didn't really need a psychiatrist to tell her that much of her distress came from her stalemated career. But he did encourage her to make peace with Jack Warner.

For more than a year Natalie turned down every script that Warner Brothers offered her. "Money wasn't the major issue," she said. "I wanted the right to do outside pictures and have more freedom. I felt that no major studio had enough good properties to keep an actress making topflight movies."

The only project that Natalie later regretted turning down was *A Summer Place*, for which Warner Brothers ended up "borrowing" Sandra Dee from Universal. Though nothing more than hokey soap opera, it became a box-office smash and the stimulus for Sandra Dee's career that *Marjorie Morningstar* might have been for Natalie's.

In her battle with Warner Brothers, Natalie had the support of the Screen Actors Guild and its president, Ronald Reagan. A onetime Warner contractee himself, Reagan had targeted that studio for reform, hoping that the rest of the industry would fall into line afterward. Actors felt they were underpaid and overworked, treated like sweatshop slaves and restricted from seeking outside employment.

But Natalie had taken on a fierce adversary in Jack Warner, whom Humphrey Bogart once nicknamed "the warden of San

Quentin." Not until gossip columnist Louella Parsons inter-
vened did Natalie make any headway.

Parsons adored Natalie, whom she'd first met as a child actress working for producer-daughter Harriet Parsons in the
movie *Never a Dull Moment.* Natalie's mother and eventually
Natalie herself nurtured the relationship by making sure that
Louella always got an "exclusive" on major developments in
her life and career. As a result, Parsons considered herself
Natalie's starmaker and took a protective attitude toward her.

The Hollywood-fixated news hen considered it a national
tragedy that Natalie Wood had been missing from theater
screens for so long. She put the heat on Jack Warner by threatening to drop all mention of Warner movies from her widely
syndicated column if he didn't sit down at the bargaining table
with Natalie and treat her fairly.

In March 1959, fourteen months after being suspended, Natalie finally got a new five-year contract from Warner Brothers.
Her salary was raised to $1,000 a week, with provision for grad-
ual increases to $7,500 a week by the last year. More impor-
tantly, for every Warner picture she made, she was free to make
one outside picture of her own choosing.

Natalie was overjoyed, although Jack Warner hadn't really
surrendered that much. But he earned points with the Screen
Actors Guild and also a commendation from Louella Parsons,
who, not surprisingly, hailed him as a great humanitarian.

To show that he had no hard feelings, Jack Warner gave Natalie the best-appointed dressing room at the studio, which had
once belonged to Joan Crawford. When Crawford heard about
it, she sent Natalie a congratulatory telegram: "It was right
after I moved in that I got an Oscar for *Mildred Pierce.* I just
hope the dressing room is as lucky for you as it was for me."

Crawford's good wishes seemed unlikely to have any effect in
the immediate future. Natalie's comeback movie was *Cash Mc-
Call,* primarily designed to capitalize on the popularity of
James Garner, hotter than a pistol at the time, owing to "Mav-
erick," his Warner-produced TV series. Natalie couldn't very
well refuse the assignment, but it was an undemanding role as
the sweetheart of a ruthless business tycoon who's regenerated
into a modern Wall Street version of Robin Hood.

While Natalie made *Cash McCall,* her husband was rarely far away. Between pictures for the moment, it had become his turn at mate-sitting. Natalie didn't like the decor of her new dressing room, so R.J. supervised the repainting in her favorite colors of beige and gold. Everybody thought the couple looked adorable as they sat around between takes like a pair of teenagers, laughing at their own jokes and playing records on a portable stereo.

Everybody, that is, except James Garner. He felt extremely embarrassed whenever the script called for him to make ardent love to Natalie while her husband watched from the sidelines. Afraid of losing the Wagners' friendship by confronting them directly, Garner complained to Jack Warner, who not too politely told R.J. that he had five minutes to sling his ass off the premises.

Natalie got into similar trouble while hanging around the set of R.J.'s next movie at 20th Century-Fox. It was a radical departure for him, a gaudy backstage musical with the quasi-religious title of *Say One for Me*. R.J. needed all the prayers he could muster as he made his singing and dancing debut alongside two experienced costars, Bing Crosby (as a priest with a congregation of Broadway show folk) and Debbie Reynolds.

Natalie didn't fancy the idea of R.J. working with one of his previous girl friends. Especially one who'd just figured in the biggest romantic scandal of the decade and might very likely be on the prowl for a husband to replace the one she'd lost to Elizabeth Taylor.

In the past, directors usually tolerated Natalie's hovering about. But this one, Frank Tashlin, flew into a towering rage and banned her permanently from the set. "In my pictures," Tashlin glowered, "I don't allow wives to coach husbands from the sidelines." That still didn't stop Natalie from meeting R.J. in the studio commissary every lunchtime.

Neither *Say One for Me* nor *Cash McCall* clicked at the box office. *Variety*, the entertainment industry's bible, listed them both among the biggest losers of 189 movies released by the major Hollywood studios during 1959.

Gloom set in at the Wagner household. Natalie and R.J. fell into a pattern of constant bickering, which seemed a healthy way of working off the frustration and disappointment they both felt while watching their careers going from bad to worse.

Their marital spats made juicy fodder for the gossip columns, but the couple laughed them off as a necessary component of their relationship.

"We'll probably go on fighting—and making up—until we're ninety," Natalie said.

FIVE

Playing House

NATALIE WOOD AND ROBERT WAGNER belonged to a rapidly vanishing breed—movie stars who were polished to glossy perfection on the studio assembly lines under exclusive, long-term contracts. "Since I was four," Natalie said in 1959, "the studios have been my home, and R.J. never acted anywhere else either. In fact, he was a star before he could act!"

As part of that upbringing, you were expected to pursue the ultra-glamorous lifestyle that was synonomous with Hollywood, regardless of whether or not you could actually afford it. Although Natalie and R.J. resisted it for a long time, they finally took the plunge in the autumn of 1959 by purchasing a $150,000 mansion in Beverly Hills.

But Natalie wasn't content with just acquiring an address on Beverly Drive, one of the poshest on the celebrity circuit. She wanted a showplace that would establish Mr. and Mrs. Robert

Wagner as paragons of the community. R.J. shared that view. Their hopes and dreams all came out of the fan magazines that they read from cover to cover while they were growing up.

They started out with a stately colonial house that reminded Natalie too much of a residence for senior citizens. After renovations that were never fully completed, the couple ended up with a Greco-Roman extravaganza of the Cecil B. DeMille school of architecture.

For months, walls were ripped down, put back up and rooms rearranged. Natalie hired and fired three decorators before she decided she could do it better herself. The bills were fantastic. Bathroom fixtures alone cost $50,000.

Construction problems were endless. The ornate central staircase wobbled at the slightest footstep. The antique balustrade, salvaged from Marion Davies' legendary Santa Monica beach castle before it was demolished, kept falling apart. Natalie's sunken marble bathtub tore loose from its mounting and crashed through the ceiling into the living room below. Another faulty ceiling collapsed and buried the Wagners' enormous canopied bed. Fortunately, it was vacant at the time.

To create a Greek temple effect, white pillars surrounded the exterior of the house. Floors were covered with white marble. A special ventilation system was installed in the master bedroom, which had no windows. The couple knew that the scandal magazines would pay a fortune to any photographer who could catch them in bed together.

Gilt moldings, smoked mirrors and velvet draperies abounded. Natalie spent weeks scavenging through antique shops for paintings and bric-a-brac to make up for the couple's lack of such treasures of their own. Crates of secondhand books were purchased to fill the shelves of R.J.'s wood-paneled den, which also served as a library and office.

The house's most flamboyant feature was the outdoor lanai and swimming pool, the latter divided into his-and-her sections. At Natalie's end stood a statue of a Greek goddess; R.J.'s, naturally, had a Greek god. Salt water filled the pool, reportedly a first for Beverly Hills. Frank Sinatra sent a hundred-pound sack of sea salt as a housewarming gift.

By January 1960, Natalie and R.J. found themselves so deeply in remodeling debts that they needed money desperately. Having already drawn substantial advances against their Warner and Fox contracts, the only way to generate extra income was through outside work. Since neither of their home studios had any projects ready for them at the moment, they were able to negotiate waivers to work elsewhere in the interim.

When they got married, Natalie and R.J. said they would never try to capitalize on their relationship by appearing in a movie together. But when you're in financial straits you learn to be flexible. While shopping around for projects, they discovered that they could get $50,000 more as a team than they could individually.

The offer came from MGM, which wanted them for the film version of Rosamond Marshall's bestselling novel, *The Bixby Girls*. Apart from the money involved, the Wagners could soothe their consciences with the fact that their relationship in the film could never be mistaken for the one they had in real life.

For 1960, the movie was considered quite daring. Cast as young Texas "white trash," Natalie and R.J. are lovers just long enough for her to get pregnant and introduce the first plot complication. Rather than face a life of poverty with R.J., she snares a millionaire husband, convincing him that he's the father of the yet unborn child. Meanwhile R.J. has a disastrous affair with a black nightclub singer, using her as a stepping-stone to a career as a jazz musician. In the bizarre conclusion, he marries Natalie's spoiled-rotten sister-in-law, thus becoming "uncle" to his own child.

"You might say that the picture was ahead of its time," R.J. quipped years later.

Starring opposite Natalie and R.J. were George Hamilton and Susan Kohner as the wealthy brother and sister, and Pearl Bailey as R.J.'s ill-fated mistress. The innocuous title, *The Bixby Girls*, was changed to the more startling and enigmatic *All the Fine Young Cannibals*.

Presumably the implication was that love destroys, turning people into human flesh-eaters. MGM hoped that the public might mistake it for the handiwork of Tennessee Williams, whose current hit movie, *Suddenly Last Summer*, dealt with cannibalism in the more literal sense.

All the Fine Young Cannibals was directed by Britain's Michael Anderson, best known for Mike Todd's spectacular *Around the World in 80 Days.* He hardly seemed the ideal choice for a movie about young Texans, so it wasn't surprising that the movie often seemed like a parody of Tennessee Williams.

"We all dripped Southern accents, paraded around in wigs and tried to look terribly, terribly decadent," Natalie remembered.

Critics eventually upchucked all over *All the Fine Young Cannibals,* pelting it with snideries ranging from "a caldron of overcooked garbage" to "not fit for human or animal consumption." Even the industry trade papers, which tended to be lenient because they were almost totally dependent on the film companies for advertising, called it the worst release from a major studio that year. The public stayed away in droves, flocking instead to *Psycho, Ocean's Eleven* and *The Apartment,* all of which opened around the same time.

All the Fine Young Cannibals was probably the most dreadful film that either Natalie Wood or Robert Wagner ever made. It was even more unfortunate that they had to share it. The experience deeply upset them and put their careers in jeopardy.

R.J. was in an especially vulnerable position. Associated with 20th Century-Fox for ten years, he was nearing the end of the second of his five-year contracts. Since he'd not had a really successful picture for ages, his bargaining power at renewal time would be virtually zero. The studio could pretty well dictate its own terms if he wanted to stay on there.

He wasn't sure that he did. While the guarantee of a hefty weekly paycheck offered more security than free-lancing, R.J. saw slight chance of getting better roles than he had in the past. Once the Fox management pigeonholed you in a certain category—R.J.'s seemed to be Smiling Joe Juvenile—little variation was permitted. You just went along until you grew too old and were replaced. R.J. found himself losing ground to more recently signed contractees like Paul Newman, Bradford Dillman, Richard Beymer, Stuart Whitman, Anthony Franciosa, Don Murray, Stephen Boyd and Pat Boone.

Right after he finished *All the Fine Young Cannibals,* Fox wanted R.J. to appear with Elvis Presley in *Flaming Star.* The Western would mark Elvis' debut as a straight actor, in the role of a half-breed Indian warrior no less! R.J. saw no way of shining in the decidedly secondary role of cavalry officer adversary, so he refused the assignment and was immediately suspended.

With renovations at the Beverly Hills house still draining the Wagners' joint bank account, R.J. couldn't afford to be off salary very long. Pleading for mercy, he persuaded Fox to reassign him to *Solo*, a semimusical about a success-hungry jazz musician in the vein of *Young Man With a Horn*.

The potential for a career turnaround was there. Dick Powell, who'd squeezed such a fine performance out of R.J. in *The Hunters*, would produce and direct. André Previn was composing the music.

Meanwhile a full year had passed since Natalie made her last movie for Warner Brothers, *Cash McCall*. She kept rejecting the scripts offered her, which tended to be slurpy soap operas that eventually became vehicles for other Warner contractees like Connie Stevens, Angie Dickinson and Diane McBain.

Now twenty-two years old, Natalie had become fed up with the fan magazines still calling her "a promising young star of tomorrow." In the five years since *Rebel Without a Cause*, she'd been hovering on the brink of major stardom without ever finally breaking through.

She blamed it on Jack Warner's failure to consider her for truly mature parts or to let her work with any directors beyond the usual studio hacks. She couldn't understand why Warner had to "borrow" Audrey Hepburn for Fred Zinnemann's *The Nun's Story*, for example, or Leslie Caron for Josh Logan's *Fanny* when they already had Natalie Wood under contract.

Through an act of God, Natalie finally got the opportunity she wanted. Lee Remick became pregnant and had to be replaced in her starring role in *Splendor in the Grass*. After going over the list of Warner contractees, producer-director Elia Kazan decided that Natalie was the only possibility, but she'd have to make a test first. Could she fly to New York immediately and meet with him?

Before she could commit herself, Natalie had to talk it over with R.J. They'd promised each other that whenever they had to travel anywhere it would always be together. Further complicating matters, *Splendor in the Grass* would be produced entirely in New York City and environs. If Natalie did get the part, she'd have to be away from home for at least three months.

R.J. insisted that Natalie disregard their pact for the moment. The trip East to meet Kazan would only take a few days. And should she be hired, R.J. would try to arrange his own schedule so that he could be with her as much as possible.

The couple agreed totally that the opportunity to work with Elia Kazan, tantamount to God for the post-World War II generation of actors, couldn't be passed up. One of the founders of the revolutionary Actors Studio, Kazan's brilliant collaborations with Marlon Brando, James Dean, Tennessee Williams and Arthur Miller, were responsible for scores of Tonys and Oscars. For Natalie it could be the fulfillment of a dream to someday give a performance equal to that of her idol, Vivien Leigh, in *A Streetcar Named Desire*, which Kazan had directed.

For her initial meeting with Kazan, Natalie traveled to New York alone. She hoped to avoid publicity in case the director decided she wasn't good enough. Such a rejection could be extremely damaging to her professional standing if not kept secret, she believed.

After settling into a Waldorf-Astoria suite paid for by Warner Brothers, Natalie sought help from her actress friend, Norma Crane, an Actors Studio alumna well trained in the Kazan-Lee Strasberg Method. Natalie asked Crane to breeze through the script for *Splendor in the Grass* and suggest ways of playing some difficult scenes that she'd underlined with a red grease pencil.

Norma Crane stuck around while Natalie dressed for her appointment with Kazan. "The girl in *Splendor* was the purest, most virginal young thing in the world, and there was Natalie putting on mascara, six-inch spike heels, false eyelashes, bracelets, rings," Crane remembered. "I said to her, 'You're going to meet Kazan. *The big part*, remember?' She replied, 'I'm Natalie Wood and this is how I look when I go out.' "

Natalie needn't have worried about not getting the part. Kazan had been wanting to work with her ever since he'd seen her performance in *Rebel Without a Cause*.

"But everybody at Warner Brothers kept warning me against her," Kazan remembered. "They pointed out that she had made so many lousy pictures and that she was getting worse and worse."

When Kazan met Natalie, he was impressed by her energy and ambition. "She told me she wanted a new career," Kazan said. "She had tremendous will power to be good. So many actresses, you feel they have a private life, a husband and kids, and acting has a place. But, with Natalie, acting was her whole life."

For the screen test Kazan banished the Hollywood version of Natalie Wood from the set. "I used paint remover on her, took off her glamorous clothes and put her in front of the camera, naked and gasping," he said.

"I decided that if she worked hard and listened to me I could probably free her from all the bad acting habits she'd picked up in her many years in the business," Kazan continued. "She could cry on cue, for example, but only with her eyes. The rest of her face remained an impassive mask."

Natalie was so ecstatic over Kazan's acceptance that she could have flown back to Los Angeles under her own power. Further good news, at least for Natalie, was that R.J.'s next picture, *Solo*, had been postponed until autumn. Unless Fox handed him an interim assignment, which seemed highly unlikely, he'd be able to accompany her to New York when *Splendor in the Grass* started up in May.

With remodeling of Chez Wagner still going on—R.J. wondered how much longer he had to put up with loose plaster sprinkling his cornflakes every morning—the couple couldn't get away fast enough. They hired extra workmen to make sure that the job would be completed by the time they returned.

Since the story of *Splendor in the Grass* took place mainly in Kansas at the end of the roaring twenties, why did it have to be filmed in New York? First, Elia Kazan loathed working under the antiquated Hollywood system, by which movies were churned out like cars on an assembly line.

Second, Kansas lacked adequate production facilities. To save the enormous expense of transporting equipment, actors and crew there, it was better to use a New York City studio, with parts of Staten Island and Westchester County doubling for the Sunflower State in exterior scenes.

Under the terms of her contract, Natalie had to be paid regu-

lar salary plus a weekly living allowance of fifty percent while
working outside Hollywood, so the Wagners' temporary move
to Manhattan didn't add to their financial problems. They
rented a furnished apartment on the Upper East Side, bringing
with them just enough things to fill seventeen wardrobe
trunks, plus a portable stereo given to them as a going-away
present by their newlywed friends, Elizabeth Taylor and Eddie
Fisher. So they'd feel more at home, R.J. taxied to Colony
Records on Broadway and spent $750 buying duplicate copies
of favorite albums they'd left behind.

In all the excitement of moving and getting ready to start
Splendor in the Grass, Natalie hadn't bothered much with finding
out production details. But she did know that Jack Warner had
plunked down the enormous sum of $250,000 for the script, the
first written expressly as a movie by Pulitzer Prize-winning
playwright William Inge. Author of such hits as *Picnic, Bus Stop*
and *Come Back, Little Sheba,* Inge ranked with Tennessee Williams and Arthur Miller as one of the foremost theatrical writers of the time. Natalie realized that the chance to work with
both Elia Kazan *and* William Inge was rare indeed and that
she'd better not blow it.

Had it been up to Jack Warner, Natalie's leading man in
Splendor in the Grass would have been the studio's top pinup boy,
Troy Donahue. But Kazan and Inge vetoed that suggestion immediately, with Inge insisting that they hire a young protégé of
his who'd never acted in a movie before. Inge delivered such an
effective sales pitch on the actor ("He's going to be bigger than
Marlon Brando and James Dean put together!") that Jack
Warner signed him for $200,000, an astonishing fee for a new-
comer. His name was Warren Beatty.

According to rumors circulating at the time, the homosexual
Inge had fallen passionately in love with Beatty, who encouraged the attachment in order to advance his career. The exact
nature of the relationship between the middle-aged playwright
and the twentyish ex-high school football star may never be
known, but Inge's circle of gay friends jokingly dubbed him
"Warren's fairy godfather." He not only launched him in films,
but the previous year he had also given Beatty his first big
professional chance with a top role in *A Loss of Roses.* Unfortu-

nately the play became Inge's first Broadway flop, closing after three weeks.

Natalie and R.J. both had a nodding acquaintance with Beatty, a well-known Hollywood party crasher who used the fact that he was Shirley MacLaine's younger brother as his calling card. Once past the door, he usually headed straight for the piano, where he ended up charming everybody with his talent for mimicking the styles of jazz greats like Art Tatum and Erroll Garner.

R.J. became apprehensive about Natalie working with Warren Beatty. For all the whispers about his relationship with William Inge, Beatty also had a reputation as a lady-killer. It was common knowledge that his current mistress was none other than Joan Collins, who had once caused tension between the Wagners.

A closely guarded secret, however, was that Collins had recently undergone an abortion because Beatty felt he wasn't ready to take on the responsibilities of husband and father. It must be remembered that in the strict moral climate of 1960 couples weren't even supposed to live together, let alone have babies, outside marriage.

Joan Collins seemed to be as concerned as R.J. over the possibility of something developing between Natalie and Warren. On the day that *Splendor in the Grass* started filming, all four were on the set. R.J. hardly left Natalie's side during the production breaks.

"R.J. couldn't seem to keep his hands off Natalie," a crew member recalled. "He was always kissing and hugging her, as if to show that he loved her so much that he'd punch the first guy that even winked at her."

Not to be outdone, Joan Collins clung to Warren Beatty like Saran Wrap. Anticipating that everybody was in for a long and bumpy ride, the production manager ordered name-embossed canvas folding chairs for R.J. and Collins to use on the set, something usually done just for key members of the cast and staff.

In *Splendor in the Grass,* Natalie and Beatty portray a pair of high school sweethearts whose sexual yearnings are frustrated by the puritanism of Middle America in the 1920s. When Natalie refuses to "go all the way," Beatty drops her and takes up with the school slut. Natalie starts to have a mental breakdown upon discovering that he's been unfaithful to her. She eventually lands in the county asylum when a near rape by another beau causes her to go raving mad.

Although Natalie and Beatty never make it to bed together in the film, the script called for passionate kissing and dry humping galore. With that stickler for realism Elia Kazan calling the shots, they had to do endless takes and retakes as he goaded them to fever pitch.

Eventually the make-believe embraces turned into a real affair, but whether it actually started then could be answered only by the two participants. However, the unit publicist recalled that "Bob Wagner and Joan Collins were around so much that it would have been impossible for Natalie and Warren to be alone together long enough for even a quickie."

Still, someone buzzed into the ear of Dorothy Kilgallen, who wrote in her nationally syndicated column that "Natalie and Warren are staying up nights rehearsing the next day's love scenes." The Wagners' attorney sent Kilgallen a telegram demanding a retraction, claiming that the item was "defamatory and untrue." Kilgallen refused to back down.

Joan Collins left New York before *Splendor in the Grass* finished. In order to be with Warren Beatty, she'd turned down a picture at 20th Century-Fox and been placed under suspension. Since Beatty wasn't the most spendthrift of lovers, her money eventually ran out and she had to accept Fox's next assignment, *Esther and the King*, an Italian coproduction being made in Rome.

Fox apparently wasn't as eager to put Robert Wagner back to work. He seemed to spend a lot of time playing errand boy for his wife. One day Kazan noticed his absence from the set and asked Natalie, "Where's R.J?"

"Oh," she replied with a yawn, "he's gone to Bergdorf's to buy me a scarf."

Another time R.J. arrived on the set and found Beatty standing with his arm wrapped around Natalie's waist while they waited for the electricians to shift some of the lights for the next take.

"What are you doing, Bob, keeping tabs on me?" Beatty said,

loudly enough for everybody around to hear. R.J. laughed, but his face turned a reddish mixture of embarrassment and rage.

Whenever Natalie and Beatty had to play a love scene R.J. retreated to his wife's dressing room until he heard Kazan yell, "Cut!" R.J.'s standard explanation was that he didn't want to inhibit their performances: "Clark Gable once told me that he used to break out in a cold sweat and blow all his lines whenever Carole Lombard came around to watch him working with Lana Turner."

But R.J. also had his own feelings to consider. "R.J. was a very sensitive guy. It really killed him to watch Natalie and Warren turning on the heat, even if they were only doing it to win Kazan's approval," a friend said. "But there was nothing R.J. could do about it except look the other way and wait for the day when he could take Natalie home to L.A."

Natalie seemed to be transformed into a new woman while making *Splendor in the Grass.* Although she'd been prone to tardiness and sloppy preparation on some of her previous films, she now always arrived on time and knew her lines. Was it Elia Kazan's influence or Warren Beatty's? Probably a combination of the two.

Kazan gave Natalie the "Big Star" treatment and she loved it. "Before I did a scene, Gadge [Kazan's nickname] would always ask me how *I* thought it should be done," she remembered. "No one had ever flattered me like that before, so for me this was the greatest director in the world!"

But Kazan could also be a mischief-maker. Natalie was terrified of deep water and didn't want to do a scene that, in retrospect, turned out to be somewhat prophetic. In a state of hysteria after fighting off a would-be rapist, she plunges dazedly into a reservoir and nearly drowns.

"Gadge kept telling me not to worry: 'All you have to do is jump in and we'll use a double to finish out the scene,' " Natalie said. "While waiting for the crew to arrange things, I saw this girl who weighed about two hundred pounds sitting on a rock. I went over to her and asked what she was going to do in the movie.

" 'I'm going to double for you,' she said. 'But there's only one problem. I'm terribly scared because I don't know how to swim.' Naturally, I wound up doing the entire scene. I'm positive that Gadge did that deliberately, knowing how I'd react."

Natalie felt no inhibitions, however, when Kazan asked her to appear stark naked for the scene in which, after an angry screaming match with her mother, she had to leap from the bathtub and race down the hallway to her bedroom. It would be a "first" for a major Hollywood film. Nudity was forbidden under the industry's system of self-censorship, which hadn't yet evolved to using ratings such as "G," "R" or "X." Without the Motion Picture Association of America's "Seal of Approval," the picture couldn't be released.

R.J., who deplored the idea of his wife baring everything, insisted on being on the set with Kazan when the filming took place. Except for the cameraman and a few technicians, no visitors were permitted. Warren Beatty reportedly watched through a peephole cut in the wall.

Kazan shot the nude scene without informing Jack Warner. When the rushes were flown to California, Warner nearly had a heart attack at the screening. Although Warner Brothers had introduced talking pictures, he wasn't going to let it become the first Hollywood studio to make a skin flick. Warner insisted that the scene be cut, but he later relented by permitting it to be included in prints shown in foreign countries, where the MPAA censorship code didn't apply.

When *Splendor in the Grass* finally wrapped in August, R.J. breathed a sigh of relief as Warren Beatty left for Europe for a new project. William Inge had persuaded his close friend Tennessee Williams to request Beatty for the role of the Italian gigolo in the film of Williams' novella, *The Roman Spring of Mrs. Stone*. R.J. did not find it amusing when Natalie jokingly begged Beatty to take her with him so that she could get to meet his leading lady and *her* favorite actress, Vivien Leigh.

Natalie and R.J. intended to cruise back to California by passenger freighter via the Panama Canal for a leisurely ten days of sun and relaxation. But they canceled at the last minute because of a phone call that Elia Kazan received from director-choreographer Jerome Robbins, who was preparing the movie version of his hit Broadway musical, *West Side Story*.

Robbins wanted to know if Kazan could suggest an actress for the role of Maria, a Puerto Rican cousin of Shakespeare's

An intimate family portrait of Natalie with her parents, Maria and Nicholas Gurdin, and baby sister Svetlana, who later became an actress under the professional name of Lana Wood. (Museum of Modern Art/ Film Stills Archives)

In Miracle on 34th Street, *her most memorable movie as a child actress, Natalie has her first meeting with Edmund Gwenn, an elderly gentleman who may really be Santa Claus. (AP/Wide World Photos)*

Teenaged Natalie's most publicized romance was with Elvis Presley. He took her to Memphis to meet his family, but she returned to Hollywood bored and disillusioned. (UPI/Bettmann Newsphotos)

R.J. with his parents, Robert and Hazel Wagner. The family residence bordered on the Bel-Air Country Club, where the adolescent R.J. caddied for movie stars like Clark Gable and Alan Ladd. (Museum of Modern Art/Film Stills Archives)

Studio publicity shots like this made Robert Wagner the rage of the teen set. The ermine bow tie he's modeling cost a princely fifteen dollars at the time. (AP/Wide World Photos)

R.J. started attracting the most fan mail of any 20th Century-Fox contractee after portraying a shell-shocked GI in With a Song in My Heart. *Susan Hayward, as singer Jane Froman, cures his amnesia by recalling an earlier encounter between the two. (Museum of Modern Art/Film Stills Archives)*

A hairstylist makes a last-minute adjustment to R.J.'s Prince Valiant *wig, which once caused Dean Martin to mistake him for Jane Wyman. (AP/Wide World Photos)*

During filming of **Broken Lance**, *R.J. gets some much needed professional instruction from veteran co-star Spencer Tracy, who became a lifelong friend and adviser. (AP/Wide World Photos)*

Natalie with Sal Mineo and James Dean in a scene from **Rebel Without a Cause**. *Because all three stars died young and tragically, a Hollywood legend has developed that they were the victims of an evil curse on the production. (Museum of Modern Art/Film Stills Archives)*

Natalie and leading man Gene Kelly attend a Passover seder in Marjorie Morningstar. *Despite the tremendous popularity of Herman Wouk's novel, the movie bombed and failed in its attempt to make Natalie a major star. (Museum of Modern Art/Film Stills Archives)*

The newly engaged-to-be-married sweethearts proudly show the ring to Frank Sinatra on the set of Kings Go Forth, *the World War II drama in which Natalie co-starred with Sinatra and Tony Curtis. (AP/Wide World Photos)*

Natalie and R.J. were married for the first time in a private ceremony in Scottsdale, Arizona, on December 28, 1957. Photos like the above, intended solely for a family keepsake album, caused trauma when a friend sold them to the fan magazines. (UPI/Bettmann Newsphotos)

Natalie and R.J. ended their honeymoon trip in New York, where press photographers rarely left them alone. Whether she clobbered any of them with that copy of Marjorie Morningstar *is unknown. (AP/Wide World Photos)*

Juliet. When Kazan said, "How about Natalie Wood?" Robbins replied, "Oh, no, we want a complete unknown. We've already tested about a hundred girls."

"How unknown can you get after being buried in bombs like *All the Fine Young Cannibals?*" Kazan asked. "Let me arrange for you to see some film. You'll never believe how this kid has developed." Robbins was sufficiently impressed by the footage from *Splendor in the Grass* to ask Natalie to return to the West Coast immediately to meet with him and his codirector, Robert Wise.

Her confidence bolstered by approval from recognized geniuses like Elia Kazan and Jerome Robbins, Natalie arrived back in Hollywood ready to assume what she believed to be her rightful place as a full-fledged star. Unfortunately, at the same time, R.J. had no reason to be optimistic about his own position. Although he was thrilled for Natalie, he also couldn't help feeling envious. Except for the disastrous *All the Fine Young Cannibals*, he hadn't worked for more than a year.

And then there was the matter of Warren Beatty. Was R.J. just imagining it or was something really developing between Natalie and Warren? Without any concrete evidence, R.J. didn't want to risk offending Natalie by asking her. It seemed a betrayal of the trust that a man and his wife were supposed to have in each other.

SIX

Stormy Weather

BY THE AUTUMN of 1960, Natalie and R.J. had been married nearly three years. On the surface, everything appeared rosy.

"Marriage has given us a sense of security. We're more relaxed now. You have a tremendous amount of inner confidence because someone really believes in you," Natalie told a reporter. R.J. mumbled agreement, about all he could do with Natalie sitting in his lap and hugging him around the neck throughout the interview.

But tensions had been building for a long time. For one thing, Natalie and R.J. had totally different temperaments. She was full of ambition, he more interested in having a wife than another star around the house. Furthermore, Natalie started drawing assignments of consequence while he remained mired in pretty-boy roles that provided almost no chance to prove himself as an actor.

It was an altogether sticky situation. The couple's conviction that their marriage could sustain two separate but equal careers had a serious flaw. How do you cope with one partner suddenly becoming more successful than the other? Brought up to believe in the dominance of the male, R.J. found such a reversal harder to accept than Natalie might have if it had happened to her.

The marriage received its severest test when Natalie and R.J. returned from New York. The moment they walked in the door of their house they discovered three months' accumulation of refuse and faulty workmanship. The living room and dining room were still in such shambles that they looked as if Laurel and Hardy *and* the Three Stooges had been the contractors.

Since Natalie did all the hiring and planning, R.J. blamed her for the fiasco and refused to take any part in making it right. Eventually he had to take over anyway when Natalie became involved in a career contretemps that nearly killed her.

It all started harmlessly enough when Jerome Robbins and Robert Wise decided to sign Natalie for *West Side Story*, a United Artists release. That meant "borrowing" Natalie from Warner Brothers, which turned out to have plans of its own for her.

Jack Warner, who'd been foiled once already in an attempt to make a romantic team of Natalie and Troy Donahue in *Splendor in the Grass*, insisted on pairing them in *Parrish*, scheduled for production at the same time as *West Side Story*.

After Natalie read the script of *Parrish* she ripped it to shreds and threw it out with the trash. She would portray one of three girls in love with the rebellious stepson of a wealthy tobacco planter. The trite melodrama was hardly the quality material she thought she deserved after working with Elia Kazan and William Inge. It could turn her career right back in the opposite direction, straight down the drain.

Natalie had been through so many battles with Jack Warner that she knew exactly how he'd react if she refused to make *Parrish*. He'd put her under suspension for at least as long as *Parrish* took to film. That meant that she'd lose *West Side Story* because UA couldn't afford to postpone the $10 million production until she became available.

Rather than turn down *Parrish*, Natalie invoked the "act of God" clause in her contract, which provided that she could be excused from an assignment without penalty for reasons such as pregnancy, a serious illness or accident. She decided to have her tonsils removed, which would keep her hospitalized and convalescing just long enough to miss the starting date of *Parrish*.

Years later Natalie could joke about it: "I was saving my appendix for something really terrible, like *Bride of Godzilla!*" But at the time it became no laughing matter.

Since tonsillectomies are performed mainly on children, Natalie thought it was just about the safest operation. She didn't realize that an adult's body is less resilient, increasing the chances for infection or other serious complications. Her doctor, one of those celebrity sycophants whose creed seemed to be "the patient is always right," failed to warn her of that.

In exchange for a perfectly healthy pair of tonsils, Natalie developed pneumonia and nearly died. She remained on the critical list for three days before antibiotics finally stemmed the infection.

It was an exorbitant price to pay to avoid making an unwanted film. Natalie remained in delicate health for months afterward, incapable of coping with being wife, homemaker and movie star all at the same time. Some things had to be shunted aside or given less than their usual devotion. Unhappily, Natalie's priorities were such that R.J. found himself taking second place more often.

Nothing now stood in the way of Natalie being signed for *West Side Story*. If Jack Warner caught on to her subterfuge, he didn't try to block the loan-out by forcing her to do another studio project in place of *Parrish*. Perhaps he thought her illness punishment enough for the time being.

Some of Natalie's suffering was alleviated when the Mirisch Company and Seven Arts, the producers of *West Side Story*, offered to pay her in one of two ways: a lump sum of $250,000, or $50,000 and five percent of the profits. Either way, it put Natalie Wood into the big-money class for the first time in her career.

She took the quarter million. It would enable the Wagners to add even more improvements to their house and also to catch up on settling their debts.

Natalie and R.J. both thought that a percentage was too much of a gamble. No matter how successful the movie became, producers were notorious for "creative" bookkeeping that, at least on earnings statements, swallowed up all the profits. Natalie had no guarantee that she'd ever receive anything beyond that initial $50,000, which in itself wasn't enough to solve any of the Wagners' current financial problems.

Since *West Side Story* had already earned a reputation as one of the greatest musicals in the history of the American theater, many people wondered why Jerome Robbins and Robert Wise selected Natalie Wood, neither a singer nor a dancer, to star in the film. The answer is as cockeyed as anything that ever happened in Hollywood.

To begin with, all the leading players of the original 1957 Broadway cast, including Carol Lawrence, Larry Kert and Chita Rivera, were ruled out for the movie. Jerome Robbins wanted to work with new people who would bring a fresh interpretation to the roles.

Had it had been up to Robbins, he would have hired the most talented "unknowns" he could find. But executive producer Walter Mirisch felt that, without stars in the cast, a tragic dance musical about New York street gangs would not attract large audiences in the hinterlands. Mirisch wanted Elvis Presley for Tony (Romeo), with other current pop idols like Frankie Avalon, Fabian and Paul Anka as members of the rival Jets and Sharks.

Robbins nearly quit over that suggestion, but a compromise was finally reached, starting with Natalie Wood. The other major roles went to Richard Beymer, George Chakiris and Russ Tamblyn (all very popular with the fan magazine set at the time), and Rita Moreno, Hollywood's reigning Latin sexpot.

Natalie's latest coup caused further unrest on the home front. Nobody offered her husband impressive projects like *West Side Story*. R.J. just sat around waiting for the phone to ring. When it finally did, he started foaming at the mouth.

After stalling him for more than a year while *Solo* underwent script revisions, 20th Century-Fox wanted R.J. to start work on it immediately. However, what began as a $4 million project had been revamped into a low-budget "quickie" featuring a flock of rock 'n' roll recording stars and the mammaries of Jayne Mansfield, who would be R.J.'s leading lady.

He refused to make the movie. Fox suspended him for what turned out to be the balance of his contract, which had nearly expired anyway.

Having made all but four of his twenty-two movies for 20th Century-Fox, R.J. had a sentimental attachment to the studio and felt sad about leaving. Irrational though it might seem to anyone who didn't know that Spyros Skouras was verging on senility, Fox's sixty-seven-year-old president wanted him to stay. At the end of R.J.'s suspension, Skouras offered him a new five-year deal worth over a million dollars, but without script approval or the right to do outside pictures.

Natalie advised R.J. not to sign. So did his old friend Spencer Tracy, who told R.J. that breaking his own twenty-year bondage to MGM had been the smartest and most lucrative decision he'd ever made.

When R.J. turned down the new Fox contract, Spyros Skouras called him an ungrateful s.o.b. and invoked the dreaded Mogul's Curse: "We made you and we'll break you. You'll never work in this town again!"

Within a month R.J. signed a three-picture, nonexclusive deal with Columbia. His remuneration was kept secret, apparently to spare him embarrassment over its being far less than what his wife could command at the time. But it was believed to be $2,500 a week plus a percentage of the profits, if there were any.

R.J. wasn't thrilled with the first project that Columbia handed him, but the front office told him to trust them. They knew what the public wanted and this would be a blockbuster: a wacky crime caper called *Sail a Crooked Ship*, with the outrageous Ernie Kovacs as R.J.'s costar.

The assignment put a damper on Natalie and R.J.'s togetherness policy. For the first time since they married, work schedules conflicted. Neither seemed perturbed. In fact both were starting to realize that too much togetherness could be destructive. When they ran out of things to talk about they turned to bickering, often for no other reason than to keep a dialogue going. But when not held in check the bickering tended to intensify into quarreling and the quarreling into screaming matches.

The togetherness during working hours had also caused wounds, especially to R.J.'s pride and to his reputation around the studios. For an obviously chauvinistic reason, it was acceptable for a woman to dance attendance on her husband. But when a man did it he became the butt of jokes as "the star's husband" or, even worse, "Mr. Natalie Wood."

Yet the handholding did have value as a morale booster. It was too bad that R.J. couldn't have been with Natalie throughout the making of *West Side Story*, the most difficult undertaking of her entire life. He stuck by her side for part of the filming but eventually had to stay away when he started *Sail a Crooked Ship*.

Helping to calm Natalie's jitters in R.J.'s absence was Mart Crowley, a former production "gofer" on *Splendor in the Grass*, whom she'd brought to California to work as her personal secretary. A close, almost sisterly bond had developed between Natalie and the young Southern homosexual. Fanatic about the movie love goddesses of the past and extremely knowledgeable about clothes and makeup, he seemed the right person to help Natalie become one of the present crop. Crowley aspired to be a screenwriter; in return for his assistance, Natalie gave him a chance to learn the business from the inside.

On the first day of shooting *West Side Story*, Natalie turned up an hour late, radiating the hauteur of a true movie queen. She wore a skin-tight dress with plunging neckline, with a cossack's hat made of monkey fur perched on her head. Trailing behind her in single file were Mart Crowley plus her makeup man, wardrobe mistress and hairdresser. A few minutes later R.J. arrived, leading their gray poodle, Gigi, on a leash.

Although it appeared that Natalie Wood had "gone Hollywood" in a big way, she was also covering up for the inner fear and inadequacy that she felt over her ability to play the role of Maria. As the modern-day Juliet, she had to sing, dance and speak with a Latin accent.

With relentless perfectionist Jerome Robbins as tutor, Natalie worked sixteen-hour days and weekends to catch up with the professional dancers in the cast. Rita Moreno, an old friend from the Marlon Brando-James Dean circle of acolytes, coached her on the accent.

But Natalie proved hopeless as a singer of intricate ditties by Leonard Bernstein and Stephen Sondheim. Her vocal equipment wasn't that strong to begin with, and her recent tonsillectomy didn't help. Later, during the editing of the movie, Marni Nixon would dub new voice tracks for Natalie. But in the meantime she still needed to learn and perform all the numbers, no matter how awful she sounded. Pity the people on the set within earshot, especially when Natalie dueted with Richard Beymer, another deficient singer who required dubbing!

Natalie's problems were compounded by having to take orders from two directors. Although Jerome Robbins had been the sole director on Broadway, he'd never made a movie before except as a choreographer. The Mirisch company insisted that he share the responsibility with an experienced Hollywood hand.

For all his slave-driving tactics, Robbins, who handled the musical numbers, seemed genuinely to like rehearsing and working with actors until they felt comfortable in what they were doing. But the director of the dramatic scenes, Robert Wise (once Orson Welles's film cutter on *Citizen Kane*), was more technician than helpmate. He often brought Natalie to tears with his lack of finesse and patience.

To avoid having a nervous breakdown, Natalie grew fanatic about her psychoanalysis. While working, she took two-hour lunch breaks in order to drive to the analyst's office and back. If she couldn't be spared from the set she locked herself in her dressing room, stretched out on the sofa and had her daily session by telephone.

Although life for the Wagners seemed to contain more smog than sunshine, a hurricane was about to wreak further havoc. It blew in not from the tropics but from the nearby Hollywood Hills, where Warren Beatty had resumed living with Joan Collins in her rented house above the Sunset Strip.

After nearly two years of keeping steady company, Beatty and Collins had become officially engaged, but their frequent quarrels made marriage seem unlikely. Ironically, the root of their problems was similar to that of the Wagners: Beatty's career skyrocketing while Collins' plummeted. Like R.J., Collins had also ended her long association with 20th Century-Fox. But for a beauty pushing thirty, leading roles were harder to come by than for a man of like age. She'd been unemployed for a year.

Beatty wasn't working either, but only by choice. Although *Splendor in the Grass* and *The Roman Spring of Mrs. Stone* were still unreleased, the enormous advance publicity, plus all the gossip about his liaison with Joan Collins, had turned him into a major celebrity before the public had even seen his work. Though offers poured in at the rate of $350,000 a picture, he opted to wait for his mentor, William Inge, to finish writing a new screenplay for him based on James Leo Herlihy's novel, *All Fall Down.*

Warren Beatty had a favorite opening line that later became the title for a movie: "What's new, pussycat?" When he phoned Natalie one day on the set of *West Side Story* to reestablish contact after being away in Europe, he caught her at an especially vulnerable moment. She'd just had a screaming match with Robert Wise and spilled out her problems to Beatty, who listened intently and with disarming sympathy.

"It might have ended there, because it was not in Natalie's nature to be unfaithful," said one of her closest friends. "But Warren in heat is irresistible. His approach is direct and totally unconventional. He plays it for shock. He doesn't waste time on amenities. He appeals to the feminine wish to be engulfed."

With R.J. and Joan Collins to consider, the affair was played out in secret. How frequently or where Natalie and Beatty met was known only to the lovers, but they eventually started stepping out publicly in the spring of 1961.

No one thought anything about it at first because it was supposed to be for the sake of promoting the imminent release of *Splendor in the Grass.* When they turned up together for press screenings or interviews, it appeared to be simply an arrangement of the Warner Brothers publicity department.

But R.J. grew suspicious. Natalie had completed *West Side Story,* so she wasn't working. There was a limit to the amount of publicity that she could do for *Splendor in the Grass* and she rarely visited him on the set of *Sail a Crooked Ship.* What was she up to? Certainly not attending to finishing the remodeling of the house, which had a backyard filled with marble and wood-work still waiting to be installed. The answer finally came.

During all the movies they'd made since they started going together, the Wagners had kept up a practice of hosting a party for the production workers and technicians on their last day on the set. There would be an open bar, with Natalie and R.J. fixing drinks and passing around plates of expensive hors d'oeuvres from Chasen's. It was their way not only of saying thanks but also of keeping up an image as nice folks who weren't above fraternizing with subordinates.

For R.J., the party at the end of *Sail a Crooked Ship* became an especially important one. Working at Columbia for the first time, he wanted to make a good impression on all the new people he'd met. But, much to his embarrassment, Natalie wasn't there to assist him. She failed to arrive at the appointed time, so the party started without her.

Half an hour later Natalie strolled in with Warren Beatty. Heading straight for R.J., she threw her arms around him and apologized for being late. She and Beatty had been detained at Warner Brothers shooting publicity stills, she claimed, so she decided to invite him to the party in return for his driving her there.

"R.J. looked fit to be tied," a Columbia executive recalled. "He took Natalie into a corner and apparently read her the riot act. She circulated among the crowd for a bit, but then she and Warren left, announcing that they were going over to another sound stage to say hello to Jane Fonda and would be right back. I didn't make the connection at the time, but in retrospect that's pretty funny. Jane had been one of Warren's girls before Joan Collins. Maybe Natalie wasn't aware of that."

An hour elapsed before Natalie and Beatty returned to the party, which was rapidly winding down. This time Joan Collins accompanied them, linked arm in arm with Beatty while Natalie walked beside her.

En route to visit Jane Fonda, Beatty had stopped at a telephone booth and summoned Collins to the scene after Natalie grew panicky over R.J.'s angry reaction. Beatty's waltzing in with Collins and acting very attentive toward her was intended to dispel any suspicions that something might be going on between him and Natalie.

Given the charged atmosphere of the evening, it would have been wise for the two couples to go their separate ways when the party ended. But Natalie insisted that they make it a foursome for dinner at Villa Capri, a current hot spot.

As two couples often do for the sake of conversation, Natalie sat facing Beatty, while R.J. was opposite Collins. Somewhere between the antipasto and the main course, R.J. got the distinct impression that Natalie and Beatty were playing touch-me games underneath the table. They were giggling far too much for the insipid dialogue going on at the same time.

Of course R.J. could be imagining things, or they might just be drunk, but he wasn't taking any chances. He told Natalie he wanted to go home. She insisted on finishing her meal first.

Right now, R.J. demanded. Natalie grew furious but realized the packed dining room was no place for squabbling. She finally stalked out, with R.J. right behind her.

What transpired when the Wagners got home can only be guessed at. But R.J. finally walked out and went to stay on their boat at Newport Beach.

Around dawn the next morning Natalie turned up on the doorstep of her parents' house in Van Nuys. She was crying, with one hand wrapped in a silk scarf to stop it from bleeding. While arguing with R.J., she had become so agitated that she vented her feelings by grabbing the nearest object—a delicate crystal goblet—and squeezing it until it shattered.

Later that day in June 1961 the Wagners' public relations representatives, Rogers & Cowan, dispatched a terse announcement that the couple was going through a trial separation but that they had no immediate plans for a divorce: "Both are hopeful that the problems that exist between them can be worked out satisfactorily."

The news media and the public alike were shocked. During the three and a half years they'd been married the Wagners had been Hollywood's darlings, almost like two nice kids from the neighborhood who had wed with everyone's blessings. For the Heddas and Louellas of that world, it was the worst romantic tragedy since Mary Pickford and Douglas Fairbanks split, way back in 1933!

That great marital expert, Elizabeth Taylor, was so upset and disillusioned by the news that she popped two tranquilizers and went to bed. Taylor had been convinced that, out of all the Hollywood marriages she'd known, the Wagners' had the best chance for surviving the usual pitfalls and living happily ever after.

When informed of Taylor's pill taking, Natalie asked, "Why does *she* need sedating? It's *my* marriage that just collapsed!"

SEVEN

Moving On

DESPITE THE CLAIM of their separation announcement, Natalie and R.J. couldn't work out a solution to their problems. In fact Natalie hardly bothered to make the effort. She was so infatuated with Warren Beatty that nothing else mattered, not even her career. After *West Side Story,* she didn't work for a year so that they could be together.

"R.J. didn't stand a chance of getting his wife back while Warren was on the scene," a close friend of the couple recalled. "R.J. was too conservative, a square, really. Natalie got bored with him. A woman who's an actress usually craves excitement and conflict, even brutality, in her relationships. Warren gave her that. He was the exact opposite of R.J.: dominating, ruthless, greedy to have it all."

The Wagners' separation meant that a decision had to be made about their joint financial arrangements. Neither wanted the house in Beverly Hills, which stood as a monument to all their mistakes, so they put it up for sale. No one was eager to buy the neo-Greco-Roman monstrosity. It remained on the market for ages, finally selling for $155,000, a fraction of what the couple invested in it.

Most possessions were also disposed of: cars, household effects and, last of all, the boat on which they had spent their happiest moments. Monies were divided evenly. R.J. got half of what Natalie earned for *West Side Story*, while she was to receive half of whatever he took from his percentage deal on *Sail a Crooked Ship*.

By the time the community property settlement was finalized in August, rumors circulated that Natalie would get a Mexican divorce and marry Warren Beatty. She didn't. Instead, she rented a house high up in the hills of Bel Air, where it was so sylvan that deer roamed free and lovers could live together unnoticed. Beatty moved in after brokenhearted Joan Collins kicked him out and returned to England to try to revive her career.

In September, Natalie threw convention to the wind (this was 1961, remember) by accompanying Beatty to Florida while he worked on location scenes for his new movie, *All Fall Down*. When he finished, they flew to one of the nearby Bahama islands for a weekend.

The lovers managed to keep out of the glare of publicity until they turned up in New York in October. Supposedly Natalie and Warren were there individually to publicize the release of *Splendor in the Grass*. Warner Brothers put them up at the Plaza Hotel in separate suites on different floors, standard procedure when a male and female star who weren't married to each other traveled together.

Soon after they checked in Beatty got stopped by a house detective while using an emergency staircase in the middle of the night. With his shirttails hanging sloppily out of his trousers, he was apparently making his way back to his quarters from Natalie's. After someone informed the press, Natalie and Beatty were constantly harassed by reporters and photographers whenever they went out. Toward the end of their visit they took evasive action by moving to an apartment borrowed from a friend, which caused further shock waves among the moral guardians of the day.

Columnist Dorothy Kilgallen, whose earlier allegations of an affair had been denied, now sniffed, "The way Natalie Wood and Warren Beatty are carrying on around Gotham, it's a wonder they have time to eat."

According to an assistant who worked for Kilgallen at the time, "She'd been tipped off that the couple was so active sexually that the Plaza maids had been going in five or six times a day to change the sheets. Of course, no newspaper then would dare print such an item, so Dorothy had to phrase it in such a way that you could read between the lines."

Meanwhile Robert Wagner kept strangely silent. Legally, Natalie was still his wife. If he wanted to divorce her he seemingly had sufficient proof to sue on grounds of adultery, yet he didn't. Instead he retreated into himself and started drinking heavily, not an uncommon reaction for a man whose wife is making a fool of him by openly consorting with another.

"In the end, I was almost destroyed," he remembered.

"The saddest thing was that R.J. treated it like a bad dream that would suddenly end with Natalie galloping back to him," said an intimate. "I think he had really come to believe all that fan magazine crap about the Great American Dream Couple. R.J. couldn't admit to himself that there was never going to be a Camelot."

Some of R.J.'s friends tried introducing him to other women, hoping that a new relationship might end his unhappiness, but it proved futile. "R.J. couldn't think straight. He had no plans, no strategy for a future without Natalie," said director Richard Sale. "There was no way he could become involved with someone else while he still hoped for a reconciliation."

But circumstances only drove Natalie and R.J. further and further apart. When *Splendor in the Grass* was released, followed only a month later by *West Side Story*, Natalie Wood catapulted to the topmost rung of movie stardom.

"Many consider her the freshest and most exciting talent to emerge since Elizabeth Taylor," said *Newsweek*. "Hollywood will have a tough time deciding which of those two impressive performances will win Natalie Wood her first Oscar," *Life* predicted.

How unfortunate that R.J.'s *Sail a Crooked Ship* came out at the same time, promptly sinking in a hale of critical fusillades like "tedious and unseaworthy" and "a witless comedy best suited to kiddie matinees." Although it flopped at the box office, it earned a macabre place in movie history as the last film of R.J.'s friend and costar, forty-two-year-old Ernie Kovacs, who died in a car crash shortly after its release.

With R.J.'s career hitting bottom, his confidence over winning Natalie back also faded. Why did she need him, a near Hollywood has-been, when she had Warren Beatty, who'd just been dubbed "the most exciting American male in movies" by *Life* magazine?

R.J. finally decided it was time to try to make a fresh start elsewhere. The Hollywood studios were in a state of flux and financial crisis owing to dwindling audiences and spiraling production budgets. More and more movies were being made abroad, especially in England, France, Italy and Spain, where costs were much lower and also could be split with local coproducers.

In a moment of despair R.J. had contacted his former boss, Darryl F. Zanuck, about the possibility of appearing in *The Longest Day*, the $15 million epic of the Normandy invasion. Zanuck cabled back from France that he'd be delighted to have him. It salved R.J.'s ego considerably because *The Longest Day* was one of the most prestigious projects of the time, featuring a huge cast of American, British and European stars and based on Cornelius Ryan's global bestseller.

The overseas trip proved a real tonic. R.J.'s role in *The Longest Day* amounted to just a "cameo," but the first day's rushes turned out so well that Zanuck ordered additional scenes written for him by James Jones, author of *From Here to Eternity*, who served as coscenarist and technical adviser on the film.

R.J. had barely returned to Los Angeles when Columbia assigned a starting date to the second project of his three-picture deal with the studio. As luck would have it, it turned out to be another World War II drama, this one based on John Hersey's novel *The War Lover* and to be filmed in England.

Seeing the handwriting on the wall, R.J. became determined to resettle abroad. "It's a point that everyone reaches sooner or later," he recalled. "You find you're standing still—and not intentionally. You're getting nowhere. You have to move. You have to grow. You have to flip that page or flip your lid. I chose to do the former."

Elizabeth Taylor and Eddie Fisher, preparing to leave for Europe themselves for the resumption of *Cleopatra* after it had been shut down by her nearly fatal illness, gave R.J. a farewell party. Natalie didn't attend, nor was she invited, since she and Warren Beatty were out of town.

The next day R.J.'s parents drove him to Los Angeles Airport. "As departures go, it was a quiet one," he remembered. "I just got on that plane and got out. I brought nothing with me, nothing permanent. The few possessions I had, I left in storage. I even gave away my dog, Conroy. I intended to be away for a long, long time."

R.J. left with one string untied. He still had a wife. "He hadn't seen Natalie for months, but they talked on the phone now and then," said a legal adviser of the time. "R.J.'s position was that he wasn't going to divorce her. First, he still loved her. Second, he belonged to the old school that said that, for the sake of a lady's reputation, a man never sued in matters of the heart. If Natalie wanted to divorce *him*, he wouldn't stand in her way, but he wasn't going to take the initiative."

But divorce seemed the last thing on Natalie's mind as she traipsed everywhere with Warren Beatty. Fan magazines breathlessly reported that Beatty had given Natalie a Chihuahua pup instead of an engagement ring, that the couple had become addicted to the twist while visiting New York's Peppermint Lounge, and that Beatty lovingly wiped the cement from Natalie's feet after she became the one hundred and thirty-sixth star to be immortalized in the forecourt of Grauman's Chinese Theater.

The press delighted in the fact that Natalie and Beatty were fundamentally different from each other. She flourished in the limelight, adored putting on the ritz and socializing with glamorous friends. He preferred privacy and looked annoyed whenever approached.

"Warren was far more impetuous, unpredictable and intense than R.J., a nonconformist out of the Jimmy Dean school," said Natalie's friend Norma Crane. " 'Isn't he a wonderful actor?' she'd say to everyone she met. Warren's incessant nose-picking, hair-scratching and staccato vocabulary of four-letter words didn't bother her in the least. She was charmed by it."

During a newspaper interview in New York, Natalie had to leave the room to keep from laughing at Beatty's answer to a reporter's question about his piano playing. "Piano? Yeah, I slop around on it, hit the tree with it," Beatty said. After her careful studio upbringing where somebody always coached her on what and what not to say to the press, Beatty's rebellion against all the accepted rules fascinated her.

In February 1962, the lovers had their first falling out when Natalie received an Oscar nomination for *Splendor in the Grass* and Beatty didn't. He wasn't even mentioned on the preliminary ballot for nominees, since Warner Brothers opted to push him in the Best Supporting Actor category for *The Roman Spring of Mrs. Stone*, which needed help at the box office.

Beatty felt so demeaned by being reduced to supporting actor status (made possible by Vivien Leigh having sole star billing) that he informed the Motion Picture Academy that he'd decline the nomination. He didn't have to carry out his threat. The selectors were turned off by his arrogance and he never got on the ballot.

For a change, Natalie got angry too. Winning a nomination for Best Actress was something she'd been dreaming about all her life. She thought Beatty should be grateful for any honor that the Academy gave him in what was only his first year of making movies. They quarreled and Beatty walked out, but he returned the next day.

"Warren was never gone for very long when he had a lady who was paying the rent," a friend said.

All seemed serene by the time Natalie and Beatty turned up for the Academy Awards telecast in April. They created a stampede among photographers when they arrived at the Santa Monica Civic Auditorium. Natalie wore a slinky evening gown and white mink stole. Beatty sported a tuxedo for the first time that anyone could remember.

As the evening progressed, Natalie began to wish that she'd been nominated for *West Side Story* instead of *Splendor in the Grass*. By the time it came around to presenting the Best Actress award, *West Side Story* had won nine Oscars, including those to Rita Moreno and George Chakiris for best supporting performances. *Splendor in the Grass* had received only one, for Best Original Screenplay.

Sitting in an aisle seat, Natalie slumped in her chair, one hand over her mouth to choke her excitement, while Burt Lancaster read off the nominees for Best Actress. Her competition was Audrey Hepburn in *Breakfast at Tiffany's,* Piper Laurie in *The Hustler,* Sophia Loren in *Two Women,* and Geraldine Page in *Summer and Smoke.*

When Lancaster forgot to mention Loren, people in the front rows called it to his attention while he reached for the envelope with the victor's name. "And Sophia Loren for *Two Women,*" he hastily added, having to repeat himself when she turned out the winner. With Loren in Rome, Greer Garson accepted in her place, pointing out that it was the first Oscar ever given to a performance in a foreign-language, English-subtitled movie.

Natalie's disappointment was cushioned somewhat by *West Side Story* going on to cop a tenth Oscar for Best Picture of 1961. Although she'd won no laurels herself, she'd starred in the biggest multi-winner in the then thirty-four-year history of the presentations. That alone gave her agents basis for doubling her previous asking price of $250,000 per picture.

"There'll be another day," Natalie said when a reporter asked her how it felt losing to Sophia Loren.

Superpatriot Hedda Hopper, who deplored the increasing foreign influence on Hollywood filmmaking, had the last word on the subject. "Natalie Wood was robbed," Hopper screamed in her column the next day. "But at least she got the nicest consolation prize—Warren Beatty."

Privately, however, Hopper told Natalie that it was high time she married Beatty, that their living together wasn't setting a good example for the youth of America.

Although Natalie debated Hopper on that point, she did want to marry Beatty. Whether *he* wanted it was another question, but for the present she couldn't marry anyone as long as she remained Mrs. Robert Wagner.

To remove that technicality, Natalie filed for divorce in Santa Monica Superior Court on April 17, 1962. The Wagners' separation had been in effect since the previous August. Natalie claimed there was no chance of a reconciliation.

The divorce hearing was rushed onto the court calendar in an unprecedented ten days, Natalie pleading that she had to leave the country to attend the Cannes Film Festival. She did not, however, state that the reason for the trip was simply to be with her lover, whose latest movie, *All Fall Down,* happened to be an American entry.

Since R.J. was working abroad at the time, he did not attend the hearing nor did his attorney contest Natalie's charges of mental cruelty. Dressed in a black silk suit and matching turban, she strolled into Judge Allen Lynch's chamber on April 27 and testified that "During the last year of our marriage, my husband became very cold and indifferent. He was very critical of my friends. He criticized my management of the household. He would go off by himself. He said he preferred to play golf rather than stay home with me."

Natalie also claimed that R.J.'s behavior caused her to drop ten pounds from her normal ninety-eight. That caused some snickers among friends of the couple, who knew that the real reason for the weight loss had been Natalie's illness following her tonsillectomy.

The marriage had lasted three years, seven months and eighteen days. It was dissolved in eleven minutes. As Natalie left the courthouse, she told reporters, "Everyone searches for happiness. I guess I just haven't found it yet."

She refused to answer queries about whether she intended to marry Warren Beatty. The question was a bit presumptuous anyway. The interlocutory decree wouldn't become final for another year, in April 1963.

The Wagners' divorce started rumors that if and when R.J. got married again it would be to Warren Beatty's former fiancée, Joan Collins! While R.J. was making *The War Lover* in London he and Collins kept the Fleet Street pack busy by turning up together at all the "in" night spots and theater openings.

Gossip about that unlikely coupling swelled into scandal-sheet headlines like "Natalie and Joan's Strange Love Swap." But the truth was that R.J. and Collins were simply two lonely ex-Hollywooders who needed cheering up at a low point in both their lives.

"Although he was very attractive, I was still neurotic enough to be truly interested only in complex, difficult men—and R.J.

was gentle and sweet and too nice for me," Joan Collins re-called. "We were—hello, cliché!—'just good friends.' The tab-loid-reading public, however, found it hard to believe that an attractive man and woman could merely be friends."

The dating ended when R.J. took Collins to see the smash West End musical, *Stop the World—I Want to Get Off.* Afterward they went backstage to congratulate its charismatic star-writer-composer, Anthony Newley, who invited them to join him for dinner. A passionate affair developed between Collins and Newley. They were eventually married after his wife, actress Ann Lynn, divorced him for adultery.

Crossing out Collins' entry in his little black book, R.J. started keeping company with two other women he'd first met back in Hollywood. One was actress and jet-set playgirl Linda Christian, the second of the three wives of his great friend Tyrone Power. The other was Marion Marshall, a former Fox starlet recently divorced from Stanley Donen, the London-based American film director.

Although his relationship with Marion Marshall would grow stronger with time, R.J. still carried a torch for Natalie. "He had many pictures of his former wife about the house," said the butler who worked in his rented maisonette on London's Brompton Square. "One thing he would not tolerate, however, was having newspapers or magazines around that contained anything sensational about Miss Wood and Warren Beatty. That would send Mr. Wagner into an absolute fury."

By the spring of 1962 it was hard to pick up a news publica-tion anywhere without finding something about Natalie and Beatty. When they arrived at the Cannes Film Festival in May the press pursued them like jackals.

After Beatty's movie, *All Fall Down,* failed to win any prizes, the couple took off for Paris and Rome. Although they took separate hotel suites wherever they stayed, everybody jokingly called them "the honeymooners."

"If they're not married, they're doing an awfully good imita-tion," said columnist Sheilah Graham, who also dubbed them "the poor man's Liz and Burton." Ironically, that sizzling ro-mance was going on simultaneously. The two couples often seemed to be competing for the same space in the headlines.

Reporters hanging around the Grand Hotel in Rome noticed

considerable dissension between Natalie and Beatty. "They'd enter the hotel smiling like newlyweds," said a former UPI correspondent. "But when they went out, they were often fighting like people on the verge of a divorce. Knowing Warren's reputation as a cocksman, we assumed that Natalie didn't want to spend *all* of her time in bed."

By a strange coincidence, Robert Wagner also happened to be in Rome, shopping for an apartment. Besides being the center for European filmmaking, the Italian capital had also become the new home of his friend Marion Marshall, who fled there from London with her two sons in the midst of a custody battle with ex-husband Stanley Donen.

One night R.J. and Marshall were dining at a trendy Roman night spot when Natalie and Beatty walked in. R.J. beckoned them to his table and ordered a round of drinks.

"Almost perversely, R.J. ordered Natalie's favorite wine," said their writer friend Thomas Thompson, who learned of the incident years later. "They passed that evening staring and not staring at each other, talking and not talking to one another, dancing but almost afraid to touch. Hovering between them was what Natalie later described to me as 'a bond of sadness,' a sudden feeling that the divorce had been a terrible mistake."

Later that same night R.J. tried to telephone Natalie at her hotel to propose a reconciliation, but he kept getting a busy signal. Warren Beatty, who didn't let bedroom games prevent him from conducting business on the phone at the same time, had the line tied up for hours with transatlantic calls. R.J. finally gave up in frustration and had argued himself out of the idea by the next morning.

"I never knew R.J. tried to call me until years later," Natalie told Tommy Thompson. "For weeks after that encounter in the club, I got weepy every time I thought about it. If R.J.'s phone call had come through, I think I would have dropped everything and gone running back to him," she said.

EIGHT

Warren and Marion

IF NATALIE was having second thoughts about her relationship with Warren Beatty, it didn't look that way when they returned to California in June 1962. Badgered by Louella Parsons for some inside dirt, she would only say, "Love is the most important thing there is in life. I don't see how people can enjoy life or even exist without love. I know I can't."

The lovers moved into a new house that Natalie rented in Benedict Canyon. A spectacular fountain-waterfall in the garden sent a stream rippling through the interior and out again via a channel in the floor.

"Southern California has such a monotonous climate that you have to create your own changes of environment by switching houses every once in a while," Natalie told a visitor. Unluckily, she and Beatty suffered such an invasion by mosquitoes that the indoor waterway had to be filled in with cement.

Since sex dominated the relationship, the couple stayed home much of the time. When they did go out, Natalie spent hours beforehand glamorizing herself, wasted effort really. Excessive makeup, plus her fondness for flamboyant clothes and accessories, caused her to look considerably older than twenty-four. She held a high place on the list of "Hollywood's Ten Worst-Dressed Women."

Beatty, however, had a standard uniform of sports shirts and gabardine slacks. While he waited for Natalie to emerge from her boudoir he played the piano or read a book.

Soon after they returned from Europe, Beatty took Natalie to the Pink Pussycat, a sleazy nightclub where the star attractions were two strippers using the names Fran Sinatra and Natalie Should. Beatty hoped the visit would provide Natalie with some ideas on how to play her next movie role, as Gypsy Rose Lee in *Gypsy*. But as it turned out the trip was in vain. Because of the movie censorship of the time, Natalie couldn't strip beyond bra and bikini and also had to have her navel covered by a jewel or flesh-colored fabric.

If Natalie Wood seemed a strange choice to portray the most celebrated burlesque queen of all time, she got roped into it by Jack Warner and his lack of faith in the box-office drawing power of Rosalind Russell, who would play the pivotal role of Gypsy Rose Lee's monstrously domineering mother.

More than a year had passed since Natalie made her last movie, *West Side Story*. Remembering her difficult experience then, she shied away from taking on another musical but couldn't afford to turn it down. Not only was money running low, but her Warner contract also prohibited her from working elsewhere until she fulfilled her studio obligation for that year.

Because she'd already rejected two other Warner films, Natalie faced another suspension if she didn't change her attitude. The semitravelogue *Rome Adventure* had been a third attempt to team Natalie with Troy Donahue, so she wasn't sorry to lose that one to Suzanne Pleshette. *Days of Wine and Roses*, which went to Lee Remick, was different. Natalie coveted the role of the alcoholic wife, but she withdrew when the producer rejected some script "improvements" written at her request by her personal secretary, Mart Crowley.

In lieu of a project that might have suited Natalie better,

Gypsy was certainly not an opportunity to pass up. Written by Arthur Laurents (who also did *West Side Story*), with a musical score by Jule Styne and Stephen Sondheim, it created a sensation on Broadway in 1959 with Ethel Merman as the quintessential stage mother, Mama Rose, and newcomer Sandra Church in the title role.

Gypsy had been such a personal triumph for the legendary Merman that her fans were shocked when Rosalind Russell landed the movie version. But Merman had a poor track record in films, and Russell also shrewdly eliminated any competition by having her husband, producer Frederick Brisson, buy the screen rights.

With some musical experience on Broadway in *Wonderful Town* nine years earlier, Rosalind Russell thought she could belt her numbers at least as well as Ethel Merman. But when she heard the rehearsal playbacks, she changed her mind. Stage and nightclub star Lisa Kirk took over as voice double, with Russell talk-singing some of the quieter moments, which weren't many.

Because Gypsy Rose Lee had never been noted for her vocalizing, Natalie could do her own singing, though she needed some dubbing help from Marni Nixon on the high notes.

Since Natalie had been helped tremendously by Jerome Robbins on *West Side Story*, she was disappointed when he didn't get to repeat his Broadway staging of *Gypsy*. But Rosalind Russell wanted a director she could dominate and who wouldn't give her a hard time. She opted for her friend Mervyn LeRoy, who had previously helped her get through *A Majority of One*, though not with any distinction.

With Rosalind Russell pretty much running the show, she and her younger (by thirty-one years), independent-minded co-star were bound to clash. "Roz was very jealous of Natalie and gave her a really hard time," the unit publicist recalled. "You could understand Roz's resentment because Natalie had everything she didn't—youth, gorgeous looks and Warren Beatty providing stud service.

"Furthermore, Roz had practically killed to make *Gypsy*, believing it would send her flagging career back into orbit. She feared it would all be for nothing, because most of the publicity and promotion was being centered around Natalie. Jack

Warner insisted on that, because Natalie was one of the hottest stars in the business right then. Roz's fans were mainly older people who rarely went to movies anymore."

From the first day of rehearsals the set bristled with hostility. In retaliation against Rosalind Russell's frosty attitude toward her, Natalie kicked up a fuss by demanding a larger dressing room, comparable in size and furnishings to the one that Russell had. Whenever they had scenes together, Natalie kept Russell waiting by arriving last.

"Natalie's behavior was quite unprofessional and incensed Roz even more, which I'm sure was what Natalie intended," the publicist said.

To avoid confrontations with Rosalind Russell, Natalie stayed in her dressing room as much as possible, coddled by a constantly growing entourage. The charter member was her mother, Maria Gurdin, on the studio payroll for $100 a week as a sort of matron in waiting for the duration of filming. Howard Jeffrey, a choreographic assistant to Jerome Robbins on *West Side Story*, had become Natalie's new secretary, replacing Mart Crowley when he quit to write the Great American Screenplay. Bob Jiras, another alumnus of *West Side Story*, was Natalie's makeup consultant.

Natalie kept getting into trouble with the Make-up Artists Guild over Jiras, who wasn't a union member and had to be listed on the crew sheet as a production assistant to prevent a work stoppage. After being made up by one of the studio artists, Natalie would return to the privacy of her dressing room and have Jiras alter or touch up anything that either of them didn't think suited her.

Missing, of course, from Natalie's entourage was Robert Wagner, who, in that instance, had no replacement. The professional togetherness she'd practiced with R.J. did not spill over into her affair with Warren Beatty or at least not on his part. Although he often called for Natalie when she finished work, he told her that he had more important things to do than sit around the studio all day holding her hand.

Beatty had been rejecting job offers left and right, including the role of World War II Navy officer John F. Kennedy in *PT 109*, which the President's supporters took as an insult when they heard about it. Because he wasn't working, Natalie grew wary of Beatty's activities during the times they weren't together. All too aware of his reputation as a womanizer, she suspected him of cheating on her. Nothing he said could convince her otherwise.

If Beatty was late returning from somewhere he'd gone on his own, Natalie would get restless and keep checking her watch every few minutes. One night while sister Lana visited her, the minutes stretched into hours and Natalie became so upset that she started to cry. When Beatty finally arrived—too late to take Natalie to a dinner party to which they'd been invited—a terrible row erupted.

"When the screaming became too much, Warren slammed the door and left again and did not return that night," Lana Wood remembered. "Natalie, weeping, went to bed and I could not console her."

Because of the success of *Splendor in the Grass*, Jack Warner wanted to re-team Natalie and Beatty in *Youngblood Hawke*, based on the novel by Herman Wouk, author of *Marjorie Morningstar*. For a change, Natalie couldn't have been happier: working side by side with her lover would keep him under her constant surveillance.

Beatty, however, vetoed the idea, claiming that Warner Brothers only wanted to capitalize on the notoriety of their affair. Unwilling to allow Beatty even more freedom to roam while she worked at the studio, Natalie dropped out of *Youngblood Hawke* as well (James Franciscus and Suzanne Pleshette played the parts).

As a result, *Gypsy* was Natalie's only movie in 1962. Released at Christmas, her second attempt at a musical role earned her better critical notices than *West Side Story*. The Los Angeles *Times*, for example, called her transformation from wide-eyed innocent to brassy stripper as an ecdysiast, "rather amazing and right on the button."

But success tends to run in cycles and the public had started to tire of splashy musicals based on Broadway hits. *Gypsy* did only fair business, not helped by Rosalind Russell's performance, which critics considered vastly inferior to Ethel Merman's on the stage.

With her career now seemingly of second importance to being with Warren Beatty, *Gypsy* turned out to be Natalie's last film for over a year. Gossip columnists who didn't know any better speculated that she'd be marrying Beatty as soon as her divorce from Robert Wagner became final.

Except through lawyers, Natalie had lost contact with R.J. Friends and relatives rarely heard her mention his name. He seemed a part of her life that was finished and best forgotten.

Perhaps if R.J. had been on the Hollywood scene the situation would have been different. But moving to Europe had seemingly proved the right decision. He felt no compulsion to return to a place that still held bitter memories.

R.J.'s spirits were soaring. The very first movie he'd made abroad, *The Longest Day*, broke box-office records all over the world. While it could hardly be called a Robert Wagner showcase—the cast boasted over forty stars, including John Wayne, Robert Mitchum, Henry Fonda, Richard Burton and Sean Connery—just being in such an enormous and prestigious hit restored R.J.'s self-confidence and seemed a lucky omen for the future.

Unhappily it wasn't. R.J.'s second overseas film, *The War Lover*, in which he costarred with the up-and-coming Steve McQueen, was released by Columbia at the same time as Fox's *The Longest Day* and couldn't stand up to the competition. Although it contained some of the most realistic World War II aerial combat scenes ever filmed (R.J.'s stunt "double" was killed in a parachute jump over the English Channel), the hackneyed plot of two pilots in love with the same woman bored critics and public alike.

R.J. and McQueen, who became good friends during the making of *The War Lover*, both blamed Columbia for the movie's failure. "Steve and I thought it was a fine novel but a terrible adaptation," R.J. remembered. "We were willing to sit it out until a better script could be developed. But the head of the studio said, 'Trust me, a picture with two great guys like you can't miss.' It did."

Although R.J. no longer had a contract with 20th Century-Fox, he still "owed" them one picture under his old deal. After *The War Lover*, Spyros Skouras insisted that he make *The Condemned of Altona*, although R.J. hardly needed his arm twisted. It seemed one of the best assignments Fox had ever given him, costarring with Fredric March, Sophia Loren and Maximilian

Schell. Oscar laureate Abby Mann wrote the script, based on a play by the venerated Jean-Paul Sartre. Last but not least, the director was one of the great European masters, Vittorio De Sica.

But for all its potential, *The Condemned of Altona* turned out to be one of R.J.'s worst filmmaking experiences. "I was really nervous going into that movie," he remembered. "Here am I working with De Sica, for chrissakes, and with Freddie March, who had an Oscar and with Loren and Schell, who'd just won the top acting Oscars for that year.

"Well, the night before a crucial scene, Schell comes to my room and gives me this big talk about our playing brothers and getting into the *essence* of the relationship—you know, that actors' bullshit talk. So the next day I start my scene, and Schell takes a script and goes over behind the camera and shakes his head the whole time I'm working.

"Can you imagine?" R.J. said. "In all my years, I've never seen *anybody* do something like that. What was really pissing him off was that I was having this thing with Sophia. She liked me, and that drove Max *wild*."

R.J.'s "thing with Sophia" apparently did not develop into an affair. "They were very obviously attracted to each other, but Sophia's husband, Carlo Ponti, just happened to be the producer and was always coming around," said writer Abby Mann. "I think R.J. was afraid to make a move, because Ponti was one of the most powerful men in the European film industry at the time. He could have really made it tough for R.J. if he caught him fooling around with Sophia."

The story of the disintegration of a Krupplike German dynasty following the defeat of the Nazis in World War II, *The Condemned of Altona* turned out so poorly that Fox kept it on the shelf for a year before finally releasing it in September 1963. "This film is such a hopeless mess that it is difficult to know where to begin criticizing," said one of the unanimously negative reviews. Box-office takings were equally bad.

But that discouraging result was still in the future. During the making of *The Condemned of Altona*, R.J. became convinced that resettling abroad had been the right career move. Europe was such a wide-open field for independent filmmakers that it also rekindled his interest in producing, which had been dormant since the formation of the ill-fated Rona Productions.

While working with Vittorio De Sica, R.J. was delighted when the director offered to school him in all aspects of making the film. "The maestro really took me under his wing, let me work beside him in story conferences, and even in the cutting room," R.J. said.

In his spare time R.J. wandered around Rome and mingled with the *dolce vita* set in the sidewalk cafes along the Via Veneto. "I fell in love with the entire city . . . the people, the colors, the piazzas, the way of life," he said. "The Romans love life and love to live it to the hilt."

R.J.'s happiest moments were spent in the company of his American friend, Marion Marshall. If anybody could replace Natalie Wood in his life, she seemed to have the inside track.

A vivacious blue-eyed blonde, Marion was then thirty-three, a year older than R.J. Born Marion Tanner, she was a successful model and a 20th Century-Fox starlet by the age of eighteen. Like her close chum Marilyn Monroe, with whom she once roomed at the young women's residence known as the Hollywood Studio Club, Marion owed her Fox contract to friendship with Joseph M. Schenck, the studio's cofounder. Over seventy years old and in failing health, Schenck often sent his limousine to bring the two girls to his Beverly Hills mansion to dine, play gin rummy and whatever with him and some of his mogul cronies.

Briefly married to actor Allen Davey, Marion used the name Marion Davey when she joined Fox. To avoid confusion with Marion Davies, the legendary movie-star mistress of William Randolph Hearst, the studio changed it to Marion Marshall.

Unlike her pal with the same MM monogram, Marion Marshall never became a star, although publicists dubbed her a likely successor to Carole Lombard, whom she somewhat resembled. Starting with *The Snake Pit* in 1948, she played minor roles in about twenty Fox movies. In 1951 she signed a contract with Paramount producer Hal Wallis, who teamed her with Polly Bergen as romantic foils for Dean Martin and Jerry Lewis in *That's My Boy* and *The Stooge*.

R.J. first met Marion in 1950, when she portrayed a nurse in his initial Fox film, *Halls of Montezuma*. But at the time Marion only had eyes for Howard Hawks, one of Hollywood's foremost directors and her senior by more than thirty years.

Marion lived with Hawks for several years, helping him to get over the heartbreak of losing his wife, celebrated fashion model Nancy "Slim" Hawks, to agent-producer Leland Hayward (who divorced movie and stage star Margaret Sullavan to marry her).

Marion finally walked out on Hawks when she got fed up with his frequent but unkept promises to legalize their relationship. On the rebound, she became involved with a much younger director, Stanley Donen, himself trying to forget a disastrous romance with Elizabeth Taylor, who jilted him to marry Michael Wilding. In the interim, Donen had been divorced by dancer wife Jeanne Coyne, who cited Taylor as the "other woman"!

After a whirlwind love affair Marion and Donen were married in 1952, when she decided to end her acting career to raise a family. They had two sons: Peter, born in 1953, and Joshua, born two years later. During that time Marion became one of the most envied Hollywood wives as her husband directed such hit musicals as *Singin' in the Rain, Seven Brides for Seven Brothers* and *Funny Face.* By 1956, Donen's stock within the industry had risen so high that Cary Grant took him on as equal partner in an independent company called Grandon Productions.

In 1957, Marion Donen stayed home with the children when her husband went to England to make a Cary Grant-Ingrid Bergman comedy that turned out to be rather aptly titled *Indiscreet.* Donen fell in love with American-born Lady Adelle Beatty, one of the leading hostesses of the London smart set. Their romance ended one that she'd been having with Donen's longtime friend, Frank Sinatra, who introduced them!

Marion found herself left in the lurch when Donen completed *Indiscreet* and decided to shift his production activities to London so that he could be with Lady Beatty. After a long battle in which she finally won full custody of their two sons, Marion divorced him in 1959. He married Lady Beatty the next year.

Since Marion felt no compulsion to resume an acting career that had never really amounted to much, she found it difficult to raise two sons in the accustomed Beverly Hills style, even with a divorce settlement that included $60,000 in cash, $14,000 annual alimony and $10,800 a year in child support.

To conserve resources and also to spare the boys from being shuttled back and forth between Los Angeles and London for court-stipulated visits with their father, Marion moved them abroad. She shrewdly realized that her funds would have at least twice the purchasing power that they had back home because of a highly favorable exchange rate for the American dollar at the time.

It was easy to see why R.J. and Marion finally fell in love after being casual friends for years. Outsiders living in a foreign country, their Hollywood backgrounds gave them a common bond of interests and acquaintances.

Professionally speaking, they were not in competition with each other. Although she'd been shabbily treated by Howard Hawks and Stanley Donen, Marion was still a thoroughly maternal type of woman, one who, to feel complete, needed a husband and children to care for.

While R.J. probably could have had the pick of any woman he wanted, Marion was more limited in her choice of partners. Many men would try to avoid getting seriously involved with an over-thirty, twice-divorced woman with two kids. But, for R.J., that became a real turn-on. Being with Marion and the boys gave him something he'd never had with Natalie: a feeling of family.

As he matured, R.J. grew even more handsome. Bizarre though it might seem, Marion's exquisite facial features resembled his so much that some of their friends jokingly called her "R.J. in drag." Whether that was part of their physical attraction to each other is a question that could only be answered by a psychiatrist.

But it was an intense, sexually charged relationship. "Since their respective divorces, Marion had been celibate and R.J. nearly so," a friend said. "They had a lot of catching up to do. Even out of the bedroom they couldn't keep their hands off each other, and you could easily see why. R.J. had so much charisma. Marion, despite being the mother of two, never lost that sensuous glamor she had as a Hollywood starlet."

Unlike Natalie and Warren Beatty, R.J. and Marion conducted their relationship very discreetly. Stanley Donen had

put up such a fight over the children's custody that she couldn't
risk losing it by giving him grounds for having her declared an
unfit mother. A quick solution to the problem would be for R.J.
to marry Marion, but he couldn't until his divorce from Natalie became final in the spring of the following year.

For the sake of appearances, R.J. rented a suite in a residen-
tial hotel in an ancient district near the Roman Forum, a respectable distance from Marion's apartment. Although R.J.
spent most of his time at Marion's, they went to his hotel when
they wanted to be alone together.

Aspiring screenwriter Mart Crowley served as sort of a live-
in baby-sitter for R.J. and Marion in Rome. The lovers took
Natalie's ex-secretary under their wing after he turned up des-
titute and needing a place to stay while trying to overcome a
severe case of writer's block.

"R.J. and Marion kept me alive for what seemed a very long
Roman winter," Crowley recalled. "I was so broke that they
used to take me to Gucci's to buy me shoes. I slept on Marion's
living-room sofa."

Although R.J. moved to Europe in hopes of better career
opportunities, things weren't turning out that way. After *The
Condemned of Altona*, he went jobless for six months. Unemploy-
ment might have continued even longer if Marion hadn't persuaded him to swallow his pride by taking what amounted to a
supporting role as David Niven's nephew in *The Pink Panther*.
The offer came from director Blake Edwards, a longtime Hollywood friend who intended to make the film at Rome's
Cinecittà studio.

Because of unexpected problems behind the scenes, R.J. had
to wait another two months before shooting actually began.
Peter Ustinov and Ava Gardner, two of the other stars, quit at
the last moment in contract disputes. Germaine Lefebvre, professionally known as Capucine, took over for Gardner, but
finding a replacement for Ustinov as Inspector Clouseau wasn't
so easy. Peter Sellers finally took the part after it was completely rewritten for him so that the originally serious and dignified detective became a comical, pathetically lovable bungler.

Working alongside David Niven and Peter Sellers proved a
great restorative for R.J. at a time when he was starting to lose

confidence in himself and his future as an actor. "Niven really saved me," R.J. remembered. "I genuinely loved that man. He took me around Rome while we were filming and taught me a sense of style."

R.J. credited Sellers with curing him of one of his worst habits. "Peter kept saying to me, 'What the hell are you doing with your eyes?' I was hooding them, you see, because I was so scared of the camera. And that was about twelve years after I started working in pictures," R.J. said.

Although *The Pink Panther* turned out to be one of the biggest box-office hits of Robert Wagner's career, he came close to being permanently blinded while making it.

Stripping down to the bare minimum and taking a foamy bath in the same tub with Capucine might seem like an actor's dream come true, but not in this case. Technicians added a powerful chemical to the water to create the suds. To spare the stars from worrying, they told them it was only gentle baby soap.

"That stuff was so strong it practically took the skin off Capucine," R.J. said. "Christ, it got in my eyes and burned my corneas. They sent me home to recuperate, but when I woke up the next morning I couldn't see. I thought I was really finished."

But doctors believed that R.J.'s vision could be restored if he used eye drops fortified with vitamin A, rested quietly and stayed away from bright light. They also said it might take as long as a month. When the budget-conscious producer heard that, he wanted to keep the few scenes that R.J. had done so far and eliminate the character from the rest of the script.

Luckily, R.J. had some staunch friends to help him through the crisis. Marion Marshall took on the nursing responsibilities. David Niven, Peter Sellers and Blake Edwards went on strike, refusing to go back to work until the producer agreed to "shoot around" R.J. for as long as he needed to recuperate. Thanks to his strong will power and positive attitude, he needed a week less than the doctors anticipated.

Although R.J. regained his sight, the ordeal left him in emotional turmoil. Suppose he hadn't been so lucky? How would he have managed for the rest of his life? He had no savings or investments to fall back on, and no vocation other than acting. He realized it was time to make some major changes as insurance against future bad luck.

NINE

Transitions

AS 1963 BEGAN, gossip columnists started taking bets on who would be the first to remarry when their divorce became final in April: Natalie Wood or Robert Wagner?

Everybody gambling on Natalie lost. Her affair with Warren Beatty, the sole candidate for bridegroom, terminated explosively about a year after they started living together. The parting was one of the most traumatic experiences of Natalie's life. She never forgave Beatty for the way he treated her.

It happened during dinner at Chasen's, a classic Beverly Hills eatery reputed to have the best and most expensive chili on earth. The restaurant is a favorite of the Hollywood establishment, and a fair share filled its pine-paneled main room that night, including Mr. and Mrs. Alfred Hitchcock, the James Stewarts and the Gregory Pecks.

While Natalie and Beatty were finishing their meal he excused himself to go to the men's room. Ten minutes passed and he did not return. Assuming that he'd probably stopped to make one of his endless phone calls, Natalie ordered another coffee and waited.

Still no Warren. She sent the headwaiter to get him. When owner Dave Chasen came to her table instead, Natalie knew something was wrong. After she discovered what it was, she wished instead that Warren Beatty had dropped dead.

He had propositioned the restaurant's voluptuous blond checkroom attendant into walking off the job and going away with him on what turned out to be a three-day revel.

With more important things on his mind, Beatty also departed via a back door without paying the check. Natalie signed for it and left, forcing a big smile at everybody to hide her inner agitation.

Natalie Wood exiting Chasen's by herself after arriving with Warren Beatty was bound to cause comment. By the next morning it was all over town that he'd ditched a world-renowned star for an unknown 38-23-34 floozy. Being publicly humiliated only added to Natalie's personal heartbreak.

Gossip columnists had a field day. Dorothy Kilgallen facetiously lumped all the current headline romances together, predicting that "Warren will take Marion Donen away from Robert Wagner, Natalie will steal Tony Newley from Joan Collins, then Joan will console Richard Burton after Liz Taylor runs off with R.J."

About a week later Beatty turned up at Natalie's house to pick up his clothes and belongings. She refused to see him and he left empty-handed. Nothing of his remained anyway. Natalie had chucked it all into the incinerator.

Beatty's terminating the affair so brazenly may have been due to the fact that Natalie, as well as the press, had backed him into a corner. He had to either marry her or burn all his bridges behind him.

"Marriage has never been part of Warren's life plan," another discarded mistress said. "His habit is to love them and then leave them as soon as they start wailing the wedding bell blues. Also, Warren's a terrible user of people. He'd gotten all the publicity mileage he could from the relationship. When it started, nobody ever heard of Warren Beatty. By the time he left Natalie they were calling him the hottest star since Brando."

The breakup hit Natalie very hard, making her even more fanatic about her psychoanalysis. "I could feel the bell jar closing in," she said later. "I was shaking, and I knew that if I didn't hold on—just hold on—then I'd go over the edge."

A confidante during that time was actress friend Hope Lange, who had suffered similar trauma following her divorce from Don Murray.

"Nat and I would sit around the house a lot and talk about men, what might happen, what we wanted to happen," Lange remembered. "We were both in analysis and always analyzed things. We called it 'channelizing'—put it in the channel and look at it. I would call up and say, 'I want to channelize something.' We'd get together and talk, about the men I was going out with and vice versa. This would get a lot of laughter. We'd also laugh at ourselves—at what asses we were."

According to columnist Sheilah Graham, a friend since childhood, "Natalie wanted a strong, commanding man who would take her by the hand and lead her around by her beautiful nose. That was where Robert Wagner failed her. When Warren came along she mistook his ruthlessness for strength. She was shattered when he dumped her. It shook her confidence as a woman. Afterward, she became rather busy in the romance department. It was a gesture to prove that Natalie Wood could get any man she wanted in spite of Warren, for whom she divorced Bob Wagner."

No one was surprised when Natalie soon became involved with producer Arthur Loew, Jr., celebrated in Hollywood circles as a knight gallant to ladies in distress. Twelve years older than Natalie, Loew was the millionaire grandson of movie pioneers Marcus (MGM) Loew and Adolph (Paramount) Zukor.

Loew was the man who sheltered Elizabeth Taylor after husband Mike Todd died in a plane crash; who consoled Janet Leigh following the breakup of the second of two marriages she had prior to Tony Curtis; who took in—inevitably—Joan Collins after she divorced her first husband, British actor Maxwell Reed.

Loew's most famous act of gallantry (if it can be called that) was toward Debbie Minardos Power, the wife of Tyrone

Power, who died of a heart attack at age forty-four in the midst of filming a dueling scene for *Solomon and Sheba*. Loew not only married the young widow but also adopted Tyrone Power, Jr., born two months after his father died.

Loew and Minardos also had a son of their own before being divorced in December 1962. The divorce was convenient for Natalie; it happened only a few months prior to Warren Beatty's exit. Loew was looking for a new wounded starling to take under his protection.

For Natalie, the urbane world of Arthur Loew, Jr., was a welcome change from living with nonconformist Warren Beatty. A gourmet and arts connoisseur, Loew was also a natural, easygoing person, with a sharp wit and penetrating insight.

"Arthur could make Nat laugh over a serious problem that might be bothering her. Not by being facetious, but in a way that helped her to deal with it more easily," said Norma Crane. "Arthur's lack of heaviness could work miracles. It was not disregarding a problem. It was meeting it head on through humor."

Loew, as well as Natalie's analyst, thought it would be good therapy for her to go back to work as soon as possible. While involved with Warren Beatty, her career had taken a distant second place. Nearly a year had passed since she finished her last movie, *Gypsy*.

Fortunately the layoff had been by choice and not for lack of job offers. Next to Elizabeth Taylor, she was the most sought-after female in movies, inspiring an industry maxim, "If Liz won't, Natalie would."

Director Billy Wilder said, "Natalie is a powerful little broad who has a stranglehold on every young leading-lady part in town. If a role calls for a woman between fifteen and thirty, you automatically think of her."

Natalie had a high-powered cabinet of advisers, including William Morris agents Joe Schoenfeld and Norman Brokaw, attorney Greg Bautzer and business manager Andy Maree. Through their joint efforts, she could obtain total approval of script, director, leading man, supporting cast, makeup artist, hairstylist and costume designer.

"I have the longest contract in town, and it gets longer with every picture," Natalie said. One of the most unusual clauses was that, as part of her wardrobe, the producer had to provide bracelets of appropriate design to cover her deformed left wrist.

Natalie's deal with Warner Brothers was amended so that she effectively became a "free agent." She owed them one picture a year for four years, with the terms for each movie to be negotiated as they came up, rather than a blanket contract.

With her newfound independence, Natalie reactivated Rona Productions, which she had received as part of the community property settlement with R.J. Intending to package her own movies, she started by optioning the film rights to Dorothy Baker's novel, *Cassandra at the Wedding.*

But the first movie actually made by Rona was Paramount's *Love With the Proper Stranger,* a coproduction with Alan J. Pakula and Robert Mulligan, the producer-director team from the highly regarded *To Kill a Mockingbird.*

The bittersweet comedy about an affair between a Macy's sales clerk and a jazz musician appealed to Natalie because it differed from anything she'd done before. It also promised to be highly controversial, focusing on the delicate subjects of unmarried pregnancy and abortion. Filming would be done entirely on location in New York City in a gritty black and white style comparable to the French "New Wave" that was all the rage at the time.

Natalie wanted Paul Newman for leading man, but when he opted to make *The Prize* instead, she happily settled for Steve McQueen. Whether she also considered McQueen a likely replacement for Warren Beatty in her personal life is another question. But as soon as *Love With the Proper Stranger* entered production, Natalie's staunchest moral critic, Dorothy Kilgallen, predicted another romantic contretemps similar to the one that developed during *Splendor in the Grass.*

Besides being a gorgeous hunk, it's easy to see why Natalie might fancy McQueen. After being jilted by Warren Beatty, latching on to Steve McQueen would salve her wounded pride and bolster her public image as a sex symbol. McQueen also happened to have a wife. That gave Natalie an opportunity to prove that she could get any man she wanted, even if it meant breaking up a marriage.

Whether an affair actually took place between Natalie and

McQueen is doubtful. "I saw Natalie and Steve working to-gether and sensed a closeness that went beyond the camera," said sister Lana Wood. "Later, when I asked, she looked up and grinned wickedly—the closest I think she could come to a leer, which was not very close at all."

But Natalie's reaction may have been pretense. According to Neile Adams (Mrs. Steve McQueen at the time), Natalie never landed him, but not for lack of effort.

"Natalie had a real crush on Steve," Neile Adams said. "She tried every which way to ensnare him short of using a butterfly net, including adolescent tricks like waiting on the steps of her dressing trailer for Steve to pass and then pretending to be talking to someone inside. It gave Natalie an opportunity to stop him and chat. Steve was amused by the methods she em-ployed and actually looked forward to the next day's shoot to see what her next move would be."

Although Neile Adams years later lost her husband to Ali McGraw, she claimed that McQueen resisted Natalie's ad-vances for two reasons. First, he was very much in love with his wife and devoted to their two children. Second, Natalie had been married to a man who was one of his best friends, Robert Wagner.

Whether R.J. would have appreciated McQueen's loyalty is another moot question. At the time R.J. had more important matters on his mind. He was unemployed, and his relationship with Marion Marshall suffered a not quite unexpected develop-ment. Marion's ex-husband, Stanley Donen, had filed suit in London for custody of their two sons, citing her illicit affair with R.J. as the reason.

R.J. hadn't worked since *The Pink Panther.* Job opportunities for an American actor in Europe were becoming scarce as the Hollywood trade unions started making wage and other em-ployment concessions to bring "runaway production" back to where they thought it rightfully belonged. Although he dis-liked the prospect of leaving Rome, R.J. realized that he'd have to swim with the tide if he wanted to stay afloat.

Marion's imbroglio with her ex-husband made it even more necessary to pull up stakes. Until R.J. became legally free to marry again, she could throw a monkey wrench into the Brit-ish court proceedings by taking the children back to the United

States, where judges tended to side with the mother in such disputes.

Neither R.J. nor Marion had the slightest doubts about *wanting* to get married. They seemed to have achieved a loving, mutually supportive relationship that augured well for the future. Furthermore, R.J. had become so devoted to the Donen boys (and they to him) that he and Marion wanted to have some more children of their own. For too many obvious reasons, they could hardly risk doing that outside wedlock.

The westward move began in the spring of 1963. R.J. installed Marion and the boys in a temporary apartment in New York City and then flew to Los Angeles alone to straighten out his own tangled affairs.

With no work on the horizon, R.J. intended to get a firm commitment from Columbia Pictures for the final movie of the three-picture contract that so far included *Sail a Crooked Ship* and *The War Lover*. Since R.J. had been ego-massaged into making those two films against his better judgment, he couldn't believe it when Columbia's production chief told him, "Well, Bob, you do have a three-picture deal. But I just don't know . . . your last two pictures bombed."

R.J. said later, "All of a sudden, they were *my* pictures! I told him I would go quietly—and gratefully." Perhaps R.J. wouldn't have reacted so altruistically if he'd known that he'd be out of work for more than two years.

But R.J. had only high hopes for the future. While negotiating with other studios, he also started looking for a place to live. With a future family to consider, it had to be a pretty large house. Anything that size in Beverly Hills or the other "A-list" neighborhoods proved far beyond what he could afford at the moment.

R.J. finally settled for a small ranch once owned by movie and TV star Robert Young. It was about twenty miles from Hollywood in Tarzana, a town that had a movie connection. The San Fernando Valley community had evolved from the baronial estate that novelist Edgar Rice Burroughs built from his *Tarzan* and other earnings.

R.J. and Marion were finally married on July 22, 1963, in a civil ceremony at New York's Bronx County Courthouse. Since they'd been living together for more than a year, a honeymoon trip seemed unnecessary. In October, when their new home became ready, they moved back to California. As a surprise for his young stepsons, Peter and Josh Donen, R.J. bought them each a pony.

Natalie reacted to the news of R.J.'s marriage with carefully disguised consternation. "She wished him well, and meant it," said Lana Wood, who believed that Natalie also wished secretly that R.J. was hers again. "My sister was not one to permit failed relationships, especially a relationship like theirs, whose success—and subsequent failure—was so very public."

Soon after R.J. and Marion were married, Natalie announced her engagement to Arthur Loew, Jr. Flashing a twelve-carat diamond ring that Loew had given her, she said the wedding would take place in January 1964.

By then things were happening so fast in Natalie's career that the wedding date was postponed indefinitely.

At Christmas, Paramount had released *Love With the Proper Stranger* in time to qualify for the 1963 Academy Awards. Natalie received rave reviews for her performance and was nominated for the coveted New York Film Critics Award as best actress of the year but lost to Patricia Neal in *Hud*.

In a special year-end 1963 edition devoted entirely to the movies, *Life* selected Natalie as the quintessential screen personality of the moment. The issue closed with a dramatic full-page photograph of Natalie gowned in satin and furs, bathed by spotlights and fussed over by a wardrobe mistress and a hairdresser.

"Natalie Wood glows with the glamour that a true star—and the movies themselves—have never lost," the caption said.

Natalie had just started her most lucrative assignment so far, *Sex and the Single Girl*. The fact that despotic Jack Warner had agreed to pay her $750,000 for ten weeks' work gave her more than just monetary satisfaction. Seven years earlier, for *Marjorie Morningstar*, she'd been lucky to get $750 a week!

According to the studio payroll records, Natalie's remuneration for *Sex and the Single Girl* was almost double the $400,000 that her leading man, Tony Curtis, received. For smaller costarring roles, Henry Fonda got $100,000, and Lauren Bacall, $50,000.

Warner Brothers purchased the screen rights to Helen Gurley Brown's bestselling sex guide for $200,000, just to use the title and the name of its author. In the fictitious plot (partially concocted by novelist Joseph Heller), Natalie played Dr. Helen Brown, a famous sex therapist whom a scandal magazine tries to expose as a virgin unqualified to discuss the subject.

In the midst of making *Sex and the Single Girl*, Natalie got nominated for an Oscar for her performance in *Love With the Proper Stranger.* Since she'd been twice defeated in past Academy Award derbies, her old friend Louella Parsons threw caution to the wind and picked her as the odds-on favorite to win in the Best Actress category.

Natalie and Arthur Loew, Jr., arrived at the awards telecast on April 13 just as the orchestra started the overture. Natalie had deliberately planned it that way to deprive reporters and photographers of an opportunity to arrange a lobby grouping with Warren Beatty and current flame Leslie Caron, who she knew would also be there.

Ironically, Natalie found herself competing that night not only with Caron (nominated for *The L-Shaped Room)* but also with Warren's sister, Shirley MacLaine (*Irma La Douce).* The other nominees were Rachel Roberts (*This Sporting Life)* and Patricia Neal (*Hud*). Neal, of course, turned out the winner.

A month after Natalie's Oscar disappointment, Robert Wagner reached a milestone in his life. At age thirty-four, he became a father for the first time with the arrival of a daughter, Katharine, on May 12, 1964. Kate, as she came to be called, was named after Katharine Hepburn, devoted companion of R.J.'s great friend Spencer Tracy.

The night of Kate's birth R.J. stayed with Marion and the baby for as long as the hospital would permit, then stopped at La Scala in Beverly Hills for dinner. The show-biz hangout was always crowded with people he knew, so the proud father bought a box of cigars at the cashier's counter and started handing them around.

Since La Scala was Natalie's favorite restaurant, it wasn't such a coincidence that she happened to be dining there that night with several friends. When R.J. reached her booth there was an awkward silence between them. They stared at each other for a moment, Natalie congratulated him, and R.J. moved on.

Without intending to do so, R.J. upset Natalie terribly. He had a successful marriage *and* a baby. She had neither.

"I suppose I was happy for him," Natalie remembered. "At least I said I was. . . . But what I wanted more than anything in the world was a child, and when we had been married he insisted on waiting. And now here he was telling me about the birth of his daughter by another woman. It made me cry for myself and what might have been."

TEN

A Fork in the Road

IN THE YEARS following their divorce Natalie and R.J.'s lives proceeded in completely opposite directions. Except for working in the same business, there was no common ground. She continued merrily onward as Hollywood's most publicized bachelor girl. He became a dedicated family man. No one, not even Louella Parsons or Hedda Hopper at their most delirious, would have predicted that they'd ever get together again.

Although R.J.'s tenure in Europe drastically changed his private life, his career seemed to be in shambles. After making *The Pink Panther* in 1963 he was unemployed for two years. Marriage and family responsibilities unavoidably occupied a lot of his time, but the job offers weren't pouring in either. At least not the choice, high-powered kind he desired.

"I'm no longer the pretty boy with a beach ball in one hand and a tennis racquet in the other," R.J. said at the time, although producers had small reason to believe otherwise. When they could choose from a field of leading men like Paul Newman, Steve McQueen, Rock Hudson, Warren Beatty, Marlon Brando, Jack Lemmon, George Peppard, George C. Scott, Tony Curtis and James Garner, they were unlikely to consider Robert Wagner unless in desperation.

R.J.'s free-lance status compounded the problem. Since no studio regularly handed him projects as 20th Century-Fox once did, R.J. and his agents had to go out and find them. Also, no studio publicity department worked at keeping the name and face of Robert Wagner before the public. His personal life appeared stable and dull as dishwater. Without a movie to promote, the news media had little reason to give him coverage.

"I began to lose my self-confidence," R.J. said later. "I didn't know what I was doing. While I was making the rounds, I went to see Elia Kazan. I said, 'I can't do it anymore. I don't know what the hell I am. I've lost it!' He took a lot of time with me and suggested that I get into analysis. I did, and I started to get my confidence back, and then I was okay."

In January 1965, R.J.'s agents persuaded him to sign for a one-week stage production of *Mister Roberts* at the Pheasant Run Playhouse in St. Charles, Illinois, near Chicago. R.J. played the title role of the World War II cargo ship commander, in which Henry Fonda had scored triumphs on both stage and screen.

For an actor like Robert Wagner, who'd never worked before live audiences except in the school plays of his childhood, attempting a performance that inevitably would be compared to Fonda's was a courageous move. But R.J. realized that if he succeeded it could open up new opportunities for him in Hollywood and perhaps even in the Broadway theater.

Unhappily, it didn't. While working in movies, R.J. became accustomed to memorizing and shooting a page or two of dialogue a day, and not necessarily in chronological order. The "character" didn't really emerge until two or three months later, when all the bits and pieces were finally put together in the editing room.

But on the stage R.J. was required to do the equivalent of three months' work in two and a half hours. And not for one time only, but every night plus three matinees. He found the discipline completely beyond him. He couldn't get home fast enough when the brief engagement ended.

Through his buddy Paul Newman, R.J. finally got the professional break he needed. R.J. and Newman had become friends while both were under contract at 20th Century-Fox. When Newman was cast in *The Hustler*, R.J. got very upset because he coveted the role for himself. Newman promised to make it up to him one day and he finally delivered, though it took him five years.

The movie was *Harper*, based on Ross Macdonald's "Lew Archer" detective novel, *The Moving Target*. While it would definitely be a Paul Newman vehicle (the private eye's last name had to be changed from Archer to Harper because Newman believed "H" titles like *The Hustler* and *Hud* to be lucky for him), a number of juicy costarring roles were up for grabs. When Newman invited R.J. to join a supporting cast that already included Lauren Bacall, Julie Harris, Janet Leigh and Shelley Winters, R.J. didn't have to be asked twice.

But actually getting the role of the neurotic pilot wasn't easy. Natalie Wood's alma mater, Warner Brothers, the producers of *Harper*, thought Newman had made a rotten choice.

"Jack Warner and I had never been friendly, and he was determined that I not be in *Harper*," R.J. remembered. "Paul felt otherwise and prevailed. Thank God, Paul is quite formidable when he's on your side. That's the part that made me. For the first time, I got some damn good reviews."

Late in the movie R.J. is revealed as one of the villains in the case of a vanished millionaire. When Newman forces a confession from him, R.J. cracks up and pulls a gun.

William Goldman, who wrote the screenplay for *Harper*, movingly described the filming of the scene: "Now it's time for Wagner's close-up. The camera is on *him*, and all Newman has to do is stand out of range with the script in his hands and read his string of insults. The camera rolls, Newman reads, and suddenly, as actors say, Wagner fills the moment.

"On camera, in close-up, Robert Wagner starts to cry. This is, let me tell you, a bonus. And it's genuinely exciting. . . . And no one is more excited than Newman. In fact he's so excited at what's happening with Wagner that *Newman* begins fucking up his lines. All he has to do is stand there and read and he can't get the goddam words out right.

"It didn't matter, thankfully. They got the shot," Goldman said. "Wagner was so deep into what he was doing that the crying continued. After the shot was finished, everyone ran to Wagner and milled around, congratulating him; it was that thrilling."

Later R.J. told Goldman that a moment like that had never happened to him before. "It was also the first time in Wagner's experience that a major star had actually stayed around and stood there off camera, reading the lines with him, acting along as it were," Goldman said. "Usually, when the star is done with his shot, it's off to the dressing room, and the remaining performer gets to act with the script girl reading the star's lines. Script girls are very important on the set, they work like hell—but they are also noted for a certain woodenness when it comes to reciting dialogue. No question that Newman's presence helped Wagner fill the moment.

"And if you ever see the movie, the moment's right there. That's not glycerine on Wagner's face as he pulls the trigger. Those were very real tears."

Released in the spring of 1966, *Harper* became a huge box-office hit. Owing to the countless private eye series on television, Hollywood hadn't risked a big all-star whodunit in years, so the public responded to its fresh, sophisticated approach to a stereotyped genre.

R.J. received such excellent notices that Louella Parsons predicted that he'd win an Academy Award. "If Robert Wagner gets the Oscar he so richly deserves, it could be the start of the greatest comeback since Frank Sinatra won for *From Here to Eternity*" Parsons said.

But R.J. never got any closer to nailing that Oscar. He failed even to be nominated, again thanks to Jack Warner's grudge against him. Warner reportedly believed R.J. to be the instigator of much of the trouble that the studio had with Natalie Wood while they were married.

In the crucial electioneering prior to the Academy Award nominations, Warner Brothers put all its backing behind George Segal for Best Supporting Actor for *Who's Afraid of*

Virginia Woolf? Segal got nominated but lost the Oscar to Walter Matthau (for *The Fortune Cookie*).

Except for the flurry of attention that R.J. received from the film's release, *Harper* didn't help his career that much. Any momentum evaporated for lack of a strong follow-up. R.J.'s next movie, *The Biggest Bundle of Them All*, a caper comedy made in Italy in the summer of 1966 with Raquel Welch, Vittorio De Sica and Godfrey Cambridge as costars, turned out so badly that MGM shelved it for two years before literally dumping it on the market.

In the interim, however, R.J. made a career decision that sheltered him from the fallout of that box-office disaster. He signed a long-term contract with MCA-Universal covering both movies and television. Although R.J. had sworn never to undertake another exclusive arrangement like the one he had with 20th Century-Fox, he really had little alternative. With a family to support, free-lancing simply wasn't paying the bills.

With about two thirds of its output going directly to television, MCA-Universal was one of the few major studios that still had enough production activity to warrant the heavy expense of a contract roster. However, unlike his earlier days of servitude, R.J. had considerable freedom to choose the projects he wanted to do.

Having spent all his life struggling to become a "Big Movie Star," R.J. didn't cotton to working in TV. He believed in the Cary Grant dictum: "I don't do television, because people don't pay to see me."

But when you're getting desperate you sometimes have to make compromises. While shuddering at the thought of doing a weekly TV series, R.J. could reconcile himself to starring in some of Universal's hybrid "world premiere" features, which were launched on prime-time network showcases like "Saturday Night at the Movies" in the United States and then released theatrically abroad.

In his new deal with Universal, R.J. fluctuated between those so-called "vidpics" and conventional theatrical movies. The first for TV was a thriller called *How I Spent My Summer Vacation*, in which he costarred with Walter Pidgeon, Peter Lawford, Jill St. John and Lola Albright. Aired on NBC in January 1967, it received a critical drubbing but scored higher in the ratings than the TV premiere of the more celebrated Marlon Brando-Frank Sinatra musical, *Guys and Dolls.*

As things turned out, R.J. proved to be a much bigger draw on television than in movies. His first two Universal theatrical features were flops, starting with *Banning,* an exposé of corruption and sexual infidelity in the affluent country club set. *Don't Just Stand There,* in which he teamed with Mary Tyler Moore, was such an unbearably coy comedy that a critic who caught an airline in-flight showing wrote, "If the emergency door hadn't been locked, I would have jumped."

After the failure of those two movies, MCA-Universal became concerned about R.J.'s future with the company. "In the sixties, everybody was an antihero. There weren't many parts for a guy like me," R.J. remembered. "Lew Wasserman, the boss of MCA, who was originally my agent, called me into his office one day and pulled out *TV Guide.* 'This is where you belong,' he said. 'You'd be great in this medium.' "

Although R.J. disliked the idea, Wasserman persuaded him to star in a weekly series called "It Takes a Thief," the story of a master jewel thief and con artist who's released from prison to work as a government undercover agent. The rougish Alexander Mundy was a character similar to many played by David Niven in his prime, so R.J. consulted his friend before he accepted.

"David encouraged me," R.J. said. "He thought that on television I could use wit and style to good advantage."

Because of scheduling problems at ABC-TV, "It Takes a Thief" got off to a bad start in January 1968. "The show was put in as a midseason replacement. I thought, 'This is the end of my career. Midseason replacements usually die the death. I'm going to be slaughtered in the ratings,' " R.J. recalled.

"I was scared. Here I was, a quarterback with the whole team depending on me. If I failed—finish. Well, the series took off with a bang. They kept moving us to new time slots and the audience followed us just the same."

Variety described R.J.'s financial arrangement as the biggest television deal made by a movie personality up to that time. His salary was $10,000 a week, plus a participation in the profits.

Eighteen years after he made his first movie Robert Wagner

finally seemed to have found his professional niche. His personal life also appeared serene, although divorce rumors briefly
circulated when Marion Wagner returned to acting with a role
in *Gunn*, Blake Edwards' film derived from the "Peter Gunn"
TV series. Gossip columnists interpreted it as a sign of dissension in the Wagners' marriage, since Marion had long made it
plain that only divorce or widowhood could force her to resume her long-defunct career.

But it turned out to be a false alarm, and a rather amusing
one at that. Marion only took the part as a favor to Blake Edwards, who was hard pressed to find someone to play a male
transvestite. If he hired a man, he was afraid the audience
would catch on to the sexual disguise long before the surprising finale. To throw everybody off the track, Marion's billing
in the credits listed her as M. T. Marshall (the initials standing
for her maiden name, Marion Tanner).

While R.J.'s future never looked brighter, the same could not
be said for Natalie Wood's. Although she now earned upward
of a million dollars a year, her life was a mess. Films that
showed great promise on the drawing boards turned into critical and box-office failures. Her search for personal contentment
proved futile.

To her friend Tommy Thompson it seemed that Natalie was
riding the front car of a roller coaster whose only progression
was down, and fast.

"I remember evenings when she would disappear into her
bathroom and take her Seconals and then beseech me to sit
beside her until they took effect, until her eyelids were falling
and her words were blurring and she was finally able to
achieve a few hours of drugged blackness until an unwelcome
dawn.

"Had the headline writers found the same tragic verbs for
her as they had for Marilyn Monroe, it would have saddened
but not surprised most of her close friends," Thompson said.

A wildly eclectic assortment of men helped to fill the lonely
hours. Five months after she was supposed to marry producer
Arthur Loew, Jr., Natalie returned his ring and canceled their
engagement. Publicly, she blamed it on a conflict with her career, going from one film to another virtually nonstop.

But the real reason for the breakup was the usual one for

women who became involved with Arthur Loew. "Arthur was a very sweet guy, but like many people of inherited wealth, he was extremely lacking in drive and ambition," said one of his many exes. "He got bored very easily and couldn't sustain a relationship for more than about six months. He was the sort of man you stayed with until someone better came along."

For Natalie, that successor became thirty-year-old Ladislav Blatnik, a tall, chubby-faced Yugoslavian blond whom she met during a skiing holiday in Switzerland. Described in society columns as "The Jet Set Cobbler," Blatnik claimed to travel 500,000 miles a year peddling shoes for his family's manufacturing company, headquartered in Caracas, Venezuela.

While Blatnik seemed an oddball choice for Natalie Wood, his bankroll was a big attraction. He probably also reminded her a bit of R.J., warm and eager to please and be liked.

Blatnik also had a rather unique talent for eating glass. He could stop a party dead in its tracks by chewing and swallowing a wine goblet. Natalie didn't let him do the trick too often because he would only risk it with her finest Baccarat crystal.

In April 1965, Natalie and "Laddy" announced their engagement, adding that they intended to divide their time between Hollywood and Caracas after the wedding.

Many doubted it would ever happen. "How would a glamorous movie star ever get by with the name Natalie Blatnik? If she didn't dig Gurdin, you knew damn well she wouldn't put up with Blatnik," said columnist Earl Wilson. "And would Natalie have exchanged show business for shoe business just to live in Caracas, for Christ's sake?"

Blatnik came into Natalie's life at a time of peak activity in her career. He was with her constantly, his function seemingly as much sycophant as lover.

"Laddy made Natalie feel like a star, sending fresh flowers, candy and expensive little gifts to her dressing room every day," said her hairdresser. "During work breaks he would play Latin music on the stereo or instruct her in Spanish with records from Berlitz."

How Blatnik managed to carry on a flourishing shoe trade at the same time puzzled some of Natalie's friends, who suspected his real sources of income were on the shady side. "He was about as trustworthy as a watch purchased in a dark alleyway," said Tommy Thompson.

While Blatnik was on the scene in 1965, Natalie outdid herself by making three movies, but not necessarily by choice. Jack Warner forced her to do the first one when Columbia Pictures canceled *Inside Daisy Clover*, which she had promised to make for Alan Pakula and Robert Mulligan, the producer-director team from *Love With the Proper Stranger*.

Jack Warner offered to take over the project from Columbia if Natalie made *The Great Race* first at Warner Brothers. Not only did she long to play Daisy Clover, but she also knew that finding another backer wouldn't be easy. Columbia dropped the $4.5 million film for budgetary reasons.

Natalie became very unhappy while making *The Great Race*, not the best mood to be in for a $12 million slapstick farce being ballyhooed as the funniest movie in Hollywood history. Filmed largely on location in Europe, it meant that Natalie had to be separated from her analyst for two months.

She also didn't respond to chauvinistic needling from her two costars, Jack Lemmon and Tony Curtis, or to director Blake Edwards, who seemed more interested in staging pie-throwing contests than in helping her to give a good performance. A wardrobe of cumbersome turn-of-the-century gowns, all with tightly corseted underpinnings, didn't help Natalie's disposition either. Last but not least, she had to turn down an offer from master director William Wyler for *The Collector* because of conflicting production schedules (Samantha Eggar got the part *and* an Oscar nomination).

Finally Natalie reached the breaking point and wanted to go home to Beverly Hills. She knew enough tricks of the trade to wait until enough film had been exposed before making her move. That way it was unlikely that she'd be fired because it would be too expensive to start over with another actress.

"Natalie suddenly became very temperamental, arriving late on the set or calling in sick, claiming she was having her period," said production executive William Orr. "Then she started running up huge bills at the Paris dressmakers and charging them to Warner Brothers. The accounting department went bananas, so she was packed off to L.A. the next day.

Her remaining scenes were either cut from the script or shot with a double."

A much more dedicated Natalie became evident when she made *Inside Daisy Clover*, a vehicle that she believed could finally win her the Oscar that had long eluded her. Based on Gavin Lambert's novel about a young, Depression-era movie star reminiscent of Judy Garland and Deanna Durbin, the role had an autobiographical streak. Natalie had experienced similar situations and stresses in her own life.

"When Natalie first read my screenplay," Gavin Lambert remembered, "she said to me with a mixture of fear and admiration, 'But at every key moment of Daisy's life, she's alone!' This not only showed her intuitive grasp of the character, but it also related to a recent experience she went on to tell me about.

"A famous and talented star in her sixties, semiretired and almost wholly solitary, had invited her to dinner," Lambert continued. "The star meant to be friendly but only succeeded in being horrifying. 'So lonely and bitter,' Natalie said. 'She seemed to have a grudge against every woman we talked about, and every man she called a fag or a Commie.' If that was what it took to become a movie legend, she wanted no part of it.

"But of course she *did* want a part of it," said Lambert, who became a close friend in subsequent years. "Therein lay the tension of her life—how to reconcile her strong appetite for imaginative excitement with her need for security."

When a rising young actor named Robert Redford was signed to play opposite Natalie in *Inside Daisy Clover*, rumors circulated that he would become the next man in her personal life. A year older than Natalie, Redford certainly seemed a more suitable match than Ladislav Blatnik, her current swain. But to the gossipmongers' disappointment, only a mutually admiring friendship developed.

"Natalie went gaga over Bob Redford. What woman wouldn't?" said her secretary, Howard Jeffrey. "But Bob not only looked like Jack Armstrong, the all-American boy, he lived like him as well. He was happily married and did not play around."

Redford was also very concerned about his masculine image. Before he accepted the part as Daisy Clover's husband he insisted on a rewrite so that the character's bisexuality was treated even more ambiguously than in the original novel.

Redford's demand seemed presumptuous, given that *Inside Daisy Clover* was only his third movie and just a featured role at that. But he'd recently enjoyed a big hit on Broadway in *Barefoot in the Park,* and Hollywood tended to treat stage-trained actors with greater reverence than its own. (Not always when it came to money, however. Redford's salary was a flat $6,500 a week, while Natalie's was $33,000 a week, *plus* a percentage of the profits.)

While working with Redford on a scene in Santa Monica Bay, Natalie experienced one of those frightening encounters with the sea that, in retrospect, may have been an omen. But at the time she shrugged it off as just another peril of the job. A huge wave developed out of nowhere, separating Natalie and Redford's small boat from the one carrying the cameramen and technicians.

"There was no way we could get Natalie and Bob off the boat," said director Robert Mulligan. "And the lines to keep them in place were breaking right and left. One of the crew members broke his leg as a cable snapped and we had to rush him to the hospital.

"All the time we were worrying about Natalie and Bob and it was obvious that she was terrified and he was having a great time. When he found out about the broken leg, of course, he didn't think it was so funny, but I think his sense of fun kept Natalie from having a heart attack."

Over the years Natalie had developed a close friendship with writer Garson Kanin and his wife, stage actress Ruth Gordon. The two women had always wanted to work together, so when the role of Daisy Clover's batty mother came along, Natalie suggested Gordon. Jack Warner wouldn't hear of it, holding out for a big movie name. Gordon's last film work had been over twenty years before in supporting roles.

But Natalie fought hard for her friend, and Ruth Gordon finally got the part. Thanks to Natalie's persistence, Gordon's career was rejuvenated. At sixty-eight, she went on to enjoy greater popularity in films than she ever did in the theater.

"I learned a lot about being a movie star from Natalie," Ruth Gordon recalled. "She never threw her weight around, but one day while we were on location in Pasadena, I said, 'Oh, I forgot my lucky bracelet with my St. Christopher's medal.' Natalie said, 'Send a limo for it.' It was in my dressing room back in the Burbank studio and I said, 'Oh, no.' She said, 'That's what limos are for.' "

Ironically, Ruth Gordon—not Natalie Wood—ended up with an Academy Award nomination for *Inside Daisy Clover*. Gordon got nominated in the Best Supporting Actress category but lost to Shelley Winters in *A Patch of Blue*.

The winner for Best Actress that year was Julie Christie in *Darling*. When Natalie didn't even get nominated, she blamed it on lack of support from Warner Brothers. Angry words were exchanged with Jack Warner, and as a result *Inside Daisy Clover* was not only Natalie's fourteenth Warner Brothers movie but also her last. She never worked for the studio again.

Although Natalie received favorable reviews for her performance (particularly for the recording booth scene where she suddenly goes berserk), *Inside Daisy Clover* was both a critical and box-office fiasco. The New York *Times*'s Bosley Crowther, then considered the most influential film critic in the country, called it "fatuous and vulgar." Most of his contemporaries agreed that it missed the mark as a potentially blistering sendup of the movie business.

But that disappointment was still ahead. While making *Inside Daisy Clover*, Natalie became tremendously enthused about its future potential. When she next signed for Paramount's *This Property Is Condemned*, finally getting a long-cherished opportunity to play a Tennessee Williams heroine, it appeared that her career had hit a hot streak.

The role was Alva Starr, whose mother runs a disreputable boardinghouse in Depression-era Mississippi. "It's probably the closest I'll ever get to playing Blanche DuBois, so I'd better make the most of it," Natalie said at the time. "Alva is a great character, always ordering Sazerac cocktails and longing for the excitement of the big city. She wants out of her small town with a capital O, and she'll do anything to get away. There's plenty of room at the bottom if she stays.

"My own life hasn't been so different," she continued. "There was plenty of room at the bottom if I'd kept making those Tab Hunter movies. I had to fight for everything. . . .

You get tough in this business, until you get big enough to hire people to get tough for you. Then you can sit back and be a lady."

Natalie had enough clout now to pick her costars and director. For the leading man she again chose Robert Redford. "Natalie loved working with Bob because he doesn't come on to women like some actors do," said a friend. "Bob just does his job and is very considerate of everyone. There aren't those ego entanglements there usually are when two stars are together on a set."

Natalie had also developed such trust in Redford's judgment that, upon his recommendation, she requested that his friend Sydney Pollack be hired as the director. Although Pollack had directed only one other movie *(The Slender Thread)*, he was a TV Emmy winner greatly admired for the rapport he had with actors, which apparently came from having been one himself.

Beyond its Tennessee Williams connection, *This Property Is Condemned* had a special allure for Natalie because she replaced Elizabeth Taylor, who had intended to make it with none other than her husband, Richard Burton, as the director. When the potential bloodshed of that arrangement finally dawned on someone, the Burtons withdrew and instead acted as a team in Mike Nichols' film of *Who's Afraid of Virginia Woolf?*

Rightly or wrongly, Natalie believed that whatever was good enough for Elizabeth Taylor should be good enough for Natalie Wood. Perhaps if she'd studied the history of the project she might not have been so enthusiastic. On stage, *This Property Is Condemned* was a one-act play that ran twenty minutes. Tennessee Williams, who thought he'd said everything he wanted to in that space, refused to be involved in expanding it into a two-hour movie.

When he finally saw the result, Williams got so upset that he wanted his authorship removed from the credits. But the Williams name was too valuable a box-office drawing card. Paramount refused and finally mollified him by changing the billing from *"Based on* a play by Tennessee Williams" to *"Suggested by* a play by . . ."

The movie represented the contributions of twelve different writers, including John Huston, Francis Ford Coppola and Tennessee Williams himself (his original dialogue was used almost in toto in the film's prologue and epilogue). Sydney Pollack directed with scissors and a staple gun close at hand, putting together a shooting script from all the different versions.

"We ended up improvising, just making things up as we went along, hoping they'd add up to something," Robert Redford said.

Needless to say, *This Property Is Condemned* turned out to be Natalie's second film in a row that failed to live up to her high expectations. Bosley Crowther called it "soggy and sentimental," while *Newsweek* carped that "Natalie Wood has a few admirable moments, but most often seems a well-scrubbed debutante who has strayed into the wrong side of town."

Although Natalie's publicists tried to plant the idea with gossip columnists that her performance was Oscar caliber, she failed even to be nominated in the 1966 contest for Best Actress. Ironically, Elizabeth Taylor, whom she replaced in *This Property Is Condemned*, won for *Who's Afraid of Virginia Woolf?*

The one prize that Natalie did win in 1966 was rather dubious. That spring the *Harvard Lampoon* voted her "the worst actress of this year, next year and the following year." Much to the editors' surprise, Natalie was the first lampooned celebrity ever to actually accept the university magazine's invitation to come to Cambridge, Massachusetts, to receive the award.

A motorcycle escort of thirty Harvard undergraduates garbed in black tuxedos picked Natalie up at Logan Airport and delivered her to the campus. In an outdoor ceremony attended by the entire student body, she was presented with a gold-framed scroll citing her for "consistent but vain contributions to the cinematic industry."

The event received enormous national publicity, but Natalie's playing the good sport spared her some of the ridicule of the award itself. "I thought it was meant in fun," she told reporters. "I took it as a good-natured rib."

She was mortified, however, when a spokesman for the *Lampoon* subsequently told *Time* magazine that "It definitely wasn't meant as an honor. The editors felt Natalie had reached the pinnacle of her career and was on the way down. They wanted to let her know she wasn't the greatest actress around."

Natalie was then twenty-eight, not that much older than some of the Harvardites who panned her. She interpreted the criticism from peers as an attack on her studio upbringing and rudimentary education. Thrashing it out with her psychiatrist, she became determined to prove to herself and to her detractors that she was not one of those brainless Hollywood bimbos of legend.

In the wake of her *Lampoon*-ing, Natalie embarked on a culture kick, trading such usual haunts as La Scala and the Daisy for art galleries and the classrooms of UCLA, where she took a survey course in English literature.

"The other day I realized that I had never even read *Hamlet*," Natalie said at the time. "There are, shall we say, some educational gaps in my life. This is the first really organized reading I've ever done. It's started me on other authors, too. I'm really hooked on e. e. cummings and Pushkin."

Grateful for the experience, she showed her appreciation by endowing the Natalie Wood Performing Arts Awards at UCLA's Theater Arts Department. Each year, two $500 prizes were presented to the outstanding student actor and actress from the sophomore or junior class.

During her cultural kick Natalie's mansion in Bel Air began to resemble a museum. Adorning every room were expensive paintings, sculptures and lithographs, including works by Bonnard, Courbet and Pasternak (father of Boris, her favorite Russian writer). She also had a collection of pre-Columbian art which she once loaned to UCLA for public exhibition.

By this time Natalie had ended her affair with Ladislav Blatnik, who departed the scene for reasons and destination unknown. Natalie chose no full-time replacement but briefly had flings with actors Stuart Whitman, Tom Courtenay and Richard Johnson, the latter both Britishers who were working in Hollywood.

For a while Natalie also became the occasional companion of Frank Sinatra, then in the midst of a tempestuous romance with Mia Farrow. As part of her campaign to get Sinatra to marry her, Farrow kept dating other men to make him jealous. In retaliation the "Chairman of the Board" sometimes sought consolation with Natalie, although it's doubtful she would have become the third Mrs. Sinatra if Mia Farrow hadn't finally landed him.

In the end Natalie had Sinatra to thank for rescuing her

from a potentially dangerous involvement. At the Daisy dis-
cotheque one night she became chummy with a young screenwriter who was very much into the Ken Kesey, Electric Kool-
Aid world. When Natalie happened to mention that she'd
taken an LSD "trip" with the man, Sinatra became very concerned and made her promise never to repeat it. To make sure
that she didn't, Sinatra put one of his bodyguards on her tail
until he became satisfied that she had terminated the relationship.

While making preparations for her next movie, Natalie fell
deeply in love with the European who would direct it. A major
studio had signed the director to a Hollywood contract after
one of his films won an Oscar and numerous other honors.
Unfortunately he had a wife, so the affair caused Natalie tremendous pain.

In the beginning Natalie envisioned the movie as the one
that would finally cause critics to take her seriously as a dramatic actress. And in the internationally acclaimed director she
thought she'd found not only a potential husband but also a
Svengali, à la Ingmar Bergman and Liv Ullmann or Federico
Fellini and Giulietta Masina.

Had her lover not been married, Natalie's daydreams might
have come true. But she wasn't content to be his mistress forever and he had no intention of divorcing his wife. Like many
Continental men, he thought he could have both, but Natalie's
strict Russian-American upbringing didn't permit that.

One night Natalie went to a party and ran into the director
and his wife, who apparently knew nothing of her husband's
infidelity. Natalie managed to mask her distress but collapsed
in tears when she got home.

The next day she told her lover it was all over, and she really
meant it. Under the circumstances, working together would be
impossible, so she also withdrew from the movie. Without
Natalie's participation, the studio lost interest in the project
and it never got produced.

The breakup left Natalie deeply depressed for months afterward. It also widened a breach with her mother that had ex-
isted since the divorce from R.J. Mrs. Gurdin strongly disapproved of Natalie's illicit romances, never failing to gloat and

criticize when they ended. That was hardly what Natalie wanted to hear.

She also could not count on getting much counsel from younger sister Lana Wood, who had similar problems of her own to cope with and who was also in their mother's bad graces. Although Lana's acting career peaked with a two-year run on the "Peyton Place" TV series, she had developed quite a fanzine reputation as a sexpot because of two broken marriages and a string of lovers longer than her sister's. Intimates attributed Lana's behavior to a psychological need to prove herself better than Natalie, but it always made for a very difficult and strained relationship between them.

As she did once before, Natalie turned for consolation to former fiancé Arthur Loew, Jr. He not only recommended work as the best therapy for her depression but also came up with a firm job offer in a movie that he and Joe Pasternak were producing at MGM. For $750,000, a fee that would cure anyone's blues, Natalie signed on for *Penelope*, a caper comedy based on a novel by E. V. Cunningham (a pen name of Howard Fast).

In the title role, Natalie played a neglected housewife who embarks on a life of crime so that her banker husband will pay more attention to her. Having spent such a large chunk of their budget on Natalie's salary, the producers had to round out the starring cast with Ian Bannen, Dick Shawn, Peter Falk and Jonathan Winters, none of whom were major movie names at the time.

There's nothing worse than an unfunny comedy, and *Penelope* turned out to be the nadir of Natalie's career. "I broke out in hives and suffered anguish that was very real pain every day we shot," she remembered. "Arthur Hiller, the director, kept saying, 'Natalie, I think you're resisting this film,' while I rolled around on the floor in agony."

Mainly on the strength of Natalie Wood's drawing power at the box office, *Penelope* got booked into New York's Radio City Music Hall as the Thanksgiving holiday attraction in November 1966. Although it broke opening-day records, attendance quickly plummeted in the wake of bad reviews and unfavorable word of mouth.

Whether she deserved it or not, Natalie had to assume most

of the blame for the movie's failure. She was, after all, its principal reason for existence. After the reviews and box-office reports came out, she took to her bed and wanted to see no one except her psychiatrist, Dr. John Lindon, and her former secretary, Mart Crowley. In exchange for his companionship and general help around the house, the latter received free room and board in Natalie's guest cottage while he typed away at what eventually became his landmark homosexual play, *The Boys in the Band.*

Although Dr. Lindon and Crowley tried as best they could to snap Natalie out of her depression, she grew worse as the year drew to an end. Nineteen sixty-six had been disastrous for her in everything that mattered. Besides *Penelope*, her two previous movies, *Inside Daisy Clover* and *This Property Is Condemned*, proved bitter disappointments. The fallout from all three threatened to undermine the position she had worked so hard to achieve as a Hollywood superstar.

But nagging her even more was the fear that she'd failed as a woman. Here she was this supposedly great sex symbol and she didn't even have a man in her life. She still had crying jags and self-recriminations over her affair with the European director. Perhaps she shouldn't have broken it off so abruptly, perhaps she eventually could have coaxed him into divorcing his wife so that they could be married. She tried reaching him by phone, only to discover that he'd taken an assignment abroad and wasn't expected back for months.

One afternoon Natalie had a visitor from out of her past. Bearing no flowers, chocolates or any other gift, Warren Beatty arrived unannounced and uninvited to beg her to reconsider appearing in his next movie, *Bonnie and Clyde*. She'd already turned him down once, claiming that she couldn't risk being separated from her analyst during the required three months of location work in Texas.

Since Natalie was in even worse psychological shape than she'd been then, Beatty's pleading fell on deaf ears. Exactly what else they talked about is known only to them, but right after Beatty left the house Natalie attempted suicide by swallowing a handful of barbiturates. Apparently Beatty's visit opened up old emotional scars which, added to other more recent problems, became too painful for her to bear.

"All I know is this," said Mart Crowley, who was in another part of the house at the time and witnessed some of the events. "Warren came by and they were talking. Then I heard raised voices and Warren left. Natalie went upstairs to her bedroom. That's when she took the pills.

"Just before she lost consciousness she must have had second thoughts, because she started downstairs. I heard her call. I found her slumped on the stairs."

Crowley immediately called Natalie's psychiatrist, who told him to take her to Cedars of Lebanon Hospital in Hollywood. Dr. Lindon met them there and supervised a stomach pumping that placed Natalie out of danger. Afterward Lindon spent over an hour alone with Natalie. Both did a great deal of shouting and screaming that reverberated into the corridors.

Just to be on the safe side, Lindon insisted on Natalie remaining in the hospital overnight. Registered under a pseudonym, she stayed in a private wing. Nobody but Dr. Lindon, Mart Crowley and a few hospital staffers knew of her presence.

Fearful that her mother would come rushing to her bedside and create a big scene, Natalie didn't want her family to be notified. But Crowley felt obligated to do so and phoned Maria Gurdin anyway. She broke down when she heard the news but agreed to stay away if her visiting was going to upset Natalie that much.

Since Crowley didn't want to leave Natalie alone in the hospital, he asked Mrs. Gurdin to arrange for Lana Wood to bring some old clothes for her sister to wear when she checked out. The plan was to disguise Natalie and sneak her out a back exit so that no one would recognize her and report it to the press.

When Lana Wood arrived at the hospital she started to cry at first sight of Natalie. "Her hair was hanging into her face, she was wearing a loose hospital gown, and her face was puffy, her tiny body swollen. I kissed her, then took her hand," she recalled.

"I didn't want to live anymore," Natalie whispered, looking away.

Lana Wood reached across, took Natalie's chin and turned her face so that they were looking directly at each other.

"And now you do?" she asked.

Natalie looked away again. Her sister sat silently beside her for a long time before Natalie glanced back and spoke.

"Now I do," she said.

ELEVEN

Changing Partners

AFTER *Penelope,* Natalie Wood didn't make another movie for almost three years. Rumors started within the industry that she'd lost her box-office clout, that at age thirty she was washed up, no longer being considered for the top roles.

Not exactly true, since Natalie did reject several parts that proved very successful for other actresses, including Jane Fonda in *Barefoot in the Park* and Ali MacGraw in *Goodbye Columbus.* But at the time the offers came along Natalie was preoccupied with trying to pull herself together again after being pushed to the brink of self-destruction.

"I didn't know who the hell I was," she recalled. "I was whoever *they* wanted me to be, *they* being agents, producers, directors or whoever else I was trying to please at the time. I started putting space between myself and my work, so that I didn't start panicking when there wasn't a job to bounce to. It was mainly a matter of getting to the point where I could actually be alone and say, 'Hey, I'm not such a bad person to hang out with.' I had a lot of monkeys to get off my back."

Forever after, Natalie credited psychoanalysis with helping her to locate her own identity, separating it from the fantasy world of magazine covers and teaching her that she alone was responsible for her life and her decisions. She learned she didn't have to depend on sleeping pills or psychic energizers to help her.

"I don't mean to make it sound too terrific," she later told Tommy Thompson, "because, God knows, I don't have all the answers. But I'm as grateful for that experience as for anything that ever happened to me. If it wasn't for those years of analysis, I'd probably be dead. I'm so happy now, it's scary. I'm afraid to even talk about it for fear it will crumble or something. But every moment is precious now, and for much of my life there didn't seem much even worth losing."

When she started feeling more secure about herself Natalie took the drastic action of firing the cabinet of agents, lawyers, publicists and accountants who had kowtowed to her every whim for years. In a further show of independence, she booked herself on a flight to New York for a week of shopping and sightseeing entirely on her own.

"It must seem silly except to anyone who never did anything for herself," Natalie said, "but for me it was a step-by-step progression to normalcy."

The hardest problem she had to deal with was her lack of a deep romantic involvement. Talking about that deficiency, she often invoked the name of friend and role model Elizabeth Taylor. "Elizabeth goes with her man. That's why she's survived, if you ask me. And for a woman, what else is there?" Natalie said at the time.

The man who seemingly most suited her requirements was unavailable. One night, while Natalie and sister Lana happened to be dining at La Scala, Robert and Marion Wagner arrived with a group of friends. R.J. waved at the two women and they reciprocated.

Afterward the talkative Natalie turned silent and started to cry. Her sister squeezed her hand under the table and asked what was upsetting her.

"I'm still in love with R.J. I'll probably always love him," Natalie said. A few minutes later she insisted on leaving the restaurant, carefully avoiding the Wagners' booth on the way out.

For a short time Natalie kept company with independent producer, ex-William Morris agent David Niven, Jr., who had inherited some of his father's urbane charm but had no ambition to pursue an acting career of his own. Then, in the autumn of 1967, Natalie attended a dinner party given by publicist friend Rupert Allen and found herself placed next to a man she'd never met before.

"It was really strange," she recalled. "I sat down and we turned to look at one another. And that was it!"

Nine years older than Natalie, prematurely gray-haired Richard Gregson was the head of U.S. operations for a British talent agency, London International Artists. Born in India of British parentage, he spent most of his youth in England and Canada. After high school he traveled around the world in odd jobs for several years before becoming a literary and theatrical agent through the help of his older brother, cinema star Michael Craig.

In Richard Gregson, Natalie found both a lover and a supportive, understanding companion who wasn't intimidated by her being a wealthy Hollywood sex symbol. Married but long separated, Gregson had two young daughters and a son whom Natalie quickly took to mothering whenever they stayed with their father.

Because of his wife's exorbitant financial demands for a divorce, Natalie lived with Richard Gregson for two years before a settlement was finally reached. During that time Natalie usually accompanied him on his frequent business trips to London and the Continent, which further contributed to the long lull in her career.

With Gregson's encouragement, Natalie tried to find studio backing for two movies in which she wanted to star, *I Never Promised You a Rose Garden* and *Will There Really Be a Morning?* Not coincidentally, both concerned women with troubled psychological histories similar to Natalie's. Producers considered them too downbeat and neither got filmed until years after she gave up her options.

Instead Natalie decided to end her work sabbatical by accepting an offer from Columbia Pictures for *Bob & Carol & Ted & Alice*, costarring with Robert Culp, Elliott Gould and Dyan Cannon (then known primarily as the ex-Mrs. Cary Grant). Although she'd received $750,000 for *Penelope*, her box-office luster had dimmed in the interim and producer Mike Frankovich refused to go that high. After much haggling, Natalie agreed to accept $250,000 against ten percent of the gross.

One of the first major Hollywood films to deal with the liberated morality of the 1960s, *Bob & Carol & Ted & Alice* created a sensation by focusing on wife-swapping and group sex, which were provocatively summed up in the advertising catch line, "Consider the possibilities." Directed by newcomer Paul Mazursky, the satire won critical plaudits for its crazy, improvisational style and enjoyed an immense box-office success.

Much to Natalie's disappointment, many reviewers said she had slight flair for comedy. They compared her performance unfavorably to that of costar Dyan Cannon, who wound up with a 1969 Oscar nomination as Best Supporting Actress (losing the award to Goldie Hawn in *Cactus Flower*).

But if there was a last laugh to be had, Natalie had it, all the way to the bank. She earned over $3 million from her share of the record-breaking grosses!

While *Bob & Carol & Ted & Alice* revitalized Natalie's bargaining power within the industry and brought her a flood of new offers, she preferred to devote herself entirely to her relationship with Richard Gregson. Suddenly becoming jobless when London International Artists shut down its American branch, Gregson formed an independent company called Wildwood Enterprises in partnership with Robert Redford, Natalie's great friend as well as one of Gregson's former clients.

To help the new firm get started, Natalie pitched in by appointing herself Gregson's unofficial assistant on Wildwood's first project, *Downhill Racer*. Robert Redford had promised to make the ski thriller for Paramount Pictures in settlement of a contract dispute over his refusal to appear in *Blue*, a Western that ultimately proved a flop for his replacement, Terrence Stamp.

While *Downhill Racer* shot on location in the snow country of Utah, Colorado and Idaho, Natalie helped out by typing script revisions, shopping for wardrobe and props, touching up makeup and appearing as a well-disguised extra in several crowd scenes. She also suffered a nasty skiing accident that forced her to turn up as a presenter on the April 1969 Academy Awards telecast with her broken leg in a cast.

Happily, Natalie had fully recovered by May 30, the date that she and the just-divorced Richard Gregson set for their marriage despite warnings from Natalie's superstitious mother that May weddings brought only tears and unhappiness.

An extravagant Russian Orthodox ceremony was held at Holy Virgin Mary Church in Los Angeles. Robert Redford served as best man. Natalie's new stepchildren, Sarah, Charlotte and Hugo Gregson, marched in the procession.

With a crown of daisies and pastel ribbons streaming over her long dark hair, Natalie looked like a vision in a silk gown designed by her longtime friend, costume designer Edith Head (who also served as one of the bridesmaids).

When asked about the unique bouquet of wild flowers and sprigs of wheat that she carried in her hands, Natalie told a reporter, "That's an old Russian fertility symbol. Oh, yes, I'd like two or three children." No one was terribly surprised when, six months later, she announced that she was pregnant.

Meanwhile, what Robert Wagner felt about the latest developments in Natalie's life can only be guessed at, but he undoubtedly wished her well.

By that time R.J. had made another stab at theatrical movies, an instantly forgettable racing-car thriller with Paul Newman, Joanne Woodward and Richard Thomas. Entitled *Winning*, the movie did not help the careers of anyone involved and convinced R.J. to concentrate on television work. His MCA series, "It Takes a Thief," had entered its second year on the ABC network, garnering high points in the Nielsen ratings week after week.

In his dual capacity as star-producer, R.J. shrewdly surrounded himself with the best talent available, including his lifelong idol Fred Astaire, who played his father in occasional episodes. As two suave ex-cons, the relationship was immensely likable, one of the best elements of the series.

R.J. endeared himself to many of his coworkers by showing a consideration that he had learned under the old studio system but that had nearly vanished from the present Hollywood way of doing things. When he signed Bette Davis to play the unlikely role of a safecracker in one episode, he remodeled a dressing room for her and filled it with fresh flowers every day. Of course he had a motive for doing so, but Davis respected him. She never balked if he wasn't satisfied with a scene and requested retakes.

Almost totally obsessed with making "It Takes a Thief" successful, R.J. spent the better part of two years living in his office suite on the Universal lot. By this time he had moved his family to a bigger, more expensive house in Palm Springs, which was too far away for a daily commute.

The long separations, punctuated only by weekend visits, caused a serious breach in the seven-year-old Wagner marriage. The Universal City guard patrol noticed a sharp increase in the number of beautiful young female callers at R.J.'s office, especially after normal working hours. Gossip claimed that his lovers changed as often as his leading ladies, which was about every ten days.

One night R.J. went stag to a party at producer John Foreman's house. A few minutes later Natalie Gregson, six months pregnant and huge, also arrived unaccompanied, her husband being in London on a business trip.

"Suddenly we found ourselves off in a corner, sitting together, talking, remembering the happy times, our boat, the private moments, what few of them there were," Natalie recalled. "When we left, R.J. followed me in his car to make sure I got home safely. We stood on the front porch, and it was awkward, and I finally said, 'Well, are you happy, R.J.?' And he said, 'I'm happy that you're having a baby.' The next day he sent me flowers and it totally dissolved me."

R.J. reacted similarly. After leaving Natalie's house he experienced such strong feelings of sadness and regret that he started to cry. He finally had to pull off the road to avoid having an accident. "Oh, Jesus," he muttered to himself as he realized how much he still cared.

On September 29, 1970, Natalie gave birth to a daughter, Natasha, her original Russian name. "I can definitely say that was the happiest moment of my life," Natalie claimed later. "Once you have children, I think it changes your viewpoint forever. You look at life differently. You make different decisions because you are responsible for somebody else. That was one of the reasons I didn't work for a long time after Natasha was born. I always wanted children very much, but I didn't have them in my twenties. I had Natasha when I was thirty-two."

Natalie became a nursing mother, all but vanishing from the public spotlight. The Gregsons divided their time between a sprawling hilltop house in Bel Air and a weekend retreat at Lake Tahoe. Gregson had ended his partnership with Robert Redford to join Arthur P. Jacobs' APJAC Productions as executive vice-president, developing various projects including spin-offs of the company's blockbuster movie, *Planet of the Apes*, and a musical version of *Cyrano de Bergerac*.

While all seemed serene in the Gregson marriage, Robert Wagner's domestic problems became public knowledge when he started being seen around town with a twenty-two-year-old brunet actress named Christina Sinatra, the youngest child of a nearly lifetime friend. Although R.J. and Tina had known each other long enough for her to call him "Uncle Bob," the romance did not ignite until they started working together in an episode of "It Takes a Thief."

At the end of 1970, R.J. and Marion Wagner announced that they had separated and were consulting lawyers about a divorce.

Ironically, not long after the breakup hit the headlines, a new play opened locally in which R.J. and Marion were models for the central characters. Entitled *Remote Asylum*, it was written by Mart Crowley, who used some of his personal knowledge of the couple's tenure in Rome as the basis for the plot. It concerned two Hollywoodites who flee the country over matrimonial problems (his wife has just left him for another man, she's fighting her ex-husband for custody of their children). Somehow or other they wind up in Acapulco instead of Rome, staying with Merle Oberon and industrialist husband Bruno Pagliai in their cliffside hacienda.

"It's about people who believe that with a passport and a plane ticket you can escape from yourself," Mart Crowley told a reporter on opening night. "So you arrive at the right desti-

Natalie spent so much time visiting the set of R.J.'s In Love and War *that the production crew gifted her with her own canvas chair, with lettering amusingly suiting the occasion. (UPI/Bettmann Newsphotos)*

Natalie's make-believe flirtation with Warren Beatty in Splendor in the Grass *precipitated a real-life affair that caused her to divorce R.J. in 1962. Beatty eventually jilted her for a restaurant hat-check girl. (AP/Wide World Photos)*

R.J. married actress Marion Marshall, a divorcee with two young sons, in a civil ceremony in July 1963. Their only child, Kate Wagner, was born the following year. (UPI/Bettmann Newsphotos)

Natalie and Ladislav Blatnik, one of many suitors during her bachelor days in the mid-1960s. A shoe merchant known as the "Jet Set Cobbler," Blatnik had a unique talent for eating glass. (UPI/Bettmann Newsphotos)

Flanked by best man Robert Redford, Natalie beams at second husband Richard Gregson following their Russian Orthodox wedding in May 1969. Three of the children in the group are Gregson's from his previous marriage. (Jean Cummings)

Elliott Gould, Natalie, Robert Culp and Dyan Cannon shared the same bed in Bob & Carol & Ted & Alice. *The hit spoof of liberated sexuality made Natalie a multimillionaire through her profit participation. (Museum of Modern Art/Films Stills Archives)*

In 1970, R.J. seemed destined to become Frank Sinatra's son-in-law when he announced plans to marry twenty-two-year-old Tina Sinatra. The couple traveled everywhere together until the engagement was abruptly and mysteriously cancelled within six months. (AP/Wide World Photos)

Remarried at sea on July 16, 1972, Natalie and R.J. enjoy a champagne toast to "the second time around." Just over a decade had passed since their divorce. (Jean Cummings)

Laurence Olivier, who starred with Natalie and R.J. in the 1976 TV production of Cat on a Hot Tin Roof, *welcomed them to London when they arrived for the start of filming. Accompanying the couple were their two-year-old daughter, Courtney Wagner, and her six-year-old half-sister, Natasha Gregson. (AP/Wide World Photos)*

During rehearsals for the "Hart to Hart" TV series, R.J. and leading lady Stephanie Powers take a break with Capucine, that episode's special guest star. The two women must have had plenty to talk about, since both were mistresses of William Holden at one time or another. (AP/Wide World Photos)

Natalie and R.J. seemed to be enjoying themselves in what turned out to be one of their last photographs together, taken in 1980. (AP/Wide World Photos)

Natalie has eyes only for Christopher Walken as director Douglas Trumbull, right, tells them how to play a scene in Brainstorm, *the sci-fi thriller she was making at the time of her death. The Wagners took Walken sailing with them on that fateful Thanksgiving holiday week-end of 1981. (AP/Wide World Photos)*

Members of the Los Angeles Sheriff's Department tow the inflatable dinghy to shore after it was found near Natalie's body in the waters off Catalina Island. (AP/Wide World Photos)

*At the funeral, R.J. took a handful of gardenias from Natalie's bier
and distributed them among her immediate survivors. Afterward, he
returned to the casket, bent down and tenderly kissed it on one corner.
(AP/Wide World Photos)*

nation with the wrong person—yourself—until you decide to face yourself."

Critics expecting another probing and entertaining work from the author of *The Boys in the Band* were totally baffled and bored by *Remote Asylum* and it closed within the week. The reviewer for the *Herald-Examiner* said, "The biggest excitement of the evening comes from a dog who barks twice."

Although Crowley invited both R.J. and Marion to the opening, only she turned up. Apparently unperturbed by what she witnessed, she happily posed for pictures afterward with Anne Francis and William Shatner, who portrayed Marion and R.J. on stage.

Natalie and Richard Gregson were also in the audience. Not looking as though she'd enjoyed the evening, Natalie managed to at least crack a smile when a friend stopped her in the lobby on the way out and said, "The moral of this play is don't hire a secretary who takes notes."

R.J. had just announced his engagement to Tina Sinatra, which is probably why he didn't attend the opening of *Remote Asylum*. Gossipmongers were predicting they'd be married as soon as he got divorced.

Columnist James Bacon ran into them at a party one night and asked R.J., "In your wildest dreams, did you ever think that someday Frank Sinatra would be your father-in-law?" The lovers just stared fondly at each other and laughed.

Now that their relationship no longer had to be kept secret, R.J. moved into Tina's condominium apartment in Century City, a present from Daddy Sinatra on her twenty-first birthday. In favorable weather R.J. and Tina liked to fly kites on the community's lawns, once part of the back lot of his alma mater, 20th Century-Fox.

In the spring of 1971, R.J. received the crushing news that ABC intended to cancel "It Takes a Thief" after two and a half years on the air and that Universal-MCA would end production of the series. "I just couldn't believe they'd pulled the rug from under me. It still makes me sick," he said years later. "The show was a success, the format was perfect, the audience identification element was strong, and as a result "Thief" was the biggest show in the history of syndication for Universal. And they killed it."

Universal's executive team refused to give R.J. a reason beyond an unyielding "We've decided to go in another direction." Since his contract still had two years to run, the studio wanted to use him in telefeatures and guest spots in some of its other series.

When R.J. refused to go along with their proposals a legal dispute developed that couldn't have come at a worse time for him. Money that he'd been intending to use for the financial settlement in his divorce suddenly became unavailable pending resolution of his differences with Universal.

R.J. and Marion Wagner were finally divorced in Los Angeles Superior Court on October 14, 1971. Contrary to polite custom, the husband rather than the wife initiated the suit, citing irreconcilable differences. Marion Wagner did not appear in court to contest the claim. She reportedly still loved R.J., agreeing to a divorce only because he demanded it.

The marriage had lasted eight years. Marion received full custody of their seven-year-old daughter, Kate Wagner. R.J. had to pay his ex-wife $1,250 per month alimony, plus twelve and a half percent of his annual gross income above $150,000, plus $400 a month for child support.

With R.J. a single man again, it seemed that he would marry Tina Sinatra as soon as the divorce decree became final. But no one reckoned on some surprising developments that were taking place simultaneously in the Natalie Wood-Richard Gregson household.

On August 1 hell broke loose when Natalie discovered that her husband was having an affair. With whom exactly or for how long, she never told anyone except her psychiatrist. After confronting Gregson she became hysterical, threw him out of the house and told him never to return.

The next day Natalie hired a twenty-four-hour guard patrol to prevent Gregson from coming to pick up his belongings or to visit their ten-month-old daughter. She believed that she had every right to do so. She owned the house and had purchased it prior to becoming involved with Gregson.

Heavily tranquilized and getting up only to nurse Natasha, Natalie kept to herself for several days, then started divorce proceedings. Neither relatives nor friends could talk her out of it or even persuade her to attempt a reconciliation first.

"Everyone asked me, even my mother, to think it over, to think of Natasha," Natalie recalled. "I did, but it only made my decision firmer. It would have been worse for Natasha if Dick and I had stayed together. How can a man and woman live together without love and not communicate their antagonism? Children are perceptive; they can sense hostility faster than anyone, and that can mess them up more than growing up with a single parent."

Natalie was so furious with Gregson for deceiving her that she tried to deny him visitation rights with Natasha, for fear he would be a bad moral influence. But he finally received a court order that permitted him to see his daughter for ninety minutes twice a week on Tuesday and Friday afternoons, plus the third Saturday and Sunday of each month.

Owing to California's community property law, which required that everything the couple owned had to be divided equally, lawyers for both sides battled for months before reaching a settlement. Gregson's British citizenship further complicated matters.

Court documents revealed that at the time of separation Gregson owed Natalie more than $67,000 as part of an agreement whereby she paid their living expenses and he was supposed to reimburse her from his funds in England when they became available in the United States. Ownership of the couple's art collection, including works by Maillot, Bonnard and Braque, was transferred to a trust for Natasha in lieu of auctioning it off and dividing the proceeds.

Although there'd been no outward signs of dissension while the marriage ran its course, there had been trouble from the beginning. "My first wife wasn't in the profession, so I was unprepared for living with an actress," Richard Gregson said. "I got very upset at Natalie's temper tantrums. I couldn't cope with her ego. It took me three years to learn, and by the time I had, we were divorced.

"Natalie was pretty much hung up on herself, rather selfishly, too, until Natasha came along and broadened her. Natalie was very unwilling to accept criticism or to be told that she was wrong. She'd get angry and pout for a day or two until she realized I wasn't her enemy, that I loved her and was only trying to help. By that time she had accepted the advice, but she'd missed the point altogether."

After the split Natalie thought of every argument and fight that the couple had. "I relived the whole marriage, trying to find out what went wrong, how it went wrong," she recalled. "I was terribly depressed. I didn't want to see anybody. One day my friend Suzanne Turman phoned and said, 'Let's play tennis.'

" 'Play tennis?' I replied. 'How can I play tennis in this condition?' Do you know what she said? She told me, 'Natalie, you might as well live.' That happened to be the title of a book she was reading at the time, *You Might as Well Live.* It really made sense. I mean, what else was I going to do for the rest of my life?"

TWELVE

The Second Time Around

SOON AFTER the Gregson marriage broke up, R.J. telephoned Natalie. "He said he was sorry and that he understood what an unhappy time it was for me," she remembered. "I assumed he was just being friendly. He's very thoughtful and it was the kind of thing R.J. would do, without romantic motives. But then he started calling often, and I thought maybe he did feel something besides friendship."

But it took R.J. several months to sort out what those feelings were. At the time of Natalie's divorce he was very much engaged to Tina Sinatra. They were planning an elaborate wedding at her father's fortresslike estate in Palm Springs.

Natalie, meanwhile, was too disillusioned by her own recent experience to be fostering new matrimonial plans. "They'd have to bind and gag me, drug me and drag me before I'd even consider getting married again," she said. But as the wounds healed she began socializing again, usually with her friends Mart Crowley or Tommy Thompson as escorts.

Soon the gossip columnists were linking Natalie with California's young attorney general, Jerry Brown, whom she met at a dinner party. Although they dated several times, no romance developed with the future state governor. "He's nice, but he's boring," Natalie told a friend.

More to Natalie's taste was Steve McQueen, who'd been unresponsive to her romantic overtures when they worked together in *Love with the Proper Stranger* seven years earlier. This time the circumstances were more favorable. Having recently broken up with his wife, McQueen was on the prowl. Natalie Wood, suddenly Hollywood's number one unattached woman, was a logical and, it turned out, quite compliant conquest.

"Natalie and Steve were an item for about seventy-two hours, and then he zoomed off on his motorcycle seeking action elsewhere," said a mutual friend of the couple. "Natalie wasn't terribly upset. In fact I think she felt rather grateful to Steve for the experience. It helped to restore some of the self-confidence she lost when her marriage ended. If she could make it with a big stud like Steve McQueen, then maybe she wasn't a failure as a woman after all."

Not long after Natalie's fling with McQueen, Robert Wagner and Tina Sinatra terminated their engagement. Why that happened was never explained, but it did seem more than just coincidental that both Natalie and R.J. became free of their romantic entanglements almost simultaneously.

R.J. had just moved into a new house in Palm Springs. "At Christmas I was feeling very lonely," he remembered. "I reflected on the past, and always the good things that reared up in my mind concerned Natalie. She was all I could think about.

"After all, Natalie was my first real love, as I was hers. Once you've had that kind of marriage or relationship with your first love, that feeling never leaves you. You always feel something special for that person, because the intensity of one's first real love is so much greater."

On impulse, R.J. phoned Natalie and asked her if she'd like to come down to Palm Springs to help him decorate the house. "I thought my heart would stop when he invited me," Natalie said later. "I felt like a kid again! Then I just got on a plane and flew down there. And we were together from that moment on."

The couple lived together in secret for three months. "We hid out in Palm Springs and Lake Tahoe," Natalie said. "Although we both knew instantly that this was going to be the proverbial 'it,' we had to make sure. We spent a great deal of time talking about where we'd been and where we wanted to go with our lives.

"When R.J. and I were married we were like two children acting out a studio script. We deliberately hid our weaknesses from each other. Now we found that we could really talk to each other. We were not afraid to be ourselves. But we realized that we needed those years apart to reach that understanding."

In April 1972, Natalie and R.J. stepped out together in public for the first time in ten years at the annual Academy Awards ceremony at the Dorothy Chandler Pavilion. The reunited couple's arrival caused a bigger tremor of excitement among spectators and press photographers than that of eighty-two-year-old Charlie Chaplin, returning to Hollywood after a thirty-six-year exile to accept an honorary Oscar.

But before anyone could find out what Natalie and R.J. were up to, they skipped town and flew to New York to board the Southampton-bound *Queen Elizabeth II*. R.J. had to go to London to publicize *Madame Sin*, a TV movie he made with Bette Davis, so Natalie went along for a sort of sneak preview of an anticipated second honeymoon.

It became a near tragic experience that made them resolve to remarry and enjoy their newfound happiness for as long as fate allowed. "The morning after we sailed, a four-day storm developed that was the worst in that area of the Atlantic for a hundred years," R.J. said. "The swells were more than seventy feet high and the winds were in excess of a hundred miles an hour. The swells were so big that they activated an automatic shutoff on one side of the ship. If you lose power in that kind of storm it's very serious.

"So Nat asked me, 'Do we have any chance of getting out?' And I said, 'No,' because the decks were inaccessible. Anyway, the winds were so strong that we would just have been blown away before we could make it to a lifeboat. I must say, Nat took it like a true sailor. She just rang the buzzer and asked the steward to bring us another bottle of champagne and some caviar!"

When the weather-battered _QE II_ docked two days late at Southampton, reporters massed at the terminal were startled to see Natalie Wood and Robert Wagner come down the gangplank wrapped in each other's arms. Since no one knew that they'd been living together for months, the couple went along with the mistaken presumption that neither of them had been aware of the other's booking on the voyage and that a shipboard romance developed quite by chance.

"Timing is everything in life," R.J. told a wire service correspondent. "It just happened, and as a result we've been very happy and had a lovable, enjoyable time, despite the freak storm."

Fending off questions about a possible remarriage, R.J. finally answered: "Yes, I would think so, though it won't be right now."

Several crucial matters had to be resolved first. Natalie's divorce from Richard Gregson was still not official. There were two children to consider: Natasha Gregson and Kate Wagner.

"Natasha has started calling R.J. 'Uncle,' " Natalie said at the time. "I'm so glad she doesn't call him 'Daddy,' because Richard is her father. I feel terrible when I see little children so confused that every man who comes into the house is a potential 'Daddy.' R.J.'s Kate is eight and a beautiful girl. We've become great friends."

R.J. encouraged Natalie to be fair about sharing Natasha with Gregson. "Being able to talk with R.J., I've come to understand the man's point of view," Natalie said. "R.J. feels a lot like Richard—after all, they both have daughters who have been parted from them by divorce. When R.J. tells me how much he misses Kate when he's not with her, I sympathize with Richard's feelings all the more."

R.J. couldn't afford to take on the financial responsibilities of a new marriage. "I was in a lot of litigation at the time," he recalled. "The government was after me for back income taxes. MCA was suing me for breach of contract. I was going to produce a film, but the financing fell through and I had to pay off the people. And, of course, there was the cost of getting a divorce from Marion, so I was totally broke."

But thanks to her participation in *Bob & Carol & Ted & Alice*, Natalie was a millionaire who wouldn't let money stand in the way of a happy ending. "She really was terrific," R.J. said. "Frankly, she bailed me out, and off we started again. It was the most highly emotional and most marvelous time of my life."

This time R.J. didn't propose. No rings were hidden in the bottoms of crystal champagne glasses. Neither he nor Natalie had any doubts about getting married again—only a date and place were needed.

Over the years Natalie had often consulted Hollywood's high priest of the occult, astrologer-psychic Carroll Righter, before she made a major decision. For this all-important occasion, Righter told her that a wedding taking place on the water would bode well for the future.

Since some of the happiest times of the couple's first marriage were spent boating, Righter's advice made sense to them. They followed his recommendations of date, time and place exactly.

The wedding was held on Sunday afternoon, July 16, 1972, aboard a borrowed fifty-five-foot yacht called the *Ramblin' Rose*. To avoid interference from the press, the couple kept everything secret. A public announcement wasn't made until the next day.

Just family and a few close friends were invited. Relatives laughed and rejoiced over the rarity of getting a second opportunity at in-lawship with the same people. Any unfriendliness that might have developed between the Gurdin and Wagner clans over the breakup of the first marriage was patched up and quickly forgotten.

As soon as the wedding party boarded, the ship headed up the Pacific coastline, finally dropping anchor near Malibu in Paradise Cove. With a spectacular sunset as the backdrop, Natalie and R.J. were remarried by a county judge.

The scene differed radically from their formal wedding in Arizona fifteen years earlier. This time Natalie, who would soon turn thirty-four, wore a long gown of violet gingham with short puffed sleeves. R.J., now forty-two, was dressed in slacks and a half-buttoned shirt, with a silk scarf knotted rakishly around his neck. Kate Wagner and Natasha Gregson, products of their interim marriages, served as attendants.

Everybody wept, including the bride and groom. "It's the greatest thing that ever happened to me. There's no doubt about it. Getting that second chance is something I'll always be grateful for," R.J. said afterward.

"Our life together never really ended. It was just interrupted," Natalie added. "We had each other in our youth, and now we have each other in our prime."

Not surprisingly, the wedding's theme song was the Sammy Cahn-James Van Heusen standard, "The Second Time Around." Numerous recordings by everyone from Guy Lombardo to Frank Sinatra were played endlessly over a public address system. The song's opening line, "Love is lovelier the second time around," was printed on the party napkins and souvenir matchbooks.

Natalie's psychoanalyst, Dr. John Lindon, made the rounds with a cassette recorder, getting all the guests to tape congratulatory messages. The only photographer present was Lana Wood's third husband, actor Richard Smedley, who shot countless rolls of film at his sister-in-law's request.

"There's only one moment that will go unrecorded," Smedley kidded R.J.

"It's already happened," R.J. laughed, as Natalie overheard and poked him playfully in the ribs.

Natalie and R.J. didn't find it funny, however, when Smedley subsequently sold some of his pictures to a fan magazine syndicate for $500. Since there'd been a similar breach of privacy when they got married the first time, the Wagners felt twice betrayed. R.J. took it the hardest and iced Lana Wood for years, even after she and Smedley were divorced.

When the champagne finally ran out and the *Ramblin' Rose* returned to port, Natalie and R.J. waved everybody good-bye and headed back to sea alone. They spent several days cruising up and down the coast and over to Catalina Island. It was not only a rapturous honeymoon but also an inducement to devote more time to the nautical life.

"When it was over, we just hated to go home," R.J. said. "In the years we'd been apart, neither of us went near the water very much. We'd forgotten how important it was to our relationship. We definitely wanted to get back to sea by buying a boat of our own."

For the present, however, they hardly needed a boat in the desert resort of Palm Springs, where the Wagners decided to take up residence in the gracious old stone house R.J. moved to after his divorce. The unpolluted air of the Coachella Valley, at the foot of Mount Jacinto, seemed to have it all over Los Angeles as a place to raise a family. Apparently the family would be a large one. The house had five bedrooms plus a three-bedroom guest house adjoining the swimming pool.

Natalie wanted to have a baby as soon as possible. But while they waited for nature to take its course the couple completely remodeled the house, carefully trying to avoid all the mistakes they had made years before with their Greco-Roman monstrosity in Beverly Hills. Their one concession to Tinsel Town glitz was a *balneum* worthy of Caesar and Cleopatra, with a sauna and a huge double bathtub sunk into the floor with a Jacuzzi at one end.

For months after their remarriage the Wagners received a huge amount of mail from the public. "People have been absolutely marvelous," R.J. said. "From all the letters we've received, they seem honestly happy we're back together, and I do believe they were aghast when we parted. I guess we were like a symbol to young people. They identified with us and had a real feeling about our relationship."

"It's made me realize a sort of universal truth," Natalie said. "That everybody has loved someone in their life very much and they may have lost them in one way or another—sometimes irreplaceably or irrevocably. But there's always that first love in your life, and very rarely does anyone have the opportunity, or the good luck, or whatever you want to call it, to be able to recapture it again and make it better. And I think this is something that people feel so deeply about that, when we did get together again, they had to share their thoughts with us, because they think of someone in their own lives and they wish it could be that way again."

Except for a walk-on "cameo" in her friend Robert Redford's *The Candidate*, Natalie hadn't worked in three years, not since *Bob & Carol & Ted & Alice*. With the millions she earned from her percentage deal, she never had to make another movie if she didn't want to. Her eagerness diminished as she settled into her new life with R.J.

Not long after the remarriage, however, an offer came along
from television producers Aaron Spelling and Leonard
Goldberg that involved both of them. "We had a good TV-
movie script called *The Affair*, about a crippled songwriter falling in love with a handsome lawyer who is unaware, at first,
that she's handicapped," Leonard Goldberg recalled. "It was a
natural teaming for Natalie and R.J. But how to get them?
Natalie didn't do television. It was a time when the big movie
stars still considered TV work an open confession that their
career was on the skids."

But Spelling/Goldberg Productions sent the Wagners the
script anyway and they liked it. "The fact that R.J. and I would
be working together was an added inducement," Natalie said.
"We hoped to prove that we'd come a long way in the fourteen
years since we made *All the Fine Young Cannibals!*"

But the Wagners also saw the offer as an opportunity to reactivate their joint production company, now renamed Rona II
(*Ro*bert and *Na*talie, The Second Time Around). If they decided to appear in *The Affair*, they wanted a financial participation. Spelling/Goldberg had no alternative but to sweeten the
pot.

"On page 6 of the 180-page contract there was a provision
that within one year the Wagners could develop a series pilot,
in which neither of them had to play a role," Leonard
Goldberg said. "It was a nice gesture but there wasn't much
risk in it for us or for the network [ABC]. If nothing was sub-
mitted by the Wagners during the year, the network would
simply have to pay them an additional $25,000."

The Affair was filmed, registered well in the ratings and the
clause on page 6 was forgotten by the Wagners, who became
involved in other matters. When the year was nearly up, the
Spelling/Goldberg business affairs department asked Goldberg
if they should arrange for ABC to send the Wagners their
$25,000.

"No," said Goldberg. "We want to keep the good will of the
Wagners because we may need them again someday. So I think
we'd better go through the motions of getting some sort of
series idea over to the network."

Goldberg had come up with what even he called a "terrible"

concept, "The Alley Cats." His partner, Aaron Spelling, looked at it and said, "You ought to be ashamed of yourself."

R.J. read it and said, "That's possibly the worst idea I've ever seen in my life." But he and Natalie figured that they had nothing to lose. They'd get more than the $25,000 if a miracle happened and they wangled a development deal out of the network.

While making *The Affair* in the summer of 1973, the Wagners rented an ocean-front house in Malibu to be nearer the studio as well as to escape the blistering heat that was one of the drawbacks to year-round living in Palm Springs. On July 17 they celebrated their first rewedding anniversary. Three days later, on Natalie's thirty-fifth birthday, they received medical confirmation that she was pregnant.

"Love produces many wonderful things, the best of which is children," Natalie said at the time. "R.J. and I want to have more than one baby, so it doesn't matter what this first one will be. Boy or girl, it will be our miracle!"

During pregnancy Natalie gained an astonishing fifty pounds, giving her the appearance of what a friend called "a toothpick with an enormous olive around the middle." While working in *The Affair*, her costumes, which were fortunately of the caftan style befitting a hippie songwriter, had to be let out every few days to hide her condition.

Despite her burgeoning size, Natalie insisted on accompanying R.J. to England when he signed for the BBC-TV miniseries, *Colditz*. The World War II Nazi prison story turned out to be the highest-rated program ever shown on the network. When R.J. received the production schedule he asked to be written out of one episode because he didn't want Natalie to be that far away from her doctor so close to her due date.

"I wanted nothing—repeat *nothing*—to possibly interfere or harm Natalie, however minor the risk," R.J. said. "That way we were able to return home one full month before the baby was due. As a matter of fact airlines don't like to take women who are in the ninth month of pregnancy because the sharp increase of pressure at takeoff can induce labor. I filmed two episodes of *Colditz* at once, while dubbing the third, just so we could get the hell out of there and Natalie wouldn't have the baby on the plane!"

Natalie had had such an easy time giving birth to her first child that she wanted to have the new baby at home in Palm Springs. But at the last minute she changed her mind and decided to go to Cedars of Lebanon in Los Angeles, where she could have the same doctor who delivered Natasha.

Her second thoughts proved fortuitous when a daughter was born on March 9, 1974. "I was fully awake and watched the whole thing in a mirror until they ran into difficulties and had to perform an emergency caesarean," Natalie said later. "The umbilical cord was wrapped around the baby's neck three times. A whole team of doctors were running around in white coats yelling 'Emergency Section—Emergency Pediatric Intensive Care—get up here on the double!'

"The last thing I remember them doing is throwing a white sheet over the mirror so I couldn't see the knife. I kept yelling, 'Cut! I want a retake!' I felt like I was on the wrong set and the scene was from somebody else's picture."

Natalie learned later that if the baby had been delivered normally she might well have been strangled to death by the umbilical cord she moved through the birth canal. Happily, she was born in excellent condition and named Courtney Brooke.

Courtney just happened to be the name of the character that Natalie was portraying in *The Affair* when her pregnancy was confirmed. And Brooke? "Because we always liked the sound of it," R.J. said.

By a strange turn of events, Courtney Brooke Wagner was born in the same hospital where Natalie had been taken after attempting suicide in 1966. Discussion of that incident was forbidden in her inner circle. Whether R.J. had ever been told about it is unknown.

But one day, while R.J. was out, Lana Wood made a rare house call and boldly brought it up in the midst of a conversation with her sister. Noticing how blissfully happy Natalie seemed in her marriage and motherhood, Lana couldn't resist asking her if she would have tried to take her own life if she'd been able to foresee her present status.

Without hesitating, Natalie smiled and said, "I would have been willing to wait. I would have waited forever."

THIRTEEN

Period of Adjustment

NOT LONG after Courtney Wagner's birth Natalie started experiencing the malaise that every suburban housewife feels at one time or another, even when husband and children are the greatest. "Palm Springs is a fine place for sun and tranquillity," Natalie said. "But it got a bit *much*, you know? House guests every weekend. And then, during the week, *nobody*."

And so she persuaded a reluctant R.J. to pack up and move back to Beverly Hills, very close to all the action. For $350,000, they purchased Patti Page's Cape Cod-style home on Canon Drive. The singer originally built it with the royalties from "Old Cape Cod," the biggest of her many hit records.

"This is our last move, Nathan, until we go to the Motion Picture Relief Home," R.J. quipped, using a pet name for his wife.

Natalie gradually turned the rambling nine-room, two-story

structure into one of the most attractive houses in town, eclectically decorated with her paintings by French masters, R.J.'s collection of sculpture and drawings from the American West, and a vast array of exotic tropical plants. Prominent in the den were a poker table and bar chairs left over from their first marriage. They were returned to them by R.J.'s sister, who got them when they divorced.

Natalie often told friends that the remarriage had to be successful, that it was up to her to make sure that it turned out that way. To avoid one of the biggest problems that the couple had the first time around, Natalie decided that being a wife and mother would take priority over her career. Nothing was going to prevent her from carrying out those domestic responsibilities.

By choosing to subordinate career to marriage, Natalie realized she'd taken a decidedly antifeminist stance, but it didn't bother her. "There comes a time when you've got to recharge your batteries," she said. "I've worked steadily and consistently since I was four years old. I think, if your whole impetus and all of your priorities come from your career, there's something missing in a person. I didn't have my first child until I was past thirty. I just want to take care of a family for a change."

Whether she did it consciously or not, Natalie had also tipped the professional scale in her husband's favor. When she and R.J. were married the first time, her career overshadowed his. Now he would be the dominant star of the family. No one would ever again think of calling him "Mr. Natalie Wood."

Natalie and R.J. renewed an old promise concerning work. "We've agreed that neither of us will accept jobs that will force us to remain apart for any length of time," R.J. said. "The family unit is very important to us. I hate to be away from Nat and the kids for even a single day."

To be with her family, Natalie turned down a $250,000 offer to appear with R.J., Paul Newman, Steve McQueen, William Holden and other stars in the disaster epic, *The Towering Inferno* (Faye Dunaway, who replaced her in *Bonnie and Clyde*, replaced her again). Natalie also rejected Robert Redford's invitation to play Daisy Buchanan opposite him in *The Great Gatsby*, so the part went to Mia Farrow instead.

In the summer of 1974, when Courtney was five months old,

Natalie tried a test run to determine if she could be housewife and working actress simultaneously. The movie was *Peeper*, a spoof of private-eye mysteries, casting Michael Caine in the title role and Natalie as a nymphomaniac heiress. Besides the opportunity to work opposite one of her favorite actors, Natalie signed on because most of her scenes would be filmed on the former estate of silent film clown Harold Lloyd, less than ten minutes away from the Wagner residence in Beverly Hills.

Natalie took Courtney and Natasha to the set every day. Their grandmother, Maria Gurdin, looked after them in the dressing room while Natalie worked. The arrangement was necessitated by Natalie's membership in the La Leche League. She'd been breast-feeding Courtney since birth.

Whether at work or at home, Natalie felt no inhibitions about nursing Courtney in front of family or friends. One night she started to feed her at the table while the Wagners' dinner companions were sipping their coffee. The maternal scene prompted one of the guests, Paul Newman, to remark, "Well, the milk train certainly stops here."

Natalie attacked the role of motherhood with extraordinary zeal. "If one of her children fell down while playing and received the barest scratch, Natalie wanted to summon Dr. Christian Barnard, Michael De Bakey and the entire Mayo Clinic staff to apply a bandage," Tommy Thompson said. "After a while she got wise and became very much the modern mother, treating kids like kids. When Natasha was four and a half, she told her the facts of life."

After finishing *Peeper*, Natalie didn't work for two years, but not for lack of offers. She just got caught up in family life and in the sudden resurgence of R.J.'s TV career, which left very little time for anything else.

In 1975, R.J. finally settled a long legal dispute with MCA-Universal that had started with the abrupt cancellation of "It Takes a Thief," after which the studio wanted him to do guest shots on some of its other shows like "The Virginian." R.J. refused, holding out for another series of his own.

When they couldn't agree on a subject R.J. walked out. "Universal tried to stop me," he recalled. "They pushed me right to the wall. They wanted part of my residuals on everything I did. They wanted to slice up my salary, just to let me work at all.

Then they enjoined me from working. I had a bad, bad time. I sued them for the right to be free. I won. I went on my way. I'd had it up to here with TV. The interference. I did *Colditz* in England, then nothing."

To keep active, R.J. briefly returned to theatrical movies in *The Towering Inferno* and *Midway*. In both epics he and many other stars became merely stick figures against a backdrop of spectacular special effects. R.J. decided that maybe TV wasn't that bad after all.

Burying the hatchet with MCA, R.J. sold them on an hour-long pilot for a series called "Switch," written by his friend Glen Larson. The story—a private detective partnership between an ex-con and an ex-cop who once sent him to prison—was reminiscent of "It Takes a Thief." But then, TV has never been known for original ideas. CBS bought it straight away and wanted to pair R.J. with Eddie Albert.

"The chemistry was right. I decided I'd try again, although there were problems right away," R.J. recalled. "We couldn't get enough scripts. For the whole of the first year it was hell. I was trying to get depth into the characters and the writers were trying for situations, angles. They were so busy with connective tissue, the characterizations went out the window. There was no time to get good writing. I found myself on the phone calling up actors, saying 'I've got this script that's good for you but it's not finished.' That is not the way to run a show. The most important thing in our business is preparation. It's the cry of our whole industry."

As a pair of rogues who fleeced the fleecers and outconned the conartists, R.J. and Eddie Albert brought their own individual brands of charm to their roles. Despite a lukewarm critical reception, "Switch" enjoyed a successful three-year run, starting from September 1975.

For the premiere episode R.J. persuaded Natalie to do a walk-on bit to bring them luck. In a poolside scene where R.J. is ogling some bikini-clad beauties, he absent-mindedly bumps into Natalie, who glares back at him with a withering "get lost" look in her eyes.

As soon as "Switch" reached hit status the Wagners celebrated by purchasing the boat they'd long dreamed about. Although they had scouts out shopping for them as far away as

England and the South of France, they found exactly what they wanted twenty minutes from home at Marina del Rey, the biggest pleasure-boat harbor on the Pacific Coast. It was a 60-foot power cruiser similar to one that Ernest Hemingway, R.J.'s great seafaring hero, once owned in Cuba.

The Wagners named the yacht *Splendour* in honor of Natalie's *Splendor in the Grass*, ironic in view of what that movie contributed to the breakup of their first marriage. To differentiate between past sufferings and their newfound happiness, they deliberately chose the original British spelling used by William Wordsworth in "Intimations of Immortality," from which the film title came.

And a splendid vessel it was, with enough sleeping space for eight people and a luxurious Early American interior of dark wood and highly polished brass fittings. Natalie did all the decorating herself, right down to the hand-sewn curtains over the portholes. Above the couple's private cabin were twin brass plaques: CAPTAIN and FIRST OFFICER. R.J. liked to joke that he wasn't exactly sure who was what.

Although the *Splendour* more than lived up to its name, the Wagners bought it to simplify their lives. "We think of it more as a houseboat than a yacht," Natalie said. "The whole family can be together, relax and get away from it all." Whenever they had a free weekend they took sailing trips to Santa Catalina, San Clemente or other islands in the 150-mile-long Santa Barbara chain.

While R.J. was involved with "Switch," the family by necessity spent more time at home than at sea. "Working in weekly TV, you rarely get out," R.J. said. "It's damned hard to do. I work ten hours a day, nine months a year. On 'Switch,' the episode shown on Sundays has its final dubbing session Thursdays. The print is still wet when it goes on the air."

Natalie, meanwhile, tried to be a model housewife and mother, keeping things tidy and popping into the kitchen every ten minutes to make sure that her husband's dinner would be ready on time when he did get home. Except on board the *Splendour*, where she did salads or grills, Natalie left all the cooking to the housekeeper, Willie Mae Worthen.

Friends described Natalie as a space cadet when it came to doing anything in the kitchen. On Willie Mae's days off the

Wagners sent out or snacked on leftovers from the refrigerator. R.J. became an expert at whipping together Sunday breakfasts when Willie Mae went to church.

Because R.J. had so little time for socializing, Natalie liked to arrange small dinner parties at home. One night the guest of honor was Sir Laurence Olivier, whom the Wagners had known for years through an introduction by mutual friend Spencer Tracy.

Before Olivier's arrival, Natalie told daughter Natasha that an especially important guest was coming. "I wanted her to always remember that the world's greatest actor had been to our home," Natalie said later. "But Natasha just shook her head and said, 'Oh, no! He isn't the greatest actor in the world. Daddy is!'" (Of course R.J. wasn't really her daddy, but she had taken to calling him that.)

Later in the evening Natalie told Olivier the story. "Just as I was getting to the punch line," Natalie said, "Larry interrupted and said, 'I bet I know what Natasha said. It was, 'Daddy is the greatest actor in the world.' At that precise moment, Natasha walked into the room. She smiled and said to me, 'See! He agrees with me!'"

Olivier had flown to Los Angeles on a mission. He hoped to persuade Natalie and R.J. to appear with him in a television production of Tennessee Williams' *Cat on a Hot Tin Roof*, which would inaugurate a new series called "Tribute to American Theater."

"It was like a gift that fell out of the sky," Natalie said. "Here's Laurence Olivier asking *us* if we'd be interested in playing Maggie and Brick to his Big Daddy? It blew our minds. *Would we be interested!*"

"It's the greatest compliment we've ever had," R.J. said, "the kind of break we've been waiting for all our lives."

The telefilm was made in England as a joint production of Granada Television and NBC. Olivier arranged the shooting schedule so that R.J. could do it during his seasonal break from "Switch."

"Lord Olivier was incredible," R.J. said afterward. "He met us at the airport, at six-thirty in the morning, with flowers and champagne. We rehearsed for four weeks in London, blocked it just like a play, and by the time we got to the studio in Manchester we could have gone on stage and played it. The whole thing was taped in nine days."

Olivier equipped the Wagners' dressing room with closed circuit TV. That way, they could watch each other when they weren't on stage together and baby-sit with Courtney and Natasha at the same time.

"Working together is easier if you're married," R.J. said. "You can cue each other in bed, in the shower, over the breakfast table. What's hard is turning it off after a dramatic scene so you don't take Maggie and Brick home with you."

At the insistence of Tennessee Williams, the TV version of *Cat on a Hot Tin Roof* adhered more faithfully to his original play than the movie that starred Elizabeth Taylor, Paul Newman and Burl Ives.

"When they made the film, they couldn't deal with homosexuality, so something else had to be invented as Brick's problem," Natalie said. "Isn't it ironic that things you couldn't do in movies in 1958 you can now do on television?"

Aired in the United States on December 6, 1976, *Cat on a Hot Tin Roof* registered a high rating but received mixed reviews. Although no one thought R.J.'s performance equal to Paul Newman's, some critics preferred Natalie's work to Elizabeth Taylor's.

Judith Crist of *TV Guide* said it was "clearly the performance of her career. Her portrait of the woman who is consumed with envy and eaten up with longing is an unforgettable one."

Elizabeth Taylor received an Oscar nomination for her Maggie but didn't win. Natalie got nominated for an Emmy for her portrayal and also didn't win. However, the acclaim that Natalie received made her decide to reactivate her career as soon as the children no longer needed her twenty-four-hour attendance.

"I love my husband and I love my kids, but I don't think I have to give up acting in order to be constantly aware of my personal feelings—as well as trying to be instinctively aware of theirs," Natalie said.

Meanwhile she and several friends started a profitable sideline—buying, renovating and selling houses in the Beverly Hills-West Hollywood area. "I like to decorate," Natalie said. "I'll make suggestions about knocking down walls, removing windows, getting rid of wood planking and that sort of thing. I did it to my own house. People liked what they saw and began coming to me for advice."

Not that Natalie needed to work at all. The money kept rolling in from R.J.'s hit series, "Switch," plus an unexpected bonanza from that all but forgotten clause on page 6 in Rona II's contract for the 1973 telemovie, *The Affair.*

That development project called "The Alley Cats," which everybody thought was the worst idea they'd ever come across, became miraculously transformed into "Charlie's Angels." The crime series about a trio of jiggling detective maidens premiered on ABC in the fall of 1976, becoming the six biggest sensations of the year and enjoying a phenomenal run into 1981.

Natalie and R.J. had almost nothing to do with the show but to collect millions from Rona II's fifty percent interest. Their main creative input was R.J.'s suggestion of Jaclyn Smith, with whom he'd worked before, for one of the original leads (Kate Jackson and Farrah Fawcett-Majors were the other two).

In July 1977, Natalie and R.J. celebrated the fifth anniversary of their remarriage. Asked for the secret of their apparent success the second time around, R.J. said, "Nat and I are very positive, upbeat people. It sounds Pollyanaish to say it, but when we're alone we often talk about how incredibly lucky we are. Sometimes we'll ask each other, 'Is it really okay for us to be this happy?' Not that we expect something bad to happen. It's simply that life is filled with chance. Take a false step and you land on your face."

Natalie added, "We have a special sensitivity to each other's needs, and I don't see the remotest indication of any false steps. We live on the same rhythm. We're both very flexible and adjustable. That's one of the unexpected dividends you pick up as an actor: you're quick to adapt to the unexpected. If some long-planned event is suddenly canceled, it's okay. Or if R.J. impulsively suggests we go to San Francisco tonight and have dinner, chances are we'll be on a plane in the next hour. Conversely, we're completely happy having a quiet evening at home."

"No matter how you look at it," R.J. said, "the process is called maturity. In countless ways, small and large, we've built up a compatibility that grows better and stronger as the years go by."

The couple tried resolutely to maintain the happy medium that eluded them the first time around. While R.J. took a between-seasons hiatus from "Switch," Natalie made *Meteor*, her first movie in three years. Natasha had turned seven and Courtney three. Natalie felt no qualms about leaving them in their father's care while she was working. Sometimes she would take them with her anyway.

"I like to bring them when I first start a picture to give them an idea of what is going on and what my work is. They're old enough now to understand," Natalie said.

The girls watched Natalie begin her role in *Meteor*, but they were deliberately kept at home later to spare them the trauma of seeing their mother possibly drowned before their eyes, even though it was only make-believe.

One scene involved the flooding of a Manhattan subway station in a huge tank once used for Esther Williams musicals. The result, said Natalie, was like "being buried alive in a Mixmaster. There were over a million gallons of mud in holding containers overhead. As we swam, it came breaking through the ceiling and flying in all directions. You literally couldn't see or hear or say anything. The mud got in our eyes and mouths. The only protection we had was earplugs."

A disaster spectacle about a five-mile-wide meteor threatening to destroy the earth might have seemed an inappropriate movie for Natalie Wood as a comeback vehicle, but she got involved more by chance than choice. The part of a Russian astrophysicist called for an actress who knew the language. She turned out to be the only one of star caliber in Hollywood who did.

After she read the script Natalie knew that *Meteor* would never win any artistic awards but that it had the potential for becoming the box-office blockbuster that she needed to make her more "bankable" for future projects. Budgeted at $17 million, it was being directed by Ronald Neame, who made the smash hit *The Poseidon Adventure*. The prestigious cast included Sean Connery as Natalie's leading man, plus Henry Fonda, Karl Malden, Brian Keith and Trevor Howard.

In the spring of 1978, CBS decided to drop R.J.'s "Switch" at the end of its third season. Despite a mass protest from the readers of the *National Enquirer,* nothing could save it.

R.J. stoically blamed the cancellation on lack of upper-echelon support from MCA-Universal. "The show wouldn't have gone off the air if we had someone who was fighting our battle with the network. Because we didn't, the show's time slot was changed seven times in three years. But in spite of that we had built an audience, built a successful show that was being seen in forty-two countries. Then, all of a sudden, it's gone. No phone calls from CBS, nothing. It was just taken off the schedule, and that was sad."

Happy in one sense to be relieved of the pressures of a weekly series, R.J. decided to take things easier for a while by concentrating on specials and occasional theatrical movies. Natalie couldn't have been more supportive. It not only meant that the couple could have more time together but also gave her greater flexibility to take assignments of her own.

But when it came to obtaining work in a business with a double standard for men and women, Natalie had a problem that R.J. didn't. At age forty-eight, he was still considered a star very much in his prime, with two top-rated TV series to prove it.

At forty, Natalie had no recent hits to her credit and also had reached that awkward age between romantic leads and more mature parts. The choice women's roles (which were in short supply to start with) usually went to younger stars like Diane Keaton, Goldie Hawn, Barbra Streisand, Jill Clayburgh and Marsha Mason, or to older ones such as Jane Fonda, Anne Bancroft, Shirley MacLaine, Ellen Burstyn and Joanne Woodward.

For lack of movie offers after *Meteor,* Natalie decided to follow R.J.'s example and branch out into television. Since she hadn't been overexposed in that medium and still had a definite cachet as a major Hollywood star, producers expressed an eagerness to hire her. Without much effort, Natalie's agents landed her one of the leads in NBC's six-hour remake of *From Here to Eternity,* plus the starring role in *The Cracker Factory,* an ABC "Movie Night" feature.

The back-to-back assignments proved the first big test of the Wagners' vow never to take a job while one of them was working. R.J. had already signed for the ABC miniseries, *Pearl,* as well as Universal's theatrical movie, *The Concorde: Airport '79*. To further complicate matters, R.J. was due to film a two-hour pilot for a projected TV series called "Hart to Hart."

Although it seemed as though the Wagners had taken on more work than they could handle, they accomplished it all with a minimum of inconvenience. "If we've learned anything, it's the importance of being flexible," R.J. said. "I don't know how I could cut it without Natalie. It sure helps to be married to someone who understands the pressures, the uncertain schedules. And who bends backward to work her schedule around the family's."

When R.J. had to go to Honolulu for location work on *Pearl*, the couple took the two girls along and hired a Hawaiian tutor for them during the hours they would normally have spent in school. "I think it's good for the children to travel and be exposed to things," Natalie said. "They did learn a lot about the culture of Hawaii."

The Wagners tried to raise Natasha and Courtney as normally as possible for children of celebrities. "We'll never sign autographs when we're out in public with the children," Natalie said. "We make it a point to try to have them with us whenever possible, and to absolutely never leave them for longer than a week or two.

"And we've learned that the most important thing is to talk things out with the girls—because by doing so problems have a way of dissipating. For instance, Natasha has told me she thinks some children want to be her friend only because her mother is a movie star. She also told me she doesn't like people commenting that she looks like me, because she doesn't want to be anyone's carbon copy. And believe me, she's not."

Natasha so closely resembled her mother that a producer wanted to team the two of them with R.J. in a TV remake of *Miracle on 34th Street*, but the Wagners rejected the offer. "Both of us feel firmly that if the girls are to have acting careers it won't be while they're children. It's not that acting changes children—but it does change the manner in which they're regarded by their peers. And that isn't good," Natalie said, speaking from her own experience.

Natalie's desire to maintain family togetherness probably had as much to do with jealousy as it did with maternalism.

Robert Wagner was, after all, Prince Valiant personified to millions of women. Sooner or later someone was likely to try to snatch him away from her if she didn't keep up her guard.

A major reason for Natalie accompanying R.J. to Hawaii when he made the TV miniseries *Pearl* may have been to make sure that he didn't become personally involved with his leading lady, Angie Dickinson, who had recently separated from composer husband Burt Bacharach. Similarly, when Natalie turned up with R.J. in Paris and Washington while he did location work for *Airport '79*, rumors circulated that she feared his onscreen romance with stunning blonde Susan Blakely might develop into the real thing.

But if any woman was going to give Natalie cause for alarm, friends thought it would be Stefanie Powers, whom R.J. personally selected to play opposite him in the $2 million pilot of "Hart to Hart." At the time no one knew for sure whether ABC would order a full series, but if that happened, R.J. and Powers would be spending an enormous amount of time together.

"I never thought of anyone to play my wife other than Stefanie Powers," R.J. said after the casting was announced. "We worked together previously on an episode of 'It Takes a Thief' and I liked her a lot. Her style of acting is perfect for me. She's a terrific contributor and a total professional. I'm thoroughly comfortable working with her."

But R.J.'s real-life wife became very upset over not getting the part herself. "Natalie would have been perfect for Jennifer Hart," said Tommy Thompson. "In fact, her friend, Tom Mankiewicz, wrote the pilot script with Nat in mind, but R.J. vetoed the idea. He thought they should keep their professional and private lives separate, and he was probably right. Working under those pressured conditions, they would have been at each other's throats constantly."

Still it seemed a logical casting and R.J. became irritated whenever interviewers asked him why Natalie didn't play the role. "Both of us couldn't work on a series at the same time," became his standard reply. "We'd never have any home life. Someone has to be home. If she worked on my series she'd have to get up at six every morning and wouldn't be finished until nine at night. There wouldn't be anyone home with the kids for seven or eight months. A series is very demanding, the most demanding work any actor can undertake. It's especially hard on a woman."

Apparently R.J. meant to say a *married* woman and mother. Perhaps he thought Stefanie Powers more suited to working in a series because she was a childless divorcee. Then thirty-five, she had been involved in a long-term affair with actor William Holden, although they were having problems because of his alcoholism.

Denied one of the leading roles, Natalie settled for being a part owner of "Hart to Hart," a coproduction between the Wagners' Rona II and their "Charlie's Angels" partners, Aaron Spelling and Leonard Goldberg. To get R.J. to do the show, Spelling/Goldberg had to give Rona II a fifty percent interest plus two development projects in which neither of the Wagners had to appear.

To bring the enterprise luck, Natalie made a brief guest appearance in the pilot of "Hart to Hart." Dolled up to look like Vivien Leigh as Scarlett O'Hara for a scene taking place in a Hollywood studio, she sashayed across a set and drawled coquettishly at Lionel Stander, the Harts' chauffeur. In the credits she received billing under her real name, Natasha Gurdin.

While everybody waited for ABC to decide whether or not it wanted a "Hart to Hart" series, Natalie took advantage of the lull in R.J.'s schedule and worked harder than she had in years, making two TV movies plus a theatrical feature. The sudden burst of activity inspired a wave of "A Star Is Born Again" articles in the fan press, which interpreted it as a last-ditch effort at age forty to revive a nearly moribund career.

For her performance in the six-hour TV version of *From Here to Eternity*, aired by NBC in February 1979, Natalie received both a Golden Globe Award and an Emmy nomination. As the nympho wife (played by Deborah Kerr in the movie version) she and costar William Devane had to recreate Kerr and Burt Lancaster's famous tumble-in-the-surf episode. This time around they wanted to do it completely naked for the sake of realism.

The network censors wouldn't permit it, however, so Natalie and Devane had to wear flesh-colored body tights and do most of their lovemaking well submerged in water.

From Here to Eternity scored high enough in the ratings for NBC to commission a prime-time serial picking up where James Jones's novel left off. Since there was no way that Natalie could fit it into her schedule, her part was taken over by Barbara Hershey when the show resumed for a limited run in 1980.

Less than a month after her appearance in *From Here to Eternity*, Natalie turned up again on network television in ABC's *The Cracker Factory*, shown March 16, 1979. As an alcoholic, mentally disturbed housewife who lands in the county psychiatric center, she had one of the most emotionally demanding roles of her career. Critics including Rex Reed and Judith Crist thought it was one of Natalie's best performances ever, and she herself shared that opinion.

"I loved playing Cassie," Natalie said. "She was a hard character to shake off—I didn't want to say good-bye to her. I could really identify with her. I prefer playing a role that I personally feel close to rather than someone who is the opposite of me," Natalie said.

Apart from the still unreleased *Meteor* and the Michael Caine costarrer *Peeper* (which came and went so fast that few noticed what a clinker it was), Natalie hadn't starred in a theatrical movie for a decade, not since *Bob & Carol & Ted & Alice* in 1969. To make up for lost time she impulsively accepted an offer from Universal to team with George Segal in a sex farce entitled *The Last Married Couple in America.*

"After reading the script, I thought to myself, 'This is all about R.J. and me,'" Natalie said later. "When you're married these days, you sometimes feel like you're in the wilderness. You know, you feel you're the pioneers and the Indians are all around, shooting you down one by one. Even when R.J. and I want to go out to dinner by ourselves, people say to us, 'That's weird. What do you *talk* about?'"

With a plot reminiscent of *Bob & Carol* . . . , Natalie hoped the movie, like *Meteor*, would turn out to be one of those box-office hits she needed. She and George Segal portrayed an affluent couple who try to sustain a happy relationship while the marriages of all their friends are breaking up around them.

While *The Last Couple in America* was filming, ABC bought "Hart to Hart" for a series, which put an end to Natalie's so-called "comeback" for the time being. However, when a short-term opportunity came along that was the realization of a life-long dream to visit Russia, she persuaded R.J. to delay his work a few weeks in order to share the experience with her.

Natalie had been invited to her ancestral homeland to film a ninety-minute TV documentary about Leningrad's Hermitage Museum, to be shown in conjunction with NBC's coverage of the 1980 Moscow Olympics. For the first time Western cameras were being permitted to roam among the Hermitage's fourteen miles of corridors and 2.5 million works of art treasures.

Masterminding the project was German entrepreneur Luther Bock, known as "The Mystery Man of Europe" because he somehow managed to be involved in many of the major business deals between the U.S.S.R. and the West. To conduct the tour of what is probably the greatest museum collection in the world, Bock originally wanted Princess Grace of Monaco or Jacqueline Kennedy Onassis. When they turned him down he opted for two cohosts of Russian heritage, Natalie and Peter Ustinov.

Despite promises of deluxe accommodations and a wardrobe of Yves St. Laurent frocks and Russian sables, Natalie wouldn't accept Bock's offer until he guaranteed that she would be able to make two telephone calls daily—morning and night—to her children back in Los Angeles. For the first two days of Natalie and R.J.'s stay in Leningrad, long-distance connections were so bad that she threatened to leave. The problem was rectified immediately.

Fearful that the KGB had bugged their hotel suite, the Wagners spoke to each other in an elaborate and nonsensical code. Afterward, they wondered what the decipherers must have thought of their gibberish, which came straight from the Hollywood gossip columns.

No Leningraders stopped the Wagners on the street. Only Western tourists recognized them and asked for autographs. As far as the couple could determine, their only films shown in the U.S.S.R. were Natalie's *Rebel Without a Cause* and *West Side Story*, apparently because of their pessimistic views of American and capitalistic society.

The Wagners were profoundly disturbed by the quality of life in the U.S.S.R. "You simply can't comprehend what it's like to be there until you are there," Natalie said later. "About the age of thirty, everybody seems to get fat and dour. I guess about that time their dreams die." The biggest disappointment for Natalie was the cuisine, which she decided didn't compare to her mother's Russian cooking back home.

Clearly the U.S.S.R. wasn't the place for pampered Hollywood stars. They hated the incredibly slow service in the restaurants, where R.J.'s doling out of twenty-ruble notes to the waiters had no impact whatsoever. After Natalie finished filming, the couple went to Moscow by train and had to off-load their twenty pieces of luggage themselves for lack of portering service.

Later, as their return flight to America lifted out of the Moscow airport, Natalie didn't even glance out the window. "I'm glad I did it," she told R.J., "but I won't be coming back."

The Hermitage special turned out to be yet another of Natalie's projects with an unlucky outcome. When the United States pulled out of the Moscow Olympics after the Soviet invasion of Afghanistan, NBC put the show in the vault. It was finally given a single late-night, post-prime-time showing in April 1981.

Natalie and R.J.'s disillusioning experience in Russia was quickly forgotten when they got home. In September 1979, "Hart to Hart" premiered on ABC and became an overnight smash, promising to make the Wagners multimillionaires (again!) through Rona II's fifty percent participation in the profits.

After struggling for nearly thirty years to get there, Robert Wagner finally landed in the lofty atmosphere of Hollywood superstardom with the success of "Hart to Hart." At forty-nine, he confounded critics and public alike by looking and behaving like twenty-nine. *TV Guide* dubbed him "the Peter Pan of the sophisticated comedy-adventure genre."

R.J. portrayed Jonathan Hart, an urbane, self-made millionaire married to a journalist who shares his passion for amateur sleuthing. R.J. bristled whenever anyone suggested that the Harts were carbon copies of Nick and Nora Charles in the popular "Thin Man" series. But he did admit that the affectionate, bantering relationship between himself and Stefanie Powers resembled that of William Powell and Myrna Loy in the movies.

The breezy interplay between R.J. and Stefanie Powers as they zipped around in snazzy cars and frequently nibbled on each other's ears was undoubtedly the main reason for the popularity of "Hart to Hart." The romantic chemistry between the two stars was so strong, in fact, that as the show settled into its run gossip columnists in the *National Enquirer* and *Star* opined that it seemed too realistic to be mere playacting.

Whether Natalie had a real reason for concern or not, she spent more time visiting the set of "Hart to Hart" than any of R.J.'s previous efforts. One day she arrived with her two daughters just as R.J. started to climb into bed with Stefanie Powers.

"It was only a scene out of the script, but Natalie looked fit to be tied," said a crew member. "The kids, outraged by the sight of R.J. with another woman, started to cry. Natalie put an arm around each one and said, 'Don't worry. This is just the way Daddy makes a living.' "

A reporter visiting the studio once asked Natalie how she felt watching her husband romancing another woman. "I really don't like it," Natalie said. "It's not my favorite sight, but I realize that it's really just part of the work. If you're not a performer yourself, it seems more significant than it really is. Once you've played a love scene as a performer, it's like playing any other scene."

R.J. chimed in that he didn't much like it either. "I don't think it's ever easy watching your wife made love to. How uncomfortable I feel depends on the content of the scene. If it's just an ordinary kiss or a peck on the cheek, I'm much less likely to get upset than if it carries over into a passionate tumble in the hay."

Probably without realizing it, Natalie and R.J. had reached a straining point in their relationship almost identical to their first marriage, only this time the positions were reversed. What began with rumors about Natalie and Warren Beatty now threatened to start all over again if there was any truth to the gossip about R.J. and Stefanie Powers.

Also Natalie now had to contend with the fact that R.J.'s career had eclipsed hers. She hovered on the brink of being called a has-been. Producers weren't badgering her with offers, the same predicament R.J. had found himself in when they were married the first time.

While "Hart to Hart" was boosting R.J.'s popularity to an all-time high Natalie had to suffer the indignity of having two flop movies in a row, which seemingly scotched her hopes of a major comeback.

Held up for fifteen months owing to technical problems with the special effects, *Meteor* finally got released in November 1979 and emptied theaters faster than stink bombs. *Variety*, which said the disaster epic "makes 'Godzilla' look a masterpiece," also placed it on the newsweekly's annual list of mega-losers at an estimated $35 million (including prints and advertising).

And *The Last Married Couple in America*, one of the first movies to be released in 1980, did not indicate that the eighties would be Natalie Wood's decade. While nowhere near the box-office catastrophe of *Meteor*, the allegedly riotous comedy was demolished by the critics ("Stupid, smutty and ridiculous," said *Newsweek)* and quickly disappeared.

To add insult to injury, while Natalie tried to come to terms with the failure of those two movies, a British producer approached her about joining the all-star cast of the Agatha Christie mystery, *The Mirror Crack'd.*

Natalie wasn't interested. First of all, the role of a faded movie queen trying to make a comeback seemed like typecasting of the cruelest kind. Second, in order to be considered for the part, she first had to make a screen test, which infuriated her. Within the acting profession, the fact that you were an established star was supposed to be proof enough that you were qualified to do the job. The part eventually went to Elizabeth Taylor, who apparently wasn't so sensitive about those things.

Natalie didn't want to wind up playing hags and eccentrics as Bette Davis and Joan Crawford did. She desperately wanted to be accepted for the forty-two-year-old woman she was. "I think it's sort of embarrassing to be coy about it," she said. "Even if I wanted to shave a few years off here and there I couldn't, because I was a child actress, and everybody has kept track of my age, and that has made me deal with it.

"Jane Fonda and Vanessa Redgrave are a year older, and they

don't seem to be having difficulty finding roles. Liv Ullmann and Ali MacGraw are my age. I think there are lots of good parts, now that women screenwriters are becoming more accepted. The key is in making the transition; you have to segue into the other parts as you grow older."

But for the moment the only enticing offers coming in were for television features. She gratefully accepted the lead in CBS-TV's *The Memory of Eva Ryker*, which for the first time in her career provided an opportunity to play a dual role. She was a billionaire's daughter caught up in a mystery involving her late, ultraglamorous mother, whom she portrayed in flashbacks.

Although no one could have foreseen it at the time, *The Memory of Eva Ryker* turned out to be Natalie's last television work. Bizarrely, she ended up (as the mother) being drowned when the luxury liner she's traveling on is torpedoed by the Nazis at the onset of World War II.

FOURTEEN

Hollywood's Dream Couple

ON FEBRUARY 10, 1980, Robert Wagner turned fifty, a statistic that amazed millions of viewers of "Hart to Hart," where he easily passed for thirty-five. To celebrate his demicentenary, Natalie gave her husband a snazzy silver-gray Mercedes-Benz convertible and an extravagant surprise party at the Bistro in Beverly Hills.

R.J. had been led to expect an intimate dinner with a few friends, but it turned out that Natalie had taken over the restaurant's entire upstairs for a guest list of a hundred and twenty people. Some were relatives and business associates, but there were also many of the Wagners' celebrity friends, including Stefanie Powers, Suzanne Pleshette, Hope Lange, Christopher Plummer, Esther Williams, Fernando Lamas, Gene Kelly, Dinah Shore, Claire Trevor, Henry Fonda, Robert Mitchum, George Segal, Paula Prentiss and Richard Benjamin.

Natalie devoted weeks to organizing the affair, reportedly spending $15,000 by the time she finished. The room was lighted by hundreds of candles and decorated with umpteen bouquets of red, white and blue flowers. There were two birthday cakes, one shaped like the number 5, the other 0.

At fifty R.J. seemed a classic example of the man who has everything: a successful career, riches and a happy personal life with a beautiful wife and children. Asked for his secret formula, he said, "I've always wanted to be doing what I'm doing now. The trick is to keep your life full and keep it fresh, otherwise you become blasé and jaded. Enthusiasm is one thing you can never buy. I think that's one of the reasons I never really got crushed in this business. It can take people and beat them. It's like putting them in a Cuisinart; it chops them up and they're finished. I've always had tremendous enthusiasm. I really wanted to be an actor."

R.J. added, "One of the things that has helped the most in my life is that people have been there for me and have really cared. They've taken the time to reach out and talk to me. You can miss a lot of that if you're closed off. You can miss the hands that are out there when you've been knocked on your ass.

"Without any question, my wife has helped me more than anyone else. She's just a terrific lady. And I really realize how much I missed her when we weren't married. She is not only my lover, but she's my best friend, and I'd rather be with her than anybody else in the whole world. And that's no bullshit, that's straight out."

Both now comfortably into middle age, the Wagners were considered the king and queen of the movie and TV community traditionally called "Hollywood," though most of its denizens live in posher areas like Beverly Hills, Bel Air and Hancock Park. "Between them, Natalie and R.J. can probably claim to have more real friends than any other couple in town," said columnist Roderick Mann.

The reason for the Wagners' popularity was easy to discern, according to close friend David Niven. "It's because they're real," Niven said. "Neither of them talk much, you'll notice—and that in itself singles them out. And they're both really interested in other people."

Sir Laurence Olivier, who usually stayed with Natalie and

R.J. whenever he visited Los Angeles, called them "The most dear couple. They really care."

Because the Wagners were so well liked the industry rallied to their side in the spring of 1980 when it appeared that they had been defrauded of more than half a million dollars through "creative bookkeeping" by the producers of the "Charlie's Angels" TV series. The investigation was started by Los Angeles County District Attorney John Van De Kamp, who began monitoring what he called "shoddy business practices" in the entertainment field after he successfully prosecuted Columbia Pictures prexy David Begelman for passing forged checks in 1978.

Tipped off by a lawyer in the business affairs department at ABC Television, Van De Kamp told the press that $660,000 due the Wagners' Rona II company from its participation in "Charlie's Angels" might have been "reallocated" to the accounts of "Starsky & Hutch," another Spelling/Goldberg series.

As spokesperson for Rona II, R.J. registered surprise when informed of the investigation. He told reporters that so far Rona II had received no payments at all from "Charlie's Angels," then in its fourth year on ABC.

"But that is quite normal," R.J. said. "On TV it always takes a long time to get any return. You wait and pray for syndication, which is where the big money is."

Dubbed "Angelgate" by the news media, Van De Kamp's highly publicized probe dragged on for nearly a year before he finally terminated it for lack of sufficient evidence to bring criminal charges. Pointing out, however, that "substantial questions" had been raised relating to "fair dealings" by Spelling/Goldberg, the district attorney urged anyone with profit participations in their contracts to hire their own independent auditors to make sure that they received all monies due them.

Later R.J. said the investigation was "unfortunate" but that it "ended correctly." What else could he say, given that Rona II and Spelling/Goldberg were also partners in "Hart to Hart"? According to an associate: "If there had been any fiddling with the accounts, R.J. was too sharp a businessman to let it happen to him twice."

Although Natalie had a financial stake in "Hart to Hart," she knew that the success of the show was R.J.'s achievement and not hers. With her own career in the doldrums, it wasn't an easy time for her as she tried to cope with feelings of resentment and rejection.

During past lulls in her career Natalie hadn't been troubled because of her preoccupation with home and family. But Natasha, now ten, and Courtney, six, were usually at school or busy with an ever widening circle of friends. And, of course, while R.J. worked on "Hart to Hart" nobody saw too much of him except on weekends, when the whole family went sailing on the *Splendour*.

It occurred to Natalie that perhaps she needed to make a professional transition. Why not become a producer, a director, or a combination of both? With thirty-eight years of experience in the movie business, it wasn't an unrealistic goal, especially since feminists had opened up new opportunities in those traditionally male-dominated fields.

For starters, Natalie already had a base in Rona II. With great encouragement from R.J., who saw the importance of her becoming actively involved in something, she plunged into reading and canvassing the field for properties. To help out her friend Mart Crowley, who was in a financial and psychological crisis over his continuing failure to duplicate the success of *The Boys in the Band*, she hired him to work for her as a story consultant on the Rona II payroll.

Early in November 1980, Natalie's father, who'd worked as a propmaker at various studios for most of his life, died of cardiac arrest at age sixty-six. Natalie arranged the funeral, insisting, over the objections of the rest of the family, that Nicholas Gurdin be buried in a plain wooden coffin suiting his station as an ordinary laborer and carpenter.

Although Gurdin would be interred near San Francisco (the Russian immigrant's first home in America), the service was held in the chapel at Westwood Memorial Park, where Natalie owned a plot. Hardly more than a year later, she herself would be buried there, but none of her father's mourners could have foreseen that as she read his eulogy, quoting from the "splendour in the grass" passage of Wordsworth's "Intimations of Immortality."

Gurdin's death was not unexpected, since he had a long history of heart trouble. Whatever grief Natalie felt soon became secondary to helping her mother adjust to widowhood. Some years earlier Natalie had set her parents up for life in a West Los Angeles condominium. But now Maria Gurdin became uneasy about living there alone, so she spent most of her time staying with one or another of her three daughters.

As Mama's favorite, Natalie started to receive more visits than she thought necessary, given R.J.'s dislike of meddlesome mothers-in-law. Mrs. Gurdin had a tendency to start intrigues in which she played off one granddaughter against the other or sided with them against Natalie and R.J. She also encouraged Natasha and Courtney to have fantasies about becoming child stars like their mother, a *verboten* subject in the Wagner household.

Eventually Mrs. Gurdin's intrusiveness triggered a terrible row between Natalie and R.J. Since the couple rarely quarreled about anything, Natalie overreacted and saw them ending up in divorce court if she didn't remove the cause of the problem. In a fury, she threw her mother out, pointing Mrs. Gurdin toward the nearest bus stop to find her own way home.

If Natalie's behavior seemed more than a bit excessive, it showed that she wasn't going to permit anything or anyone— not even her own mother—to jeopardize the success of her marriage. She had lost R.J. once and she wasn't going to let it happen again. "This time it'll work. It's got to," she often told intimates.

Natalie's friend Tommy Thompson once said to her, "I hope you guys never divorce. I'd stop believing in the institution of marriage if you did."

"No chance," Natalie replied. "I'm not about to let him go again." She liked to describe the interlude between the two marriages as a *Seitensprung*, a German expression for when two dancers change partners and then reunite before the waltz is over.

"You're only allowed one *Seitensprung*," Natalie said.

As "Hart to Hart" continued to enjoy huge popularity, Natalie had to contend with an upsurge of rumors and malicious gossip that R.J. and costar Stefanie Powers were having an affair. Whether true or not, the mere suggestion of it could send Natalie into jealous rages, according to friends.

"Because their company, Rona II, owned a piece of 'Hart to

Hart,' Natalie used to see all the scripts in advance," said a production executive. "If she came across a romantic scene between Stefanie and R.J. that she thought was too steamy she'd demand that it be toned down or cut entirely."

The *National Enquirer* carried a story that the Wagners' "fairy-tale" marriage was doomed because both were incredibly jealous, possessive and distrustful of each other. According to the article, R.J. pulled out a pistol in the midst of a party and told horrified guests to keep their "prying eyes" away from his wife. Someone claiming to have witnessed a violent blowup between the Wagners in a Beverly Hills restaurant told the *Enquirer* that "Natalie stood up in the booth, hauled off and punched Bob in the mouth."

If Natalie and R.J.'s marriage was endangered, no signs were evident at the New Year's Eve dinner party they gave at the end of 1980. An annual tradition, it was described by their friend Gavin Lambert as "formal in the sense of black tie and place cards, yet relaxed and intimate. The Wagners both felt, simply, that the occasion was worth dressing up for. Beyond that, it was strictly for friends—no guests invited for publicity purposes—and a personal celebration."

Later the guests would look back on the arrival of 1981 chez Wagner with special poignancy. "Natalie toasted R.J. with adoration," said Tommy Thompson. "I forget her exact words, but I remember well what he said in response.

"R.J. lifted a glass of Dom Perignon and he peered across its rim and topped her. 'I love you, my darling Natalie,' he said. 'In fact, you take my breath away.' "

As 1981 began Natalie became more determined than ever to get her career started again. A year had passed since her last TV feature, *The Memory of Eva Ryker*, and two years since she made *The Last Married Couple in America.*

Going on forty-three years old, Natalie had a problem that most women her age would envy: she looked so young that producers rarely thought of her for mature roles. To counteract that image of herself, Natalie swallowed her pride by telling friends in the business to spread the word that she would read for a part and even make a screen test if necessary.

But the offers didn't come pouring in, and it was only by happenstance that MGM approached Natalie about appearing in a science fiction thriller called *Brainstorm*. An unexpected casting crisis had developed when Glenda Jackson resigned from one of the leading roles and Louise Fletcher stepped in. Although Fletcher and the leading man, Christopher Walken, were both Oscar winners, MGM lacked confidence in their drawing power and wanted to add a well-established name to the cast for box-office insurance.

Natalie read the script and had serious misgivings. Fletcher and Walken were supposed to be scientists conducting experiments in brain-wave perception. Natalie would be Walken's wife, a nonessential supporting role that any actress could play.

But with a budget of $15 million, *Brainstorm* seemed the sort of project Natalie couldn't afford to let pass. Awesome visual spectacles like those by Steven Spielberg and George Lucas were all the rage. This one, to be directed by Douglas Trumbull, who did the special effects for *2001* and *Close Encounters of the Third Kind*, could turn out to be the blockbuster shot in the arm that her career needed.

Natalie finally said she'd do the movie if the script was rewritten. She wanted more dialogue as well as more scenes, so that her character figured prominently in the main action. Douglas Trumbull and the screenwriters agreed to follow her suggestions, which they saw as a way of injecting more human drama into a story dominated by special effects.

While Natalie waited for *Brainstorm* to get underway, R.J. finished his latest series of "Hart to Hart" episodes, so they decided to fly to Europe to take advantage of what seemed likely to be the only open time in their schedules until the end of the year.

"We made up our minds that we wanted to just get away from it all just by ourselves, a dream we'd had for a long time," Natalie said. "We went everywhere deluxe class. Planes, hotels, restaurants. We ate in all the best places, saw all the shows and sights and had the time of our lives. It was perfection."

When the Wagners got home they decided to drive a Landcruiser up the California coast with the children and the family dog. They ate at hot dog stands and greasy spoon diners, spending the nights wherever anyone would let them park the van.

"The kids were in absolute heaven," Natalie said. "I remember thinking to myself, 'I have the best of all possible worlds.'

First, R.J. and I are touring the world at about a dollar a second and a couple of weeks later mustard on our faces and tacos and laughter and the usual family squabbles."

During a New York stopover on the way back from Europe, Natalie and R.J. had gone to see their friend Elizabeth Taylor acting on stage for the first time in a Broadway revival of Lillian Hellman's *The Little Foxes*. Although critics declared Taylor's portrayal of Regina Giddens inferior to previous ones by Tallulah Bankhead and Bette Davis, the play broke box-office records, seemingly opening up a whole new career for Taylor as a *grande dame* of the legitimate theater.

Not for the first time in her life, Natalie adopted the attitude that, if Elizabeth Taylor could do it, why not Natalie Wood? After returning to Los Angeles she met with Robert Fryer, head of the Ahmanson Center Theater Group, where she just happened to be a member of the celebrity board of directors. Fryer had long been badgering Natalie about doing a play at the Ahmanson, but it took Elizabeth Taylor's success to finally give her the courage to attempt it.

While the bitchy Southern belle in *The Little Foxes* seemed a ready-made role for Taylor, it wasn't so easy finding a vehicle for Natalie, who also wanted to do a revival rather than a new, untested play. Finally several friends almost simultaneously suggested *Anastasia*, about a woman who might possibly be the only surviving member of the assassinated Russian imperial family. Although the play by Marcelle Maurette and Guy Bolton had been a Broadway hit with Viveca Lindfors in the title role, it was best remembered for the movie version, which won Ingrid Bergman an Oscar and restored her to public favor after the scandal over her affair with Roberto Rossellini. When Bergman played Anastasia, she had been forty, three years younger than Natalie was now.

"*Anastasia* is the perfect play for me," Natalie said. "I saw it on Broadway when I was a teenager. I loved it so much I saw it twice. When I read it again recently, it was even more wonderful than I remembered. I had a strong emotional reaction to it and, perhaps because of my Russian heritage, I identified with the characters. All my life I've had my best experiences when I've responded to material with my heart before my head."

Having seen Elizabeth Taylor on stage, Natalie knew that

she'd have to work with a coach on breath control and voice projection if she wanted to avoid some of Taylor's technical weaknesses. But other than that, she envisioned no problems in making the transition from movie to stage acting.

"Films rarely shoot in sequence; plays naturally progress from beginning to end. That's really the major difference, along with the special feeling of working directly in front of an audience," Natalie said.

"Repeating the same role night after night is more of a plus than a negative. It helps to have the run of a show to perfect one's interpretation. Also, I expect that each performance will be a challenge because each audience is different, and the chemistry in the theater changes."

To give Natalie ample time to prepare, Robert Fryer scheduled the opening of *Anastasia* for February 1982, two months after she expected to finish *Brainstorm*.

As the stage production started to take shape, Natalie became more excited about it than about the movie. Through her friend Laurence Olivier she persuaded the illustrious Dame Wendy Hiller to come to Los Angeles to play opposite her as the elderly grand duchess who must decide whether or not Anastasia is an impostor. Arvin Brown, from the highly regarded Long Wharf Theater in New Haven, Connecticut, signed on as director.

When the Ahmanson made a public announcement of its plans for *Anastasia*, the response was so favorable that Robert Fryer told Natalie to expect a transfer to Broadway at the end of the Los Angeles run. Based on that enthusiasm, Natalie's agents started sounding out the studios about starring her in a new movie version of the Anastasia story. Her friend Tommy Thompson wanted to write the script.

Everything suddenly seemed to be going right for Natalie. The icing on the cake was her selection by Blackglama mink breeders for their "What Becomes a Legend Most?" advertising campaign, in which the models are always so famous that nobody has to ask their names. Natalie received a $10,000 mink coat and the can't-be-bought status of a Living Legend for posing for a full-page ad scheduled for that autumn's magazines and newspapers.

On July 16, 1981, Natalie and R.J. dropped everything and

took the children out to sea on the *Splendour* to celebrate the couple's ninth *second* wedding anniversary. In fact a whole decade had passed since their reconciliation, because they lived together for a year before remarrying. By this time they had a ready answer for questions about why the press tended to describe them as "Hollywood's Dream Couple."

"I think we're a dream couple because we do have so many things going for us," R.J. said in an interview. "We have been so lucky and so fortunate. You don't want to tamper with that too much. I have to pinch myself once in a while and say, 'My God, how lucky I am that it's all worked out, that it's all happened.'

"I don't really work that hard at making it romantic because Natalie can be so romantic anyway. I'm so in love with her, so it's just a matter of surprising her sometimes or doing things we like to do together. It's all kind of easy. I'm hooked on the lady, you see. . . . The big difference is that when we were married the first time, I was a little bit insecure in certain areas and jealous at times. Her career would be first and I would be second and I would get upset about that. It was just a matter of maturity and time going by."

"These last ten years have been like a miracle," Natalie added. "We always had love, but to make a relationship work requires understanding, a knowledge that things *can* go wrong, a sensitivity you lack when you're very young."

But as rumors continued to circulate about R.J. and Stefanie Powers, doubts were raised about the sincerity of the Wagners' frequent proclamations of wedded bliss.

"Natalie was becoming insanely jealous, not only of Stefanie but of other women," said a friend. "R.J. was one of the few stars who still had an aura of the great Hollywood romantic idols. Women of all ages absolutely adored him. Those gorgeous young things who were hired for T & A gags in 'Hart to Hart' were always coming on to him. Most men would find it very hard to resist. I doubt that R.J. was the exception."

When the Wagners got married the second time, Natalie must have known what she would be up against. Faced with the same predicament, some wives learn to accept those sudden infatuations as a risk of the acting profession and take a tolerant "this too shall pass" attitude as long as the affairs don't get serious.

But Natalie reacted differently because of what happened earlier over Warren Beatty. Friends believed that she was obsessed with the idea of history repeating itself, only this time with R.J. leaving her. Natalie's fears reportedly got worse as she grew older and saw her beauty and sexual allure slowly but surely eroding.

A month in advance of starting *Brainstorm*, Natalie went on a strict diet and exercise program to get into shape for what was to be her first theatrical movie in two years. In the guest house beside their swimming pool the Wagners had a complete gym with Universal equipment, a Jacuzzi and even a trapeze and ballet bar. According to friends, Natalie also used diuretics and diet pills, which tended to make her anxious and irritable while knocking off the poundage.

One night Natalie phoned the film's costume designer, Donfeld, to ask if her dieting would upset his schedule for fitting her wardrobe. "I told her not to worry," Donfeld remembered. "In my mind's eye, I saw women around the world longing to look like Natalie Wood, but Natalie Wood herself saw someone entirely different in the mirror."

Just before Natalie began *Brainstorm*, the Wagners invited Tommy Thompson on a weekend cruise around Catalina Island on the *Splendour*. A scuba-diving friend brought a bucket of abalone shells which everyone helped to pry open before Natalie took the fillets and sautéed them in herbs and butter. Later she grilled lobsters and tossed a spectacular health salad.

"We all stayed up through several bottles of Pouilly-Fuissé, spinning yarns and gossiping," Thompson said. "Natalie recalled that Laurence Olivier, sitting in my exact seat, once toasted her acting ability. She seemed astonished that Lord Olivier would find merit in her work. I'm not sure Natalie realized how good she was."

The next morning Thompson found Natalie on the deck yelling into the wind. "Stretching the pipes," she told him, looking somewhat embarrassed at being discovered.

"I understood immediately what she was up to," Thompson said. "The night before, Natalie said that she was 'scared shitless' about appearing on the stage in *Anastasia*. She was worried that her voice would not be strong enough for the massive auditorium."

From what he observed on that visit with the Wagners, Thompson believed that they were very much in love. "It wasn't fan magazine posing. It was real, sometimes embarrassingly so. On the boat they held hands and kissed and grabbed each other so often that I would turn away in embarrassment and try to make a joke of it by feigning gagging noises," Thompson said.

Now remarried for going on ten years, Natalie and R.J. had always been able to arrange their schedules so that they were never apart for more than a few days. But *Brainstorm* changed that because there would be at least a month of location filming at a scientific research center near Raleigh, North Carolina.

R.J., meanwhile, had to shoot new episodes of "Hart to Hart" in Los Angeles. The only way that the couple could be together was through alternating cross-country commutes at the weekends.

Friends noticed that when Natalie left for North Carolina early in September she seemed unhappy and upset. Some of it must have been motherly guilt over being separated from her two daughters just as they were starting a new school term, but there was probably more to it than that. Already worried by rumors concerning her husband and Stefanie Powers, she may have seen potential danger in leaving R.J. at a time when the two were constantly working together.

Whether the gossip about R.J. and Stefanie Powers was true or not, it may have triggered what happened after Natalie arrived in North Carolina. If, as subsequent events suggested, Natalie did have a flirtation with costar Christopher Walken, she may have done it just to get back at R.J. for what she suspected to be going on between him and Powers.

"Natalie was very good at intrigues, something she learned at an early age from her mother, who could have given Mata Hari lessons," said a longtime friend. "It is very possible that Natalie saw Chris as a means to arranging a trade-off. She'd give up Chris if R.J. also stopped playing around. To accomplish that, Natalie didn't need to have an affair with Chris. All she had to do was make R.J. believe that she was."

At the time *Brainstorm* went into production, Christopher

Walken was thirty-eight, five years younger than Natalie (and thirteen years younger than R.J.). Tall and gaunt, he has a steely-eyed, ascetic face that seems more suited to playing character parts than heroes. He won an Oscar for portraying a doped-up Vietnam veteran who earns a living by playing Russian roulette in *The Deer Hunter*. After the movie's 1979 release, Walken's portrayal was credited with setting off a public epidemic of such deaths.

A native New Yorker, Walken isn't the usual Hollywood type. All that he seemed to have in common with Natalie Wood was a career as a child actor, but in television and stage plays rather than in movies. Later he sang and danced in the choruses of Broadway musicals, quitting at age twenty-two to switch over to "serious" acting in everything from William Shakespeare to Tennessee Williams.

Brainstorm was supposed to be Walken's second shot at becoming a major movie star. He muffed it the first time by playing one of the leads in the next project of *Deer Hunter* director Michael Cimino. The $35 million Western, *Heaven's Gate*, turned out to be the biggest financial disaster in movie history.

Unlike Natalie, Walken brought his spouse along to the *Brainstorm* location in North Carolina. He'd been married for fifteen years to Georgianne Thon, a dancer whom he first met while both worked in a road tour of *West Side Story*. The couple never had any children, but Mrs. Walken eventually quit dancing to concentrate on homemaking and managing the business side of her husband's career. Although they had a New York City apartment and a country house in Connecticut, she usually accompanied Walken wherever his work took him.

Georgianne Walken stayed with her husband the whole time during the *Brainstorm* shoot in Raleigh, according to the unit publicist. Since Walken had also arranged for Georgianne to play a small role in the movie, it's difficult to imagine how he and Natalie could have carried on a romance with his wife so much on the scene. Either Mrs. Walken was an extremely tolerant wife or the subsequent rumors about an "affair" were false or grossly exaggerated.

R.J. flew to Raleigh twice for weekend visits. Although the trips had been arranged prior to Natalie's leaving for location, they were later interpreted by the press as "raids" by a jealous and worried husband. Not reported was the fact that on other weekends Natalie reciprocated and went home to Beverly Hills. Perhaps those trips should have been labeled "raids" as well, if they were to check up on R.J. and Stefanie Powers.

Interestingly, not until *after* Natalie's death were there rumors and stories about a liaison with Walken. Only then did the scandal tabloids become filled with lurid accounts of dressing-room trysts with the blinds *open,* moonlight smooching under the pine trees, and Natalie and Walken stumbling back to their hotel late at night completely stoned. It was also claimed that, when production of *Brainstorm* shifted to Hollywood, Natalie and Walken made love in the back seat of a chauffeured limousine while being driven to and from the studio every day.

Although Raleigh, North Carolina, isn't one of the major news beats, Los Angeles certainly is. Doesn't it seem more than a bit odd that such brazen, unguarded behavior between two major celebrities went totally unreported at the time it allegedly took place?

Not one person in authority on *Brainstorm* has ever confirmed the rumors that Natalie and Walken were lovers. That in itself proves nothing. But in such intimate matters, can anyone but the two people involved know the true answer? Unfortunately, one of them is dead and the other has been steadfastly silent on the question.

While *Brainstorm* was filming in Los Angeles, a tragic event occurred that some of the Wagners' intimates believe had a direct bearing on what happened later. On November 16, William Holden was found dead in his luxurious ocean-view apartment at Santa Monica.

Clad only in a pajama jacket, Holden had a deep gash in his forehead which suggested that he'd been murdered. But within forty-eight hours county coroner Thomas Noguchi determined that the sixty-three-year-old Oscar winner perished from loss of blood after tripping on a rug and hitting his head on a sharp table edge as he fell. Holden's blood test showed .22 percent alcohol, more than double California's legal definition of a drunken driver.

Since Holden's drinking problem had been fairly well known, the revelation that it probably cost him his life wasn't as surprising as the disclosure that he died at least four days before the manager of the building discovered his body. That the death of such a famous and revered man could go unnoticed that long made it seem as though he'd been abandoned by his family and friends.

The sad circumstances of Holden's passing raised questions about the status of his seven-year relationship with Stefanie Powers. Since Holden had often described the much younger woman as the great love of his life, why hadn't she been around when he needed her most, the news media wanted to know.

Stefanie Powers refused comment. But a friend blabbed that it had been a relationship in name only for a long time, that Powers had become increasingly intolerant of Holden's alcoholism and his refusal to seek a cure.

Not surprisingly, the William Holden case started a new wave of gossip about Stefanie Powers and Robert Wagner. In the past, Powers' seemingly happy relationship with Holden was supposed to be the reason why she and R.J. couldn't possibly be personally involved. But now that the idyllic image of the Holden-Powers affair had been shattered, many people—including Natalie Wood—began to wonder if there hadn't been some truth to the talk about R.J. and Powers after all.

In all the tumult over Holden's death, Stefanie Powers suffered a nervous collapse. Production of "Hart to Hart" was shut down while she recuperated. R.J. became the most frequent condolence caller at her house in Benedict Canyon. At least one person thought he was overdoing it a bit.

"Natalie was practically foaming at the mouth with jealousy," a friend said. "For three nights in a row, R.J. stayed over at Stefanie's house. You can imagine what must have been going through Natalie's mind over that. But she had to go along with it. It would have made her seem like a heartless and untrusting bitch if she didn't."

William Holden left instructions in his will that there should be no public funeral or memorial service. After cremation of the body, his ashes were scattered in the Pacific Ocean.

But on November 22, the first Sunday after Holden's death became known, Stefanie Powers held a small "farewell" gathering at her house for some of his closest friends. Besides Natalie and R.J., those attending included James Stewart, Richard Widmark, Billy Wilder, Lee Remick, Capucine, Blake Edwards, Alexis Smith, Craig Stevens and Holden's goddaughter, Patti Davis (daughter of Ronald and Nancy Reagan).

The Wagners were reportedly the last to arrive and the first to leave. "Natalie acted like she really didn't want to be there," said a screenwriter who attended. "She gave Stefanie the cold shoulder the whole evening. R.J. wanted to stay longer, but Natalie practically dragged him out the door, claiming she had to get up very early the next morning to go to work."

Natalie should have been finishing her scenes in *Brainstorm* that week, but the Thanksgiving holiday coming up on Thursday prevented that. The studio would also be closed on Friday so that everybody could have a four-day weekend.

On Thanksgiving Day, Natalie and R.J. hosted an open-house celebration. Unlike the black-tie affair that they traditionally held on New Year's Eve, this one was informal. Friends and relatives dropped by for drinks in the late afternoon and then stayed on for a buffet dinner if they hadn't already filled up on turkey elsewhere.

R.J. played bartender while Natalie held court on the brocade sofa in front of the fireplace. Some of the guests remembered her being unusually fidgety that day. Dressed in an angora sweater and matching slacks, she kept getting up to stir the fire or to check on countless Rigaud candles she kept burning to perfume the house.

Christopher Walken arrived at cocktail time. He stayed for about two hours, chatting mainly with Natalie and R.J. and leaving before dinner. Whether it was only that day that the Wagners asked him to spend the weekend on the *Splendour* or the invitation had been issued previously is unknown. Also unclear is why Walken's wife had chosen to go home to Connecticut rather than spend one of the major holidays of the year with her husband. The Walkens had no children, so that couldn't have been the reason.

After dinner, while everybody sat around talking, eleven-year-old Natasha went over to Natalie and said, "Mommy, please don't go this weekend. I feel bad I can't go with you. Go another time."

"Natasha, you and Courtney have made plans with your friends that you can't cancel, and R.J. and I have our plans too," Natalie said. "You're going to go through with your plans and we're going through with ours."

Right after that Natalie explained to the others, "R.J. and I are going out on the boat for a couple of days. Chris Walken is coming with us. The weather should be perfect." She asked friends Mart Crowley, Peggy Griffin and Delphine Mann if they'd like to join them, but they all had other engagements.

The next morning Natalie and R.J. picked up Walken at his hotel and drove to Marina del Rey to board the *Splendour*. Dennis Davern, the ship's one-man crew, met them at the pier.

As the quartet headed out to sea, none of them could have known that only three would be coming back. However, a fifth person, astrologer Carroll Righter, who regularly advised Natalie and R.J. and had once set down the conditions for their shipboard remarriage, claims to have had a premonition of danger.

"That weekend, I was doing up Natalie's chart," Righter remembered. "I was stunned. I knew she was in for a bad time. She was due for one of those weekends when it would have been best to stay in bed. Immediately, I tried to call the Wagners' home, but I was too late. They had already left for their fateful trip to Catalina."

Even more bizarrely, before the eighty-one-year-old seer could track the Wagners down, he collapsed with double pneumonia and had to be rushed to the hospital. "I feel somehow responsible for Natalie's death," Righter said. "If I had not been taken ill, I would have kept up until I reached her."

FIFTEEN

Gone Are the Days

AT 1:15 A.M. on Sunday, November 29, 1981, Robert Wagner's voice came on the harbor radio channel, trying to reach the Bay Watch, a private coast guard monitoring the Isthmus Bay area: "This is *Splendour.* We think we may have someone missing in an eleven-foot rubber dinghy."

Half an hour later boats from both the Bay Watch and the Harbor Patrol, plus U.S. Coast Guard helicopters, began crisscrossing the ocean surface with searchlights. The hunt turned up nothing and was suspended until daybreak.

At 7:44 A.M. a Sheriff's Office helicopter coming from the mainland spotted a woman's body floating face down, her hair splayed out in the water. It turned out to be Natalie Wood. She wore a red down-filled jacket, a blue flannel nightgown and knee-length wool socks.

The corpse was found near an isolated cove called Blue Cavern Point, less than a mile from where the *Splendour* had dropped anchor. Washed up on the shore about a hundred yards away was the rubber dinghy, *Valiant*, showing no signs of recent usage. The oars were tied down, the engine gear in neutral, the ignition switch still in the off position.

R.J. broke down when he heard the news. "He hugged me and cried," said skipper Dennis Davern. " 'She's gone, she's gone,' he said. 'Why did this have to happen?' "

Christopher Walken had still been sleeping when the search team came to the boat, according to Davern. Awakened by the noise, Walken went to the main cabin looking for breakfast. "What's up?" he asked.

When R.J. told him, "Chris didn't cry, but he looked depressed," Davern said.

Too distraught to go himself, R.J. asked Davern to accompany the police to identify the body before it was taken to the Los Angeles County morgue for the autopsy.

"When I saw Natalie, it was heartbreaking," Davern recalled. "Her jacket had come off when she was pulled from the water, but it was folded over her. They had removed her jewelry and showed it to me—gold earrings and a diamond ring. Her face was puffy and she looked so white. They showed me some bruises on the body, but I didn't want to look. I stayed a few minutes and left."

Like all suspicious deaths in Los Angeles County, Natalie's became a case for Chief Medical Examiner Thomas Noguchi, who less than two weeks earlier conducted the William Holden investigation. The *Splendour* was immediately impounded. Before R.J., Walken and Davern could leave the ship they had to be interrogated by Pamela Eaker, an investigator whom Noguchi sent to Catalina as soon as Natalie's death became known.

Enclosed in a hyperbaric chamber for safekeeping, the corpse was flown back to Los Angeles via helicopter. R.J. accompanied the body. After landing, he went straight home to Beverly Hills for an emotion-packed reunion with Courtney and Natasha, who were, of course, devastated by their mother's death.

By late afternoon the house was packed with relatives and close friends. R.J.'s ex-wife, Marion, who had never remarried, had rushed there from Palm Springs with their daughter Kate and his stepson, Josh Donen. Lana Wood and daughter Evan arrived, together with Natalie's half sister Olga and her family. Conspicuously absent was Maria Gurdin, confined to her bed at home after collapsing at the news of her daughter's death.

"All of us who gathered at the Wagners' nursed a common emotion: absolute anger," said Tommy Thompson. "This wasn't fair. This wasn't acceptable. No woman seemed to have a firmer grip on the fragile substance called life—and yet it slipped inexplicably through Natalie's fingers."

R.J. retreated to his bedroom upstairs and wouldn't come out. Marion Wagner and Josh Donen stood near, trying unsuccessfully to console him as he sat sobbing on the edge of the bed. His grief was impenetrable.

Making matters worse, the Wagners' longtime friend Bette Davis barged in at one point to confront R.J. with a horrifying rumor she'd heard that he pushed Natalie overboard in the heat of an argument. R.J. tearfully denied it. Davis, starting to cry herself, made a fast exit when she realized what a gaffe she'd made.

"I think R.J. looks on it as a bad movie that needs a retake," actor friend Lionel Stander told reporters as he left the house. "He's just shattered. He'll survive, but he'll never forget it."

Meanwhile the Hollywood press corps thought the tragedy had the makings of the biggest shocker since the Manson gang's massacre of Sharon Tate and friends in 1969. Sunday being a traditionally dull news day, Catalina Island soon swarmed with more reporters than tourists as the media tried to solve the mystery of Natalie Wood's death before Dr. Noguchi did.

By nine o'clock the next morning, when the coroner was just starting the autopsy, newspaper headlines were already suggesting that Natalie had either been murdered, committed suicide or died accidentally while under the influence of alcohol and/or drugs. Superstitious movie buffs believed her to be the latest victim of a curse on *Rebel Without a Cause* that had already caused the deaths of James Dean, Sal Mineo, Nick Adams, director Nicholas Ray and producer David Weisbart.

Perhaps the most grisly "revelation" was that several people on boats in the vicinity of the *Splendour* claimed to have heard a voice that might well have been Natalie's crying out for help. But not one of them attempted to go to the rescue.

On Monday afternoon Dr. Noguchi held a news conference to announce his preliminary findings. He said that Natalie slipped and drowned accidentally while attempting to enter the dinghy to leave the yacht. "There is no evidence of foul play," Noguchi said. "A scrape on her left cheek is consistent with her falling and having struck the dinghy as she went into the water."

Because of complaints he received from the Hollywood hierarchy about being too explicit in his public statements about William Holden's alcoholism, Noguchi tried to soft-pedal the information contained in Natalie's toxicological tests. Although they showed a .14 percent blood-alcohol reading (well above the .10 percent legal definition of intoxication), Noguchi believed that drunkenness did not cause Natalie to fall into the water.

"The .14 level of alcohol in the blood means she was only slightly intoxicated," Noguchi said. "She apparently was having wine, champagne—perhaps seven or eight glasses. That would certainly not cause a person to be drunk."

When a reporter asked if intoxication had played *any* role in Natalie's death, Noguchi said that it undoubtedly explained why she was unable to respond well to the emergency once she was in the water.

According to Noguchi, the down jacket that Natalie wore when she fell weighed about forty pounds in a saturated state. "The reason she drowned was the great weight of the jacket, which pulled her down when she attempted to climb into the dinghy," he said. "If she had just taken off that jacket, she might easily have made it into the dinghy and survived. That .14 percent of alcohol in her blood was, I believe, a deadly factor. She couldn't have been thinking clearly, or she would have slipped off the jacket at once."

Although it appeared that Natalie had died quickly and been spared the agony of confronting her lifelong fear of dark water, Noguchi later amended his findings after receiving a report from Paul Miller, the coroner's chief consultant on ocean accidents. Miller not only was an expert on the Catalina area but also had his schooner moored to the same buoy as the *Splendour* on the night of the tragedy.

Based on his knowledge of ocean currents and the jet stream,

Miller believed that Natalie could never have reached the point where her body was found unless she had been clinging to the dinghy and trying to propel it to shore by kicking her legs and paddling with one arm. Noguchi found this theory consistent with bruises on Natalie's arms and legs, which indicated that efforts to hoist herself out of the water and into the dinghy were defeated by its slippery rubber surfaces and the heavy weight of her jacket.

"Natalie Wood fought for her life in that cold November ocean," Noguchi said two years after the fact. "She did not give up. Instead she began to perform a feat that was both unique and gallant. And she almost achieved a miracle.

"Hypothermia caused her to lose strength, then consciousness, then finally her last feeble grip on the rubber boat. She sank beneath the waves and drowned. Only minutes later, the boat she had so painfully and courageously maneuvered for a mile landed safely on the beach."

But on the day after the tragedy reporters were more interested in finding out why Natalie Wood fled the *Splendour* than in what happened to her afterward. Noguchi's news conference turned tumultuous as questions were raised about rumors that some sort of interaction between Robert Wagner and Christopher Walken caused Natalie to leave.

Since at least two eyewitnesses, Dennis Davern and restaurant manager Don Whiting, claimed that Natalie had been flirting with Walken that night, one reporter theorized that she overdid it to a point where Walken, instead of going along with it, finally got fed up and told her to stop because (1) he wasn't interested and (2) it was only making R.J. terribly upset. Infuriated by Walken's siding with R.J., Natalie may have told the men off and then fled the boat in a temper tantrum.

Noguchi had no answers to such speculations. But his press aide, Richard Wilson, who had spoken to some of the police officers on the case, said there had been a "nonviolent argument" between R.J. and Walken.

Claiming that the dispute wasn't over Natalie, Wilson said, "They were arguing for general purposes. We don't know exactly why. There was no physical altercation. Each of the two gentlemen was examined."

Asked if Natalie left the yacht because she felt physically

threatened, Wilson said, "According to the information we have, no. She felt no danger at all. The argument was not over her."

Although the press conference ended in mass confusion, it left Noguchi deeply troubled. "The reasons for my unease were twofold," he said later. "One, the information about the argument was thirdhand, as far as I was concerned. Secondly, there was the consideration that always bedevils all medical examiners: how much information should be revealed if it is not directly relevant?

"In this case, a shouting match between Wagner and Walken which caused Natalie Wood to leave the yacht, even if true, was a peripheral matter as far as I was concerned. But the law charges medical examiners with discovery of 'the manner, cause and circumstance of death'—and such an argument could be construed as a part of the circumstance."

But Noguchi chose to consider the alleged dispute a fringe circumstance. "It might provide a reason *why* Natalie Wood wanted to take a lonely boat ride that night. But the actual reason for her death was her accidental slip. In more familiar terms, it's as if a husband and wife engage in a verbal fight, and the wife angrily runs out of the house, drives away in a car and is killed in a crash because she accidentally steps on the accelerator instead of the brake. The husband is not guilty of murder."

But an unsolved mystery is always more intriguing than one with all the answers. The next day it became even more baffling as R.J.'s attorney, Paul Ziffren, denied that a Wagner-Walken altercation had taken place. Instead, it was suggested that Natalie couldn't sleep because of noise from the dinghy bumping against her cabin wall. Going up on deck to move it, she may have slipped on algae or seaweed and fallen into the water. The reason that R.J. and Walken didn't hear anything was explained by their being down below at the other end of the ship.

Hoping to quell the controversy, Ziffren said, "The only important thing is that Natalie is gone. All the rest is ghoulish nonsense."

Unless R.J. and/or Walken opened up, the press became convinced that the only one who could provide a solution to the "mystery" was skipper Dennis Davern, the fourth person on board the *Splendour*. When Davern turned up working as a production assistant on "Hart to Hart," rumors started that R.J., either voluntarily or under threat of blackmail, had given him the job to shut him up. Later Davern dropped out of sight, ostensibly to write a book about his experiences.

What happened to the book is unknown but, in 1983, Davern sold an article to Rupert Murdoch's weekly tabloid, the *Star*, which claimed to be the true story of Natalie Wood's final hours. Whether it was or not, no one came forward to deny it, although that in itself proves nothing.

According to Davern, a contretemps developed when the quartet returned to the *Splendour* on Saturday night after dining at Doug's Harbor Reef. "Natalie lit some candles on the coffee table in the salon and she and Chris sat together on a small couch, sort of a love seat," Davern said. "I was sitting across the table from them and R.J. was standing, glaring at them. Natalie was flirting with Chris, hugging him and holding his arm. And Walken was doing nothing to discourage her."

R.J. was getting angrier by the second and finally exploded, Davern recalled. "He picked up a bottle of wine and smashed it on the table in front of Walken. The glass and wine flew everywhere. 'What are you trying to do? Seduce my wife?' he shouted at Walken. Chris jumped to his feet, and I thought they would fight. But he shrugged his shoulders and walked away."

Natalie was furious, Davern claimed. " 'R.J., I won't stand for this,' she screamed. She stalked off to the master bedroom. Those were the last words she said to her husband. It was the last time any of us saw her alive."

Davern considered R.J.'s reaction a bit strange. "It wasn't really Walken who was putting the moves on Natalie. It was she who was flirting with him. She was mesmerized by him. And I thought that R.J. must have been thinking it was like that time when he was first married to Natalie and she fell in love with Warren Beatty. Maybe R.J. was afraid history was going to repeat itself."

After Natalie stormed away, Walken went to his cabin, while R.J. and Davern sat talking and drinking wine until around midnight, the skipper maintained. "Finally R.J. went below. I

don't know where he went, or what he did, or even if he saw
anybody, Natalie or Walken. But about half an hour later, R.J.
came up on deck saying Natalie was missing. We both went
below and checked the rooms. Walken was asleep, sawing
wood, alone. Natalie was nowhere to be found."

Going back on deck, they noticed that the dinghy was missing. "R.J. didn't want to radio for a full search because he
didn't really think Natalie was in trouble," Davern remembered. "He thought she'd just gone off to shore because she was
mad at him for what happened. He wasn't really worried. And
he didn't want all the publicity—you know, searching for the
movie star's wife. So we kept on drinking, and it must have
been two hours later that he finally radioed for help. It took
him that long to believe she was in trouble."

Three days after her death Natalie was buried at Westwood
Memorial Park. Prior to the ceremony, members of the immediate family gathered at the funeral home where the body had
been taken following the coroner's autopsy.

Eddie Butterworth, Natalie's favorite makeup artist, did a
cosmetic restoration, but the casket was kept closed until seven-
year-old Courtney Wagner asked if it could be opened for a
final look at her mother. R.J. gave his permission and the two of
them went and stood beside it for a moment. The others stayed
behind, preferring to remember Natalie as she had been in life.

For the cortege, the white-and-gold-trimmed coffin was covered with a blanket of 450 white gardenias worked into candle-
light lace and set off with a nile-green ribbon. Because gardenias were out of season locally, they had to be ordered from
florists in eight states.

By the time the procession reached Westwood about a hundred relatives and friends had gathered for the service, held
outdoors under a shady camphor tree beside the gravesite. Another thousand or more spectators, including scores of photographers and reporters from all over the world, were spread out
behind the cemetery walls, thirty yards away.

Laurence Olivier had flown in from London for the funeral.
Other celebrities attending included Frank Sinatra, Elizabeth
Taylor, Fred Astaire, Rock Hudson, David Niven, Gregory
Peck, Gene Kelly and Elia Kazan. Causing considerable com-
ment among the onlookers were Stefanie Powers and Christo-

pher Walken, standing together chatting before the service began.

While the mourners formed a semicircle around the coffin, a balalaika player, symbolic of Natalie's Russian heritage, strummed traditional folk melodies. The phrases "Those were the days, my friend, we thought they'd never end," floated unsung in the air, perhaps along with the spirit of Marilyn Monroe, whose crypt just happened to be a few yards away.

After a blessing by Father Stephen Fitzgerald of the Russian Orthodox Church of the Holy Virgin Mary, eulogies were delivered by three of Natalie's closest friends, Hope Lange, Roddy McDowall and Tommy Thompson (who died of cancer less than a year later).

"Natalie, you put us to a very severe test today," Hope Lange began. "It's difficult to feel joy and laughter when you're not here to share it." The actress recalled that, "for Natalie's friends, there was no problem too great or too simple for her to share. She was a pillar of strength for us all, always wise, helpful and honest."

Roddy McDowall said, "It is a joy to think that one individual can accomplish so much beauty in so few decades. Natalie found a way to put life in her heart and to put heart into her life."

Quoting John F. Kennedy, Tommy Thompson said, "A life must be measured not by the quantity of years, but by the quality of the days." Recalling Natalie's rise from "a wide-eyed little kid" to "a world symbol of beauty and grace," he reminded the mourners "What a fabulous life she had!"

As the fifteen-minute service concluded, R.J. plucked a handful of gardenias from the blanket covering the coffin. Shuffling slowly over to the immediate family, he pressed flowers one by one into the hands of Natasha, Courtney, and Natalie's mother and sisters.

Then R.J. returned to the coffin, bent down and tenderly kissed it. His tear-filled eyes glimmered in the glare of the warm afternoon sun.

Afterward everybody drove to the Wagner residence for the Beverly Hills equivalent of a wake, with cocktails and a huge buffet prepared by the family cook, Willie Mae Worthen. A cordon of police was stationed outside the ten-foot-high iron grille fence to ward off the press and general public.

In the midst of the reception R.J. received a telephone call from President Reagan and his wife Nancy, offering their sympathies. Queen Elizabeth II sent a telegram that said, "On behalf of the Crown and the Commonwealth of Great Britain, I send heartfelt condolences to the family and friends of Mrs. Wagner. The tragic loss of great persons is felt the world over. However, loving memories of Mrs. Wagner will live with us always."

The day after the funeral Natalie's will, running to nineteen pages, was filed for probate. Although the value of her estate was stated conservatively as being in excess of $30,000, friends estimated it to be in the millions, owing to shrewd property investments that she made over the years. With R.J. as executor and sole trustee, the will stipulated that, except for certain bequests of cash or belongings, the bulk of the estate was to be divided so that Natalie's stepdaughter, Kate Wagner, got ten percent and the balance was divided equally between daughters Natasha and Courtney.

Natalie left her mother, Maria Gurdin, at least $7,500 and a maximum of $12,000 annually for life. Her half sister, Olga Viripaeff, got a flat $15,000, while sister Lana Wood received all of Natalie's furs and clothing. Lana subsequently sold the clothes for $15,000 and received an additional $20,000 from R.J. for the furs, which he wanted to keep for the three girls.

One of the most unusual clauses in Natalie's will was the wish that R.J. be appointed Natasha's legal guardian so that she, Courtney and Kate Wagner could continue to be brought up together under his parenting. Natasha's father, Richard Gregson, who resided in London, could have gone to court to regain custody of his daughter but decided to abide by the request.

"Natalie was a very good mother and she always wanted what was best for her children," he said. "I've always been able to visit Natasha whenever I've wanted and I'm sure R.J. will let that continue. He's always been very cooperative and encouraging in my relationship with Natasha."

Natalie's death had its effect on the two projects she had been involved in. Out of respect, the Ahmanson Theater canceled the entire production of *Anastasia* rather than sign another actress to replace her.

Since Natalie hadn't finished all her scenes in *Brainstorm*, MGM/UA found itself in a major crisis. Dissatisfied with the rushes and the way the movie was shaping up generally, the studio tried to use her death as an excuse to scrap the $16 million project and get its money back from the production insurance it carried with Lloyds of London. Filming was shut down pending the outcome of negotiations. (The studio finally lost its case and completed the film by rewriting Natalie's remaining scenes for another character. Released in September 1983, the sci-fi thriller received bad reviews and lost its entire investment.)

The production lull sent Christopher Walken rushing back to the seclusion of his country home in Connecticut. Except for attending the funeral, he had kept to his quarters at the Beverly Wilshire Hotel, refusing to make any public comment on the tragedy.

Not until two years later did he speak for the record, and then only briefly. "I'm sure that I will never be able to stop the rumors about Natalie's death," Walken told an interviewer. "The people who are convinced that there was something more to it than what came out in the investigation will never be satisfied with the truth. Because the truth is, there is nothing more to it. It was an accident."

But as the rumors continued to seethe after the funeral, R.J. retreated to his bedroom and tried to shut out the world.

"Losing someone you love so suddenly, so tragically, you feel like you're going to hit bottom. It's the deepest depression you can ever know. I couldn't get out of bed because I was absolutely devastated," R.J. remembered.

What kept him from totally falling apart was a doctor friend who reminded him of a line written by Eugene O'Neill: "Man is born broken. He lives by mending. And the grace of God is the glue."

"To me," R.J. said, "that meant I had an awful lot of glue around. I had my children, and I had an awful lot of people to help hold me together. I crumbled, there's no question about that. All that . . . in the newspapers every day. It was difficult and painful for all of us. It was *really* tough."

R.J. credited housekeeper Willie Mae Worthen with finally snapping him out of it: "This wonderful woman who works for us stuck her head in the door one morning and said, 'You have to get up and get going, the kids are worried about you.' So I sat down and talked to the kids. I said it was time they went back to school. And I figured if they could go back to school I could go back to work . . . and I think working saved my life."

Nine days after Natalie's death R.J. started filming a new episode of "Hart to Hart" entitled *Heart of Diamonds*. Having lost about ten pounds, he looked like hell, requiring an hour in the makeup chair instead of his usual five minutes.

Stefanie Powers helped him get through the day. "She'd had the trauma with Bill Holden's death, and she held my hand," R.J. said. "I really thank God for her. I'd go up on my lines, or get upset, or I'd lose confidence . . . no matter what, she never let me out of her sight. And it was fucking tough, believe me. But it was tougher on the kids than it was on me."

R.J.'s next move toward the family's recovery was to seek psychiatric help. Besides going into therapy himself, he sent eleven-year-old Natasha and eight-year-old Courtney to a child psychiatrist.

"The one thing I didn't want to happen was for my girls to get emotionally crushed," R.J. said. "I wanted them to let out all their anger and frustration, all their feelings of pain and loss and confusion, so they could start to accept it and live a new life. I wanted a way of monitoring them so they could survive and come through it okay."

With Christmas approaching, R.J.'s friends urged him to take the girls away for the holidays instead of staying in the house where Natalie's spirit still hovered in every nook and cranny. David Niven, Roger Moore and Blake Edwards found them a chalet in Gstaad, Switzerland. Delphine Mann, Natalie's closest friend, and Josh Donen, R.J.'s stepson, did all the packing and went along to look after them.

David Niven, a resident of Gstaad, stocked the chalet with food, supplies and logs for the fire. He lugged everything there himself despite the fact that he was seriously ill with amyotrophic lateral sclerosis (Lou Gehrig's disease).

"Because my daughters and I arrived there in a terrible

snowstorm," R.J. recalled, "Niven waited down at the bottom of the road for two or three hours to guide us and show us the way up the hill. And when we finally got there he just held me in his arms and we talked for hours about Natalie and Primmie, and what had happened to them. [Primula Niven, the actor's first wife, died in 1946 from an accidental fall down cellar stairs while participating in a party game of hide-and-seek at the home of Tyrone Power and his French actress wife, Annabella.]

"Niven had lost his wife at an early age and was left with two kids, so he *knew*, and he got to me real fast. He told me not to make any decisions; just take my feelings where they wanted to go, he said, and don't let other people intrude."

When R.J. and the children returned to Beverly Hills, certain changes in their lifestyle had to be made. The *Splendour* was put up for sale; R.J. never stepped foot on it again after the accident. "The sea no longer holds much attraction for me," he said.

Apparently the yacht's tragic history frightened away buyers. R.J. eventually donated it to the Sea Scouts.

R.J. also started shopping for a new place to live. The Canon Drive house where the family had resided for seven years not only held too many disturbing memories but also was besieged by tourists and curiosity-seekers.

"The children couldn't even go out the front door," R.J. said. "It was a nightmare."

Intending to make a complete break from the Beverly Hills–Hollywood scene, R.J. purchased a two-acre estate in a hilly secluded area of West Los Angeles near Will Rogers State Park. The house is a sprawling five-bedroom hacienda, with separate guest quarters, an office, a pondlike swimming pool, kennels and stables.

While renovations went on, R.J. and the children continued to live at the Beverly Hills house, which had been put on the market at an asking price of $2.9 million. "Natalie had decorated the house so beautifully before she died," R.J. said. "I didn't want to abruptly leave that—emotionally I couldn't do it. So we moved out very slowly. We'd drive to the new place and paint a room, move a little furniture in, a piece at a time.

"I didn't want to take their mother away from them completely, so I told the girls they could take any furniture they wanted from the old house to keep in their rooms, and if there was anything else they wanted, I would keep it for them until they grow up."

The most startling change in R.J.'s personal life was a budding relationship with red-haired actress Jill St. John. When they started appearing in public together only two months after Natalie's death, the Hollywood community was shocked, though not necessarily by R.J.'s alacrity. Many had been predicting that if he did become involved with another woman it would be with Stefanie Powers.

Insiders believed that Powers had been eliminated from the running because of the rumors that circulated about her and R.J. before the deaths of Natalie and William Holden.

"R.J. becoming involved with Stefanie would have seemed like confirmation of the gossip that they were lovers," a friend said. "Stefanie was already getting a lot of heat for having abandoned Holden in his final days. With so much of Natalie's death unexplained and hinting of marital discord, you can imagine the conclusion that the press and public would have drawn if R.J. and Stefanie got together. It would have haunted them forever, even if it wasn't true."

Forty-one at the time, Jill St. John was born two years later than Natalie Wood. One of the most publicized starlets of the fifties and early sixties, she never made it into the major ranks as an actress. Her main claims to fame were three disastrous marriages (including one to Natalie's ex-beau, Lance Reventlow), liaisons with Frank Sinatra and Henry Kissinger, and a near genius IQ that belied her appearance as a gorgeous ding-a-ling. She first met R.J. while both were under contract to 20th Century-Fox. Much later they appeared together in *Banning* and the TV movie *How I Spent My Summer Vacation*.

Playing matchmaker in the relationship was Natalie and R.J.'s longtime friend, writer Tom Mankiewicz, who invited Jill to dinner at his house in Malibu and arranged for R.J. and daughter Kate to join them.

"We had a good time at dinner," St. John recalled. "The next day R.J. called and asked me out. I was surprised because we'd known each other for so long, and there was never any hint of romance—only really good friendship. So I thought about it for a while and I decided, yes, I really like him a lot and I should see him."

The couple started dating and eventually moved in together, but it appeared that R.J.'s immediate need was just companionship and not a new wife. "I don't like solitude," he said. "I get anxious when I'm alone."

When a reporter asked him if he didn't feel guilty about "having fun" so soon after a loved one had died, he replied, "I don't give a goddamn what anyone thinks." As 1988 began, R.J. and St. John were still keeping company but remained unmarried.

A friend of Jill St. John cautioned her at the outset: "I wouldn't like to be the lady who takes Natalie Wood's place."

Any woman who became involved with R.J. had to possess a strong sense of her own identity to cope with Natalie's ghost. He still wore the wedding rings from his two marriages to Natalie, one on his finger and the other on a gold chain around his neck. Photographs of Natalie and the children abounded throughout the house and in his studio dressing room.

Years after the tragedy R.J. reflected, "When Natalie died, I was embittered. I still get angry about it and I wonder why it had to happen. I have all those feelings of grief and anger that people who've lost someone they love always have. I had lived a charmed life, and then I lost a beautiful woman I loved with all my heart.

"What gets me is that Natalie has missed so much already— seeing the kids grow up and flourish. She worked so hard all her life. Natalie had some tough times, being put out there to work at four years old, being pushed . . . working very hard on her life, on her talent, and then bang! Gone! And it's terrible.

"Natalie lived more than most of us live," R.J. continued. "She felt more. She experienced more. She did more and gave more. She created a lot of light with her life. She caught her rainbows. You know, I don't believe this is the only life when it comes to an end. I think that you go on. Something survives."

In the years since Natalie's death her centrally located grave in Westwood Memorial Park has become one of the cemetery's top attractions, along with Marilyn Monroe's harder-to-find wall crypt at the rear. The abundance of fresh flowers, wreaths and potted plants that cover every inch of Natalie's small province indicates that she hasn't been forgotten by her loved ones and fans.

Although scores of tourists and movie buffs come to gawk every day, they haven't deterred R.J. from visiting nor has he ever been bothered when he does. Sometimes accompanied by Courtney and Natasha but more often alone, he always brings a bouquet of white gardenias. As he kneels down and clears a place for them among the other tributes, it's plain that his mourning will never be over.

Acknowledgments

I WOULD LIKE to express my gratitude to the following people who kindly shared memories and information with me: Don Bachardy, James Bacon, Solly Baiano, Rona Barrett, Marcia Borie, Stan Brosette, Allan Carr, Gil Cates, Michael Childers, Joan Collins, Jean Cummings, Tony Curtis, Stanley Donen, Blake Edwards, Don Feld, Ed Feldman, Eddie Fisher, Father Stephen Fitzgerald, Robert Fryer, Wendy Goldberg, Dick Gutman, Terri Hall, Bill Hendricks, Hy Hollinger, Dennis Hopper, Tab Hunter, Henry Jaglom, Elia Kazan, Pat Kingsley, Gavin Lambert, Jean Leon, Don Levy, Mort Lichter, Arthur Loew, Jr., Roddy McDowall, Guy McElwaine, Dick Moore, David Niven, Jr., William Orr, Alan Pakula, Jerry Pam, Peter Schlesinger, George Segal, Arnold Stiefel and especially the late Thomas Thompson. Many other friends and associates of Natalie Wood and Robert Wagner also participated, but names have been withheld at their request.

My thanks also go to the staffs of the following research centers for their splendid assistance: the Library of the Motion Picture Academy of Arts and Sciences, Los Angeles; the American Film Institute Library, Los Angeles; the Special Collections Library of the University of Southern California, Los Angeles; the Performing Arts Library at Lincoln Center, New York.

A special note of gratitude to my editor, Casey Fuetsch, and her predecessor, Anne Sweeney, as well as to my agent, Daniel Strone.

For their encouragement and good cheer, my customary and heartfelt thanks to that large group of relatives and friends who know who they are by this time and no longer need to be named individually. Bless you all!

Filmography

The Films of Natalie Wood

1. HAPPY LAND (20th Century-Fox, 1943). Cast: Don Ameche, Frances Dee, Harry Carey, Ann Rutherford, Cora Williams, Dickie Moore (N.W., still Natasha Gurdin, uncredited in bit part). Producer: Kenneth Macgowan. Director: Irving Pichel. Screenplay: Kathryn Scola and Julien Josephson, from a story by Mackinlay Kantor. 75 minutes, B&W.
2. TOMORROW IS FOREVER (RKO, 1946). Cast: Claudette Colbert, Orson Welles, George Brent, Lucile Watson, Richard Long, Natalie Wood, Ian Wolfe. Producer: David Lewis. Director: Irving Pichel. Screenplay: Lenore Coffee, from a story by Gwen Bristow. 105 minutes, B&W.
3. THE BRIDE WORE BOOTS (Paramount, 1946). Cast: Barbara Stanwyck, Robert Cummings, Diana Lynn, Patric Knowles, Peggy Wood, Robert Benchley, Willie Best, Natalie Wood. Producer: Seton I. Miller. Director: Irving Pichel. Screenplay: Dwight Mitchell Wiley, from a story by Wiley and Harry Segall. 86 minutes, B&W.
4. THE GHOST AND MRS. MUIR (20th Century-Fox, 1947). Cast: Gene Tierney, Rex Harrison, George Sanders, Edna Best, Vanessa Brown, Anna Lee, Robert Coote, Natalie Wood, Isobel Elsom. Producer: Fred Kohlmar. Director: Joseph L. Mankiewicz. Screenplay, Philip Dunne, from the novel by R. A. Dick. 104 minutes, B&W.
5. MIRACLE ON 34TH STREET (20th Century-Fox, 1947). Cast: Maureen O'Hara, John Payne, Edmund Gwenn, Gene Lockhart, Natalie Wood, Porter Hall, William Frawley, Jerome Cowan. Producer:

William Perlberg. Director: George Seaton. Screenplay: George Seaton, from a story by Valentine Davies. 96 minutes, B&W (later colorized for TV).

6. DRIFTWOOD (Republic, 1947). Cast: Ruth Warrick, Walter Brennan, Dean Jagger, Charlotte Greenwood, Natalie Wood, Jerome Cowan, H. B. Warner, Margaret Hamilton. Executive producer: Herbert J. Yates. Associate producer and director: Allan Dwan. Screenplay: Mary Loos, Richard Sale. 88 minutes, B&W.

7. SCUDDA HOO! SCUDDA HAY! (20th Century-Fox, 1948). Cast: June Haver, Lon McCallister, Walter Brennan, Anne Revere, Natalie Wood, Henry Hull, Tom Tully (Marilyn Monroe's first screen appearance in bit part). Producer: Walter Morosco. Director: F. Hugh Herbert. Screenplay: F. Hugh Herbert, from the novel by George Agnew Chamberlain. 95 minutes, Technicolor.

8. CHICKEN EVERY SUNDAY (20th Century-Fox, 1948). Cast: Dan Dailey, Celeste Holm, Colleen Townsend, Alan Young, Natalie Wood, William Frawley, Connie Gilchrist, Veda Ann Borg. Producer: William Perlberg. Director: George Seaton. Screenplay: Seaton and Valentine Davies, from a story by Julius J. Epstein, Philip G. Epstein and Rosemary Taylor. 91 minutes, B&W.

9. THE GREEN PROMISE (RKO, 1949). Cast: Marguerite Chapman, Walter Brennan, Robert Paige, Natalie Wood, Ted Donaldson, Connie Marshall. Producers: Robert Paige, Monty F. Collins. Director: William D. Russell. Screenplay: Monty F. Collins. 93 minutes, B&W.

10. FATHER WAS A FULLBACK (20th Century-Fox, 1949). Cast: Fred MacMurray, Maureen O'Hara, Betty Lynn, Rudy Vallee, Thelma Ritter, Natalie Wood, Jim Backus. Producer: Fred Kohlmar. Director: John H. Stahl. Screenplay: Aleen Leslie, Casey Robinson, Mary Loos and Richard Sale, from a story by Clifford Goldsmith. 84 minutes, B&W.

11. OUR VERY OWN (RKO, 1950). Cast: Ann Blyth, Farley Granger, Joan Evans, Jane Wyatt, Donald Cook, Ann Dvorak, Natalie Wood, Gus Schilling, Phyllis Kirk, Martin Milner. Producer: Samuel Goldwyn. Director: David Miller. Screenplay: F. Hugh Herbert. 93 minutes, B&W.

12. NO SAD SONGS FOR ME (Columbia, 1950). Cast: Margaret Sullavan, Wendell Corey, Viveca Lindfors, Natalie Wood, John McIntire, Ann Doran, Richard Quine, Jeanette Nolan. Producer: Buddy Adler. Director: Rudolph Mate. Screenplay: Howard Koch, from a story by Ruth Southard. 89 minutes, B&W.

13. THE JACKPOT (20th Century-Fox, 1950). Cast: James Stewart, Barbara Hale, James Gleason, Fred Clark, Alan Mowbray, Patricia

Medina, Natalie Wood, Tommy Rettig. Producer: Samuel G. Engel. Director: Walter Lang. Screenplay: Phoebe and Henry Ephron, from a story by John McNulty. 85 minutes, B&W.

14. NEVER A DULL MOMENT (RKO, 1950). Cast: Irene Dunne, Fred MacMurray, William Demarest, Andy Devine, Gigi Perreau, Natalie Wood, Jack Kirkwood, Ann Doran. Producer: Harriet Parsons. Director: George Marshall. Screenplay: Lou Breslow and Doris Anderson, from a story by Kay Swift. 89 minutes, B&W.

15. DEAR BRAT (Paramount, 1951). Cast: Mona Freeman, Billy De Wolfe, Edward Arnold, Lyle Bettger, Mary Philips, Natalie Wood, Lillian Randolph. Producer: Mel Epstein. Director: William Seiter. Screenplay: Devery Freeman, featuring some of the characters from the play and movie, *Dear Ruth*, by Norman Krasna. 82 minutes, B&W.

16. THE BLUE VEIL (RKO, 1951). Cast: Jane Wyman, Charles Laughton, Joan Blondell, Richard Carlson, Agnes Moorehead, Don Taylor, Audrey Totter, Cyril Cusack, Everett Sloane, Natalie Wood, Vivian Vance. Producers: Jerry Wald, Norman Krasna. Director: Curtis Bernhardt. Screenplay: Norman Corwin, based on the French film, *La Maternelle*, by François Campaux. 113 minutes, B&W.

17. JUST FOR YOU (Paramount, 1952). Cast: Bing Crosby, Jane Wyman, Ethel Barrymore, Robert Arthur, Natalie Wood, Cora Witherspoon, Ben Lessy, Regis Toomey. Producer: Pat Duggan. Director: Elliott Nugent. Screenplay: Robert Carson, adapted from *François* by Stephen Vincent Benét. 104 minutes, Technicolor.

18. THE ROSE BOWL STORY (Monogram, 1952). Cast: Marshall Thompson, Vera Miles, Richard Rober, Natalie Wood, Keith Larsen, Tom Harmon, Ann Doran, Jim Backus, Clarence Kolb. Producer: Richard Heermance. Director: William Beaudine. Screenplay: Charles R. Marion. 73 minutes, Cinecolor.

19. THE STAR (20th Century-Fox, 1953). Cast: Bette Davis, Sterling Hayden, Natalie Wood, Warner Anderson, Minor Watson, June Travis, Barbara Lawrence. Producer: Bert Friedlob. Director: Stuart Heisler. Screenplay: Katherine Albert and Dale Eunson. 89 minutes, B&W.

20. THE SILVER CHALICE (Warner Brothers, 1954). Cast: Paul Newman, Virginia Mayo, Pier Angeli, Jack Palance, Walter Hampden, Joseph Wiseman, Alexander Scourby, Lorne Green, E. G. Marshall, Natalie Wood, Ian Wolfe, Albert Dekker. Producer-director: Victor Saville. Screenplay: Lester Samuels, from the novel by Thomas B. Costain. 144 minutes, CinemaScope & WarnerColor.

21. ONE DESIRE (Universal, 1955). Cast: Anne Baxter, Rock Hudson, Julie Adams, Carl Benton Reid, Natalie Wood, William Hopper, Betty Garde. Producer: Ross Hunter. Director: Jerry Hopper. Screenplay: Lawrence Roman and Robert Blees, based on *Tracey Cromwell* by Conrad Richter. 94 minutes, Technicolor.

22. REBEL WITHOUT A CAUSE (Warner Brothers, 1955). Cast: James Dean, Natalie Wood, Jim Backus, Ann Doran, Rochelle Hudson, William Hopper, Sal Mineo, Corey Allen, Dennis Hopper, Virginia Brissac, Ian Wolfe, Nick Adams, Edward Platt. Producer: David Weisbart. Director: Nicholas Ray. Screenplay: Stewart Stern, from a story by Nicholas Ray, adaptation by Irving Shulman. 111 minutes, CinemaScope & WarnerColor.

23. THE SEARCHERS (Warner Brothers, 1956). Cast: John Wayne, Jeffrey Hunter, Vera Miles, Ward Bond, Natalie Wood, John Qualen, Olive Carey, Henry Brandon, Harry Carey, Jr., Antonio Moreno, Dorothy Jordan, Lana Wood, Pat Wayne. Executive producer: Merian C. Cooper. Associate producer: Patrick Ford. Director: John Ford. Screenplay: Frank S. Nugent, from the novel by Alan LeMay. 119 minutes, VistaVision & Technicolor.

24. THE BURNING HILLS (Warner Brothers, 1956). Cast: Tab Hunter, Natalie Wood, Skip Homeier, Eduard Franz, Earl Holliman, Claude Akins, Ray Teal. Producer: Richard Whorf. Director: Stuart Heisler. Screenplay: Irving Wallace, from a story by Louis L'Amour. 94 minutes, CinemaScope & Technicolor.

25. A CRY IN THE NIGHT (Warner Brothers, 1956). Cast: Edmond O'Brien, Brian Donlevy, Natalie Wood, Raymond Burr, Richard Anderson, Irene Hervey, Anthony Caruso. Associate producer: George C. Betholon. Director: Frank Tuttle. Screenplay: David Dortort, from a story by Whit Masterson. 75 minutes, B&W.

26. THE GIRL HE LEFT BEHIND (Warner Brothers, 1956). Cast: Tab Hunter, Natalie Wood, Jessie Royce Landis, Jim Backus, Henry Jones, Murray Hamilton, Alan King, James Garner, David Janssen, Vinton Hayworth. Producer: Frank B. Rosenberg. Director: David Butler. Screenplay: Guy Trosper. 103 minutes, B&W.

27. BOMBERS B-52 (Warner Brothers, 1957). Cast: Natalie Wood, Karl Malden, Efrem Zimbalist, Jr., Marsha Hunt, Don Kelly, Nelson Leigh, Robert Nichols. Producer: Richard Whorf. Director: Gordon Douglas. Screenplay: Irving Wallace, from a story by Sam Rolfe. 106 minutes, CinemaScope & WarnerColor.

28. MARJORIE MORNINGSTAR (Warner Brothers, 1958). Cast: Gene Kelly, Natalie Wood, Claire Trevor, Ed Wynn, Everett Sloane, Martin Milner, Carolyn Jones, George Tobias, Martin Balsam, Jesse White, Edward Byrnes, Paul Picerni, Alan Reed, Ruta Lee.

Producer: Milton Sperling. Director: Irving Rapper. Screenplay: Everett Freeman, from the novel by Herman Wouk. 123 minutes, WarnerColor.

29. KINGS GO FORTH (United Artists, 1958). Cast: Frank Sinatra, Tony Curtis, Natalie Wood, Leora Dana, Karl Swenson, Anne Codee, Jackie Berthe. Producer: Frank Ross. Director: Delmar Daves. Screenplay: Merle Miller, from the novel by Joe David Brown. 109 minutes, B&W.

30. CASH McCALL (Warner Brothers, 1959). Cast: James Garner, Natalie Wood, Nina Foch, Dean Jagger, E. G. Marshall, Henry Jones, Otto Kruger, Roland Winters. Producer: Henry Blanke. Director: Joseph Pevney. Screenplay: Lenore Coffee, from the novel by Cameron Hawley. 102 minutes, Technicolor.

31. ALL THE FINE YOUNG CANNIBALS (MGM, 1960). Cast: Natalie Wood, Robert Wagner, Susan Kohner, George Hamilton, Pearl Bailey, Jack Mullaney, Onslow Stevens, Anne Seymour, Virginia Gregg, Mabel Albertson, Louise Beavers. Producer: Pandro S. Berman. Director: Michael Anderson. Screenplay: Robert Thom, based on Rosamond Marshall's novel, *The Bixby Girls.* 112 minutes, CinemaScope & MetroColor.

32. SPLENDOR IN THE GRASS (Warner Brothers, 1961). Cast: Natalie Wood, Warren Beatty, Pat Hingle, Audrey Christie, Barbara Loden, Zohra Lampert, Fred Stewart, Joanna Roos, Gary Lockwood, Sandy Dennis, Jan Norris, Crystal Field. Producer-director: Elia Kazan. Screenplay: William Inge. 124 minutes, Technicolor.

33. WEST SIDE STORY (United Artists, 1961). Cast: Natalie Wood, Richard Beymer, Russ Tamblyn, Rita Moreno, George Chakiris, Tucker Smith, Tony Mordente, Eliot Feld, David Winters, Simon Oakland, John Astin. Producer: Robert Wise. Directors: Robert Wise and Jerome Robbins. Screenplay: Ernest Lehman, from the Broadway musical by Arthur Laurents (book), Leonard Bernstein (music) and Stephen Sondheim (lyrics). 155 minutes, Panavision-70 & Technicolor.

34. GYPSY (Warner Brothers, 1962). Cast: Rosalind Russell, Natalie Wood, Karl Malden, Paul Wallace, Betty Bruce, Ann Jillian, Harry Shannon, Faith Dane, Roxanne Arlen. Producer-director: Mervyn LeRoy. Screenplay: Leonard Spigelglass, from the Broadway musical by Arthur Laurents (book), Jule Styne (music) and Stephen Sondheim (lyrics). 149 minutes, Technirama & Technicolor.

35. LOVE WITH THE PROPER STRANGER (Paramount, 1963). Cast: Natalie Wood, Steve McQueen, Edie Adams, Herschel Bernardi, Tom

Bosley, Harvey Lembeck, Penny Santon, Virginia Vincent, Nick Alexander. Producer: Alan J. Pakula. Director: Robert Mulligan. Screenplay: Arnold Schulman. 100 minutes, B&W.

36. SEX AND THE SINGLE GIRL (Warner Brothers, 1964). Cast: Natalie Wood, Tony Curtis, Henry Fonda, Lauren Bacall, Mel Ferrer, Fran Jeffries, Leslie Parrish, Edward Everett Horton, Larry Storch, Stubby Kaye, Otto Kruger, Max Showalter, Count Basie and His Band. Producer: William T. Orr. Director: Richard Quine. Screenplay: Joseph Heller, Joseph Hoffman and David R. Schwartz, suggested by the book by Helen Gurley Brown. 114 minutes, Technicolor.

37. THE GREAT RACE (Warner Brothers, 1965). Cast: Jack Lemmon, Tony Curtis, Natalie Wood, Peter Falk, Keenan Wynn, Arthur O'Connell, Vivian Vance, Dorothy Provine, Larry Storch, Ross Martin, George Macready, Marvin Kaplan. Producer: Martin Jurow. Director: Blake Edwards. Screenplay: Arthur Ross, from a story idea by same and Blake Edwards. 150 minutes, Panavision & Technicolor.

38. INSIDE DAISY CLOVER (Warner Brothers, 1965). Cast: Natalie Wood, Christopher Plummer, Robert Redford, Roddy McDowall, Ruth Gordon, Katharine Bard, John Hale, Harold Gould. Producer: Alan J. Pakula. Director: Robert Mulligan. Screenplay: Gavin Lambert, based on his own novel. 128 minutes, Panavision & Technicolor.

39. THIS PROPERTY IS CONDEMNED (Paramount, 1966). Cast: Natalie Wood, Robert Redford, Charles Bronson, Kate Reid, Mary Badham, Alan Baxter, Robert Blake, John Harding, Dabney Coleman, Jon Provost. Producer: John Houseman. Director: Sydney Pollack. Screenplay: Francis Ford Coppola, Fred Coe and Edith Sommer; suggested by the one-act play by Tennessee Williams. 110 minutes, Technicolor.

40. PENELOPE (MGM, 1966). Cast: Natalie Wood, Ian Bannen, Dick Shawn, Peter Falk, Jonathan Winters, Lila Kedrova, Lou Jacobi, Norma Crane, Jerome Cowan, Arlene Golonka. Executive producer: Joe Pasternak. Producer: Arthur Loew, Jr. Director: Arthur Hiller. Screenplay: George Wells, from the novel by E. V. Cunningham (Howard Fast). 97 minutes, Panavision & Metrocolor.

41. BOB & CAROL & TED & ALICE (Columbia, 1969). Cast: Natalie Wood, Robert Culp, Elliott Gould, Dyan Cannon, Horst Ebersberg, Greg Mullavey, Celeste Yarnall. Executive producer: M. J. Frankovich. Producer: Larry Tucker. Director: Paul Mazursky.

Screenplay: Paul Mazursky and Larry Tucker. 104 minutes, Technicolor.

42. THE CANDIDATE (Warner Brothers, 1972). Cast: Robert Redford, Peter Boyle, Don Porter, Allen Garfield, Melvyn Douglas, Karen Carlson, Michael Lerner (NW in unbilled cameo appearance as herself). Producer: Walter Coblenz. Director: Michael Ritchie. Screenplay: Jeremy Larner. 109 minutes, Technicolor.

43. PEEPER (20th Century-Fox, 1976). Cast: Michael Caine, Natalie Wood, Kitty Winn, Thayer David, Liam Dunn, Dorothy Adams, Michael Constantine, Liz Renay, Guy Marks, Margo Winkler. Producers: Irwin Winkler, Robert Chartoff. Director: Peter Hyams. Screenplay: W. D. Richter, from the novel *Deadfall* by Keith Laumer. 87 minutes, Color by Deluxe.

44. METEOR (American International, 1979). Cast: Sean Connery, Natalie Wood, Henry Fonda, Trevor Howard, Brian Keith, Karl Malden, Martin Landau, Richard Dysart, Joe Campanella, Bibi Besch. Producers: Arnold Orgolini, Theodore Parvin. Director: Ronald Neame. Screenplay: Stanley Mann, Edmund H. North. 103 minutes, Panavision & color.

45. THE LAST MARRIED COUPLE IN AMERICA (Universal, 1980). Cast: Natalie Wood, George Segal, Richard Benjamin, Arlene Golonka, Alan Arbus, Marilyn Sokol, Dom De Luise, Valerie Harper, Bob Dishy, Oliver Clark, Priscilla Barnes. Executive producers: Gilbert Cates, Joseph Cates. Producers: Edward S. Feldman, John Herman Shaner. Director: Gilbert Cates. Screenplay: John Herman Shaner. 103 minutes, Technicolor.

46. WILLIE AND PHIL (20th Century-Fox, 1980). Cast: Michael Ontkean, Margot Kidder, Ray Sharkey, Jan Miner, Tom Brennan, Julie Bovasso, Louis Guss (NW in cameo appearance as herself). Producers: Paul Mazursky, Tony Ray. Director: Paul Mazursky. Screenplay: Paul Mazursky, inspired by François Truffaut's *Jules et Jim.* 116 minutes, Color by Movielab.

47. BRAINSTORM (MGM/United Artists, 1983). Cast: Christopher Walken, Natalie Wood, Louise Fletcher, Cliff Robertson, Jordan Christopher, Donald Hotton, Allan Fudge, Joe Dorsey, Georgianne Walken. Executive producer: Joel L. Freeman. Producer-director: Douglas Trumbull. Screenplay: Robert Stitzel and Philip Frank Messina, from a story by Bruce Joel Rubin. 106 minutes, Panavision & Metrocolor.

Television Features

1. THE AFFAIR (Spelling/Goldberg, 1973). Cast: Natalie Wood, Robert Wagner, Bruce Davison, Jamie Smith Jackson, Kent Smith, Frances Reid, Pat Harrington. Producers: Aaron Spelling, Leonard Goldberg. Director: Gilbert Cates. Teleplay: Barbara Turner. 74 minutes, color.
2. CAT ON A HOT TIN ROOF (Granada TV, Ltd., 1976). Cast: Natalie Wood, Robert Wagner, Laurence Olivier, Maureen Stapleton, Jack Hedley, Mary Peach, Heidi Rundt. Producers: Laurence Olivier, Derek Granger. Director: Robert Moore. Teleplay: Tennessee Williams, from his Pulitzer Prize-winning stage play. 120 minutes, color.
3. FROM HERE TO ETERNITY (Columbia Pictures Television, 1979). Cast: Natalie Wood, William Devane, Steve Railsback, Roy Thinnes, Joe Pantoliano, Kim Basinger, Peter Boyle, Salome Jens, Andy Griffith. Producer-director: Buzz Kulik. Teleplay: Don McGuire and Harold Gast, from the novel by James Jones and the 1953 screenplay by Daniel Taradash. Six-hour miniseries, color.
4. THE CRACKER FACTORY (Roger Gimbel Productions/EMI, 1979). Cast: Natalie Wood, Perry King, Peter Haskell, Vivian Blaine, Juliet Mills, Marian Mercer. Producer: Richard Shapiro. Director: Burt Brinckeroff. Teleplay: Richard Shapiro, based on the novel by Joyce Rebeta-Burditt. 100 minutes, color.
5. THE MEMORY OF EVA RYKER (Irwin Allen Productions, 1980). Cast: Natalie Wood, Ralph Bellamy, Robert Foxworth, Roddy McDowall, Bradford Dillman, Jean-Pierre Aumont, Peter Graves, Mel Ferrer, Morgan Fairchild. Producer: Irwin Allen. Director: Walter Grauman. Teleplay: Laurence Heath, based on the novel by Donald A. Stanwood. 144 minutes, color.

Television Series

1. PRIDE OF THE FAMILY (Revue Productions/ABC Network, 1953–54). Cast regulars: Paul Hartman, Fay Wray, Natalie Wood, Bobby Hyatt. Director: Bob Finkel. Story concept: Paul Schneider, Clint Comerford. Weekly half-hour sitcom, B&W.

The Films of Robert Wagner

1. THE HAPPY YEARS (MGM, 1950). Cast: Dean Stockwell, Darryl Hickman, Scotty Beckett, Leon Ames, Margalo Gilmore, Leo G. Carroll (RW in uncredited bit part). Producer: Carey Wilson. Director: William A. Wellman. Screenplay: Harry Ruskin, from Owen Johnson's Lawrenceville Stories. 110 minutes, Technicolor.
2. HALLS OF MONTEZUMA (20th Century-Fox, 1950). Cast: Richard Widmark, Jack Palance, Reginald Gardiner, Robert Wagner, Karl Malden, Richard Hylton, Richard Boone, Skip Homeier, Jack Webb, Neville Brand, Martin Milner, Marion Marshall. Producer: Robert Bassler. Director: Lewis Milestone. Screenplay: Michael Blankfort. 113 minutes, Technicolor.
3. THE FROGMEN (20th Century-Fox, 1951). Cast: Richard Widmark, Dana Andrews, Gary Merrill, Jeffrey Hunter, Warren Stevens, Robert Wagner, Harvey Lembeck. Producer: Samuel G. Engel. Director: Lloyd Bacon. Screenplay: George Tucker Battle, from a story by Oscar Millard. 96 minutes, B&W.
4. LET'S MAKE IT LEGAL (20th Century-Fox, 1951). Cast: Claudette Colbert, Macdonald Carey, Zachary Scott, Barbara Bates, Robert Wagner, Marilyn Monroe, Frank Cady, Jim Hayward, Carol Savage. Producer: Robert Bassler. Director: Richard Sale. Screenplay: F. Hugh Herbert and I. A. L. Diamond, from a story by Mortimer Braus. 77 minutes, B&W.
5. WITH A SONG IN MY HEART (20th Century-Fox, 1952). Cast: Susan Hayward, Rory Calhoun, David Wayne, Thelma Ritter, Robert Wagner, Helen Westcott, Una Merkel, Max Showalter, Lyle Talbot, Leif Erickson. Producer: Lamar Trotti. Director: Walter Lang. Screenplay: Lamar Trotti, based on the life of Jane Froman. 117 minutes, Technicolor.
6. WHAT PRICE GLORY? (20th Century-Fox, 1952). Cast: James Cagney, Dan Dailey, Corinne Calvet, William Demarest, Craig Hill, Robert Wagner, Marisa Pavan, Casey Adams, James Gleason, Wally Vernon. Producer: Sol C. Siegel. Director: John Ford. Screenplay: Phoebe and Henry Ephron, from the play by Maxwell Anderson and Laurence Stallings. 111 minutes, Technicolor.
7. STARS AND STRIPES FOREVER (20th Century-Fox, 1952). Cast: Clifton Webb, Debra Paget, Robert Wagner, Ruth Hussey, Finlay Currie, Benay Venuta, Roy Roberts, Maude Pickett. Producer: Lamar Trotti. Director: Henry Koster. Screenplay: Lamar Trotti, based

on the autobiography of John Philip Sousa. 89 minutes, Technicolor.

8. THE SILVER WHIP (20th Century-Fox, 1953). Cast: Dale Robertson, Rory Calhoun, Robert Wagner, Kathleen Crowley, James Millican, Lola Albright, J. M. Kerrigan. Producers: Robert Bassler, Michael Abel. Director: Harmon Jones. Screenplay: Jesse Lasky, Jr., from the novel by Jack Schaefer. 73 minutes, B&W.

9. TITANIC (20th Century-Fox, 1953). Cast: Clifton Webb, Barbara Stanwyck, Robert Wagner, Audrey Dalton, Thelma Ritter, Brian Aherne, Richard Basehart, Allyn Joslyn, Frances Bergen. Producer: Charles Brackett. Director: Jean Negulesco. Screenplay: Charles Brackett, Walter Reisch, Richard Breen. 98 minutes, B&W.

10. BENEATH THE 12 MILE REEF (20th Century-Fox, 1953). Cast: Robert Wagner, Terry Moore, Gilbert Roland, J. Carrol Naish, Richard Boone, Angela Clarke, Peter Graves, Jay Novello. Producer: Robert Bassler. Director: Robert D. Webb. Screenplay: A. I. Bezzerides. 102 minutes, CinemaScope & Technicolor.

11. PRINCE VALIANT (20th Century-Fox, 1954). Cast: James Mason, Janet Leigh, Robert Wagner, Debra Paget, Sterling Hayden, Victor McLaglen, Donald Crisp, Brian Aherne, Barry Jones, Mary Philips, Tom Conway. Producer: Robert L. Jacks. Director: Henry Hathaway. Screenplay: Dudley Nichols, based on the comic strip by Harold Foster. 100 minutes, CinemaScope & Technicolor.

12. BROKEN LANCE (20th Century-Fox, 1954). Cast: Spencer Tracy, Richard Widmark, Robert Wagner, Jean Peters, Katy Jurado, Hugh O'Brian, Eduard Franz, Earl Holliman, E. G. Marshall, Carl Benton Reid, Philip Ober. Producer: Sol C. Siegel. Director: Edward Dmytryk. Screenplay: Richard Murphy (adapted from Philip Yordan's script for the 1949 filmization of Jerome Weidman's *House of Strangers*). 96 minutes, CinemaScope & DeLuxe Color.

13. WHITE FEATHER (20th Century-Fox, 1955). Cast: Robert Wagner, John Lund, Jeffrey Hunter, Debra Paget, Eduard Franz, Noah Beery, Jr., Hugh O'Brian, Virginia Leith, Milburn Stone. Producer: Robert L. Jacks. Director: Robert Webb. Screenplay: Delmer Daves and Leo Townsend, from a story by John Prebble. 102 minutes, CinemaScope & Technicolor.

14. A KISS BEFORE DYING (United Artists, 1956). Cast: Robert Wagner, Jeffrey Hunter, Virginia Leith, Joanne Woodward, Mary Astor, George MacCready, Robert Quarry. Producer: Robert L. Jacks.

Director: Gerd Oswald. Screenplay: Lawrence Roman, from the novel by Ira Levin. 94 minutes, CinemaScope & DeLuxe Color.

15. THE MOUNTAIN (Paramount, 1956). Cast: Spencer Tracy, Robert Wagner, Claire Trevor, William Demarest, Barbara Darrow, Richard Arlen, E. G. Marshall, Anna Kashfi. Producer-director: Edward Dmytryk. Screenplay: Ranald MacDougall, from the novel by Henri Troyat. 105 minutes, VistaVision & Technicolor.

16. BETWEEN HEAVEN AND HELL (20th Century-Fox, 1956). Cast: Robert Wagner, Terry Moore, Broderick Crawford, Buddy Ebsen, Robert Keith, Brad Dexter, Mark Damon, Harvey Lembeck, Skip Homeier, Tod Andrews, Carl Switzer. Producer: David Weisbart. Director: Richard Fleischer. Screenplay: Harry Brown, based on *The Day the Century Ended* by Francis Gwaltney. 94 minutes, CinemaScope & DeLuxe Color.

17. THE TRUE STORY OF JESSE JAMES (20th Century-Fox, 1957). Cast: Robert Wagner, Jeffrey Hunter, Hope Lange, Agnes Moorehead, Alan Hale, Jr., Alan Baxter, John Carradine, Frank Gorshin, Rachel Stephens, Biff Elliot, Marian Seldes. Producer: Herbert B. Swope, Jr. Director: Nicholas Ray. Screenplay: Walter Newman, adapted from Nunnally Johnson's script for *Jesse James* (20th Century-Fox, 1939). 92 minutes, CinemaScope & DeLuxe Color.

18. STOPOVER TOKYO (20th Century-Fox, 1957). Cast: Robert Wagner, Joan Collins, Edmond O'Brien, Ken Scott, Reiko Oyama, Larry Keating, Sarah Selby. Producer: Walter Reisch. Director: Richard L. Breen. Screenplay: Richard L. Breen, from the novel by John P. Marquand. 100 minutes, CinemaScope & DeLuxe Color.

19. THE HUNTERS (20th Century-Fox, 1958). Cast: Robert Mitchum, Robert Wagner, Richard Egan, May Britt, Lee Philips, Victor Sen Yung, John Gabriel, Stacy Harris, Candace Lee. Producer-director: Dick Powell. Screenplay: Wendell Mayes, from a story by James Salter. 108 minutes, CinemaScope & DeLuxe Color.

20. IN LOVE AND WAR (20th Century-Fox, 1958). Cast: Robert Wagner, Dana Wynter, Jeffrey Hunter, Hope Lange, Bradford Dillman, Sheree North, France Nuyen, Mort Sahl, Edith Barrett, Murvyn Vye. Producer: Jerry Wald. Director: Philip Dunne. Screenplay: Edward Anhalt, based on Anton Myrer's novel, *The Big War.* 111 minutes, CinemaScope & DeLuxe Color.

21. SAY ONE FOR ME (20th Century-Fox, 1959). Cast: Bing Crosby, Debbie Reynolds, Robert Wagner, Ray Walston, Les Tremayne, Connie Gilchrist, Frank McHugh, Joe Besser, Stella Stevens, Sebastian Cabot. Producer-director: Frank Tashlin. Screenplay: Robert O'Brien. 119 minutes, CinemaScope & DeLuxe Color.

22. ALL THE FINE YOUNG CANNIBALS (MGM, 1960). Cast: Natalie

Wood, Robert Wagner, Susan Kohner, George Hamilton, Pearl Bailey, Jack Mullaney, Onslow Stevens, Anne Seymour, Virginia Gregg, Mabel Albertson, Louise Beavers. Producer: Pandro S. Berman. Director: Michael Anderson. Screenplay: Robert Thom, based on Rosamond Marshall's novel, *The Bixby Girls*. 112 minutes, CinemaScope & Metrocolor.

23. SAIL A CROOKED SHIP (Columbia, 1961). Cast: Robert Wagner, Ernie Kovacs, Dolores Hart, Carolyn Jones, Frankie Avalon, Frank Gorshin, Jesse White, Harvey Lembeck. Producer: Philip Barry, Jr. Director: Irving Brecher. Screenplay: Ruth Brooks Flippen and Bruce Geller, from the novel by Nathaniel Benchley. 88 minutes, B&W.

24. THE LONGEST DAY (20th Century-Fox, 1962). Cast: John Wayne, Robert Mitchum, Henry Fonda, Richard Burton, Sean Connery, Rod Steiger, Robert Wagner, Robert Ryan, Stuart Whitman, Red Buttons, Sal Mineo, Curt Jurgens, many other American, British and European stars. Producer: Darryl F. Zanuck. Directors: Ken Annakin, Andrew Marton and Bernhard Wicki. Screenplay: Cornelius Ryan, based on his book (with additional sequences by Romain Gary, James Jones, David Pursall and Jack Seddon). 180 minutes, B&W.

25. THE WAR LOVER (Columbia, 1962). Cast: Steve McQueen, Robert Wagner, Shirley Ann Field, Gary Cockrell, Michael Crawford, Bill Edwards, Robert Easton, Louise Dunn. Producer: Arthur Hornblow, Jr. Director: Philip Leacock. Screenplay: Howard Koch, based on the novel by John Hersey. 105 minutes, B&W.

26. THE CONDEMNED OF ALTONA (20th Century-Fox, 1963). Cast: Sophia Loren, Maximilian Schell, Fredric March, Robert Wagner, François Prevost, Alfredo Franchi, Lucia Pelella. Producer: Carlo Ponti. Director: Vittorio De Sica. Screenplay: Abby Mann and Cesare Zavattini, from the play by Jean-Paul Sartre. 114 minutes, CinemaScope, B&W.

27. THE PINK PANTHER (United Artists, 1964). Cast: David Niven, Peter Sellers, Capucine, Claudia Cardinale, Robert Wagner, Brenda de Banzie, Colin Gordon, Fran Jeffries, John Le Mesurier. Producer: Martin Jurow. Director: Blake Edwards. Screenplay: Maurice Richlin, Blake Edwards. 113 minutes, Technirama & Technicolor.

28. HARPER (Warner Brothers, 1966). Cast: Paul Newman, Lauren Bacall, Julie Harris, Arthur Hill, Janet Leigh, Pamela Tiffin, Robert Wagner, Robert Webber, Shelley Winters, Harold Gould, Strother Martin. Producers: Jerry Gershwin, Elliott Kastner. Director: Jack Smight. Screenplay: William Goldman, based on Ross

Macdonald's *The Moving Target*. 121 minutes, Panavision & Technicolor.

29. BANNING (Universal, 1967). Cast: Robert Wagner, Anjanette Comer, Jill St. John, Guy Stockwell, James Farentino, Susan Clark, Howard St. John, Mike Kellin, Sean Garrison, Gene Hackman, Edmon Ryan. Producer: Dick Berg. Director: Ron Winston. Screenplay: James Lee, based on a story by Hamilton Maule. 102 minutes, Techniscope & Technicolor.

30. THE BIGGEST BUNDLE OF THEM ALL (MGM, 1968). Cast: Robert Wagner, Raquel Welch, Godfrey Cambridge, Vittorio De Sica, Edward G. Robinson, Davy Kaye, Victor Spinetti, Yvonne Sanson. Producer: Josef Shaftel. Director: Ken Annakin. Screenplay: Sy Salkowitz, from a story by Josef Shaftel. 110 minutes, Panavision & MetroColor.

31. DON'T JUST STAND THERE (Universal, 1968). Cast: Robert Wagner, Mary Tyler Moore, Glynis Johns, Harvey Korman, Barbara Rhoades, Peggy Stanton, Stuart Margolin. Producer: Stan Margulies. Director: Ron Winston. Screenplay: Charles Williams, based on his novel, *The Wrong Venus*. 99 minutes, Technicolor.

32. WINNING (Universal, 1969). Cast: Paul Newman, Joanne Woodward, Robert Wagner, Richard Thomas, David Sheiner, Clu Gulager, Barry Ford, Toni Clayton, Maxine Stuart. Producer: John Foreman. Director: James Goldstone. Screenplay: Howard Rodman. 123 minutes, Panavision & Technicolor.

33. THE TOWERING INFERNO (20th Century-Fox/Warner Brothers, 1974). Cast: Steve McQueen, Paul Newman, William Holden, Faye Dunaway, Fred Astaire, Susan Blakely, Richard Chamberlain, Jennifer Jones, Robert Wagner, O. J. Simpson, Robert Vaughn. Producer: Irwin Allen. Director: John Guillermin (action sequences by Irwin Allen). Screenplay: Stirling Silliphant, based on the novels *The Tower* by Richard Martin Stern and *The Glass Inferno* by Thomas Scortia and Frank Robinson. 165 minutes, Panavision & DeLuxe Color.

34. MIDWAY (Universal, 1976). Cast: Charlton Heston, Henry Fonda, James Coburn, Glenn Ford, Hal Holbrook, Toshiro Mifune, Robert Mitchum, Cliff Robertson, Robert Wagner, Robert Webber, James Shigeta, Monte Markham, Christopher George, Edward Albert. Producer: Walter Mirisch. Director: Jack Smight. Screenplay: Donald S. Sanford. 132 minutes, Panavision & Technicolor.

35. THE CONCORDE—AIRPORT '79 (Universal, 1979). Cast: Alain Delon, Susan Blakely, Robert Wagner, Sylvia Kristel, George Kennedy, Eddie Albert, Bibi Anderson, Charo, John Davidson, Andrea Marcovicci, Martha Raye, Cicely Tyson, Jimmie Walker, David

Warner, Mercedes McCambridge, Avery Schreiber, Sybil Danning, Monica Lewis. Producer: Jennings Lang. Director: David Lowell Rich. Screenplay: Eric Roth, from a story idea by Jennings Lang (inspired by the film based on Arthur Hailey's novel, *Airport*). 123 minutes, Technicolor.

36. THE CURSE OF THE PINK PANTHER (MGM/United Artists, 1983). Cast: David Niven, Robert Wagner, Herbert Lom, Joanna Lumley, Capucine, Robert Loggia, Harvey Korman, Ted Wass, Graham Stark, Leslie Ash, Michael Elphick. Producers: Blake Edwards, Tony Adams. Director: Blake Edwards. Screenplay: Blake Edwards, Geoffrey Edwards. 110 minutes, Panavision & Technicolor.

37. I AM THE CHEESE (Almi, 1983). Cast: Robert Macnaughton, Hope Lange, Don Murray, Robert Wagner, Cynthia Nixon, Lee Richardson, Robert Cormier, David Lange, Sudie Bond, John Fiedler, Paul Romero. Producer: David Lange. Director: Robert Jiras. Screenplay: David Lange and Robert Jiras, based on the novel by Robert Cormier. 100 minutes, color.

Television Features

1. HOW I SPENT MY SUMMER VACATION (Universal-MCA, 1967). Cast: Robert Wagner, Lola Albright, Walter Pidgeon, Peter Lawford, Jill St. John. Producer: Jack Laird. Director: William Hale. Teleplay: Gene Kearney. 100 minutes, color.

2. CITY BENEATH THE SEA (20th Century-Fox Television, 1970). Cast: Robert Wagner, Stuart Whitman, Rosemary Forsyth, Joseph Cotten, Richard Basehart, James Darren. Producer-director: Irwin Allen. Teleplay: John Meredyth Lucas. 98 minutes, color.

3. THE CABLE CAR MURDER (Warner Brothers Television, 1971). Cast: Robert Hooks, Jeremy Slate, Robert Wagner, Carol Lynley, Simon Oakland, Jose Ferrer, John Randolph. Producer: E. Jack Neuman. Director: Jerry Thorpe. Teleplay: Herman Miller. 73 minutes, color (later expanded to 96 minutes and retitled *Crosscurrent*).

4. KILLER BY NIGHT (Cinema Center, 1972). Cast: Robert Wagner, Diane Baker, Greg Morris, Theodore Bikel, Robert Lansing, Mercedes McCambridge. Producer: Fred Engel. Director: Bernard McEveety. Teleplay: David P. Harmon. 100 minutes, color.

5. MADAME SIN (ITC, 1972). Cast: Bette Davis, Robert Wagner, Roy Kinnear, Paul Maxwell, Denholm Elliott, Gordon Jackson. Producers: Robert Wagner, Julius Wintle, Lou Morheim. Director:

David Greene. Teleplay: David Greene, Barry Oringer. 73 minutes, color (88-minute version released theatrically abroad).

6. THE STREETS OF SAN FRANCISCO (Quinn Martin Productions, 1972). Cast: Karl Malden, Michael Douglas, Robert Wagner, Kim Darby, Andrew Duggan, John Rubinstein, Tom Bosley, Edward Andrews. Producers: Arthur Fellows, Adrian Samish. Director: Walter Grauman. Teleplay: Edward Hume, based on Carolyn Weston's novel, *Poor, Poor Ophelia*. 98 minutes, color (pilot for the TV series).

7. THE AFFAIR (Spelling/Goldberg, 1973). Cast: Natalie Wood, Robert Wagner, Bruce Davison, Jamie Smith Jackson, Kent Smith, Frances Reid, Pat Harrington. Producers: Aaron Spelling, Leonard Goldberg. Director: Gilbert Cates. Teleplay: Barbara Turner. 74 minutes, color.

8. SWITCH (Universal-MCA, 1975). Cast: Robert Wagner, Eddie Albert, Charles Durning, Sharon Gless, Ken Swofford, Charlie Callas, Alan Manson, Jaclyn Smith. Producer: Glen Larson. Director: Robert Day. Teleplay: Glen Larson. 78 minutes, color (pilot for the TV series).

9. CAT ON A HOT TIN ROOF (Granada TV, Ltd., 1976). Cast: Natalie Wood, Robert Wagner, Laurence Olivier, Maureen Stapleton, Jack Hedley, Mary Peach, Heidi Rundt. Producers: Laurence Olivier, Derek Granger. Director: Robert Moore. Teleplay: Tennessee Williams, from his Pulitzer Prize-winning stage play. 120 minutes, color.

10. THE ABDUCTION OF SAINT ANNE (Quinn Martin Productions, 1975). Cast: Robert Wagner, E. G. Marshall, Lloyd Nolan, Kathleen Quinlan, William Windom, James Gregory, Martha Scott. Producer: John Wilder. Director: Harry Falk. Teleplay: Edward Hume, from the novel *The Issue of the Bishop's Blood* by Thomas Patrick McMahon. 90 minutes, color (later retitled *They've Kidnapped Anne Benedict*).

11. DEATH AT LOVE HOUSE (Spelling/Goldberg, 1976). Cast: Robert Wagner, Kate Jackson, Sylvia Sidney, Joan Blondell, Dorothy Lamour, John Carradine, Bill Macy, Marianna Hill. Producer: Hal Sitowitz. Director: E. W. Swackhamer. Teleplay: Jim Barnett. 78 minutes, color.

12. THE CRITICAL LIST (MTM Productions, 1978). Cast: Lloyd Bridges, Melinda Dillon, Buddy Ebsen, Barbara Parkins, Robert Wagner, Ken Howard, Scott Marlowe, Richard Basehart, Ben Piazza. Producer: Jerry McNeely. Director: Lou Antonio. Teleplay: Jerry McNeely, from the novels *Skeleton* and *Critical List* by Dr.

Marshall Goldberg. 180 minutes, color (two pilot films strung together).

13. PEARL (Warner Brothers Television, 1978). Cast: Angie Dickinson, Dennis Weaver, Robert Wagner, Lesley Ann Warren, Tiana Alexandra, Gregg Henry, Katherine Helmond, Brian Dennehy. Executive producers: Stirling Silliphant, Franklin Konigsberg. Producer: Sam Manners. Director: Hy Averback. Teleplay: Stirling Silliphant. Six-hour miniseries, color.

14. HART TO HART (Spelling/Goldberg/Rona II, 1979). Cast: Robert Wagner, Stefanie Powers, Lionel Stander, Roddy McDowall, Jill St. John, Eugene Roche, Clifton James, Stella Stevens (N.W. in walk-on, billed as Natasha Gurdin). Producers: Aaron Spelling, Leonard Goldberg. Director: Tom Mankiewicz. Teleplay: Sidney Sheldon and Tom Mankiewicz, based on a story by Sheldon. 100 minutes, color (pilot for the TV series).

15. TO CATCH A KING (HBO, 1984). Cast: Robert Wagner, Terri Garr, Horst Janson, Barbara Parkins, John Standing, Jane Lapotaire, Barry Foster. Producer: Robert E. Fuisz. Director: Clive Donner. Teleplay: Roger O. Hirson, based on the novel by Harry Patterson (a.k.a. Jack Higgins). 113 minutes, color.

16. LIME STREET (RJ Productions/Columbia Pictures Television, 1985). Cast: Robert Wagner, John Standing, Julie Fulton, Anne Haney, Samantha Smith, Maia Brewton, Lew Ayres, Hurd Hatfield, Christopher Neame, Patrick Macnee. Executive producers: Robert Wagner, Harry Thomason. Director: Ray Austin. Teleplay: Linda Bloodworth-Thomason. 70 minutes, color (pilot for the TV series).

17. THERE MUST BE A PONY (RJ Productions/Columbia Pictures Television, 1986). Cast: Elizabeth Taylor, Robert Wagner, Chad Lowe, James Coco, William Windom, Edward Winter. Producer: Howard Jeffrey. Director: Joseph Sargent. Teleplay: Mart Crowley, based on the novel by James Kirkwood. 100 minutes, color.

18. LOVE AMONG THIEVES (Papazian Productions, 1987). Cast: Audrey Hepburn, Robert Wagner, Jerry Orbach, Ismael Carlo, Samantha Eggar, Christopher Neame, Patrick Bauchau. Producer: Robert A. Papazian. Director: Roger Young. Teleplay: Stephen Black, Henry Stern and Sally Robinson. 100 minutes, color.

19. WINDMILLS OF THE GODS (ITC Entertainment/Dove Productions, 1988). Cast: Jaclyn Smith, Robert Wagner, Ruby Dee, Ari Meyers, Susan Tyrell, David Ackroyd, John Pleshette. Executive producer: Sidney Sheldon. Producers: Michael Viner, Deborah Raffin. Director: Lee Philips. Teleplay: John Gay, from the novel by Sidney Sheldon. Four-hour miniseries, color.

TV Series

1. IT TAKES A THIEF (Universal-MCA, 1968–70). Cast regulars: Robert Wagner, Malachi Throne, Fred Astaire, John Russell, Susan Saint James, Edward Binns. Executive producers: Frank Price, Gordon Oliver. Producers: Jack Arnold, Glen Larson. Story concept: Roland Kibbee. Hour-long adventure series in color.
2. COLDITZ (BBC-TV/Universal-MCA, 1972–73). Cast regulars: David McCallum, Robert Wagner, Jack Hedley, Edward Hardwicke, Christopher Neame, Bernard Hepton, Hans Meyer, Anthony Valentine. Producer: Bernard Glaister. Story concept: Brian Degas and Bernard Glaister. 28 fifty-minute episodes in color (never shown in the United States).
3. SWITCH (Universal-MCA, 1975–78). Cast regulars: Robert Wagner, Eddie Albert, Sharon Gless, Charlie Callas, William Bryant, James Hong. Producer: Glen Larson. Story concept: Glen Larson. Hour-long detective series in color.
4. HART TO HART (Spelling/Goldberg/Rona II, 1979–84). Cast regulars: Robert Wagner, Stefanie Powers, Lionel Stander. Producers: Aaron Spelling, Leonard Goldberg. Story concept: Sidney Sheldon and Tom Mankiewicz. Hour-long adventure series in color.
5. LIME STREET (RJ Productions/Columbia Television, 1985). Cast regulars: Robert Wagner, Samantha Smith, Maia Brewton, Lew Ayres, John Standing, Anne Haney. Executive producers: Robert Wagner, Harry Thomason. Producer and story concept: Linda Bloodworth-Thomason. Hour-long sitcom in color (production terminated following the death of thirteen-year-old Samantha Smith in a plane crash).

Index

ABOUT THE AUTHOR

WARREN HARRIS is the author of *Gable and Lombard, The Other Marilyn: The Life of Marilyn Miller* and *Cary Grant.* He resides in New York City.